G.I. JOE

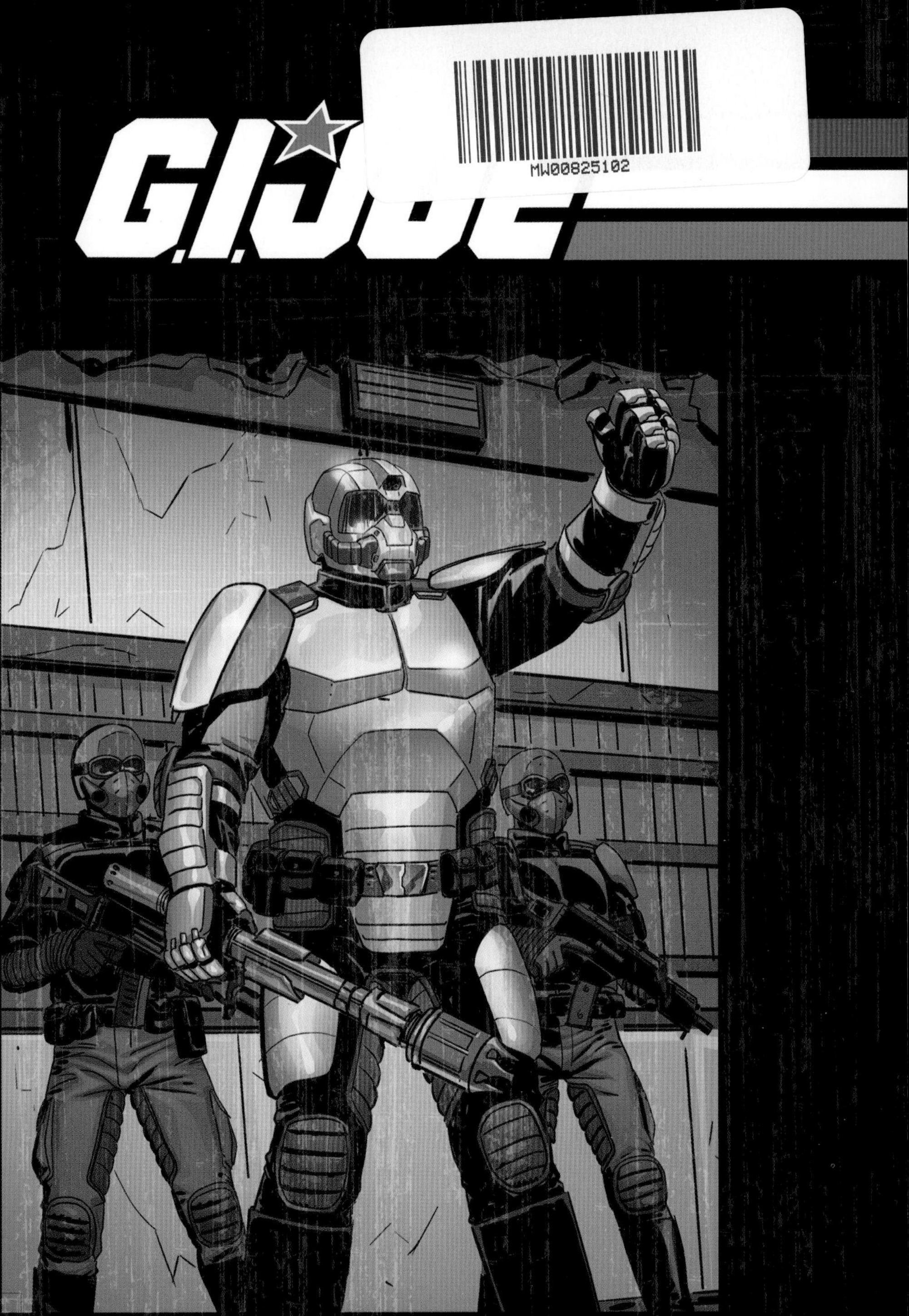

G.I. JOE

WRITER: **CHUCK DIXON**

ARTIST: **WILL ROSADO** AND **ALEX CAL** (ISSUE #17)

COLORIST: **ROMULO FAJARDO, JR.**

LETTERS: **NEIL UYETAKE** AND **SHAWN LEE**

SERIES EDITORS: **JOHN BARBER** AND **CARLOS GUZMAN**

COVER ARTIST: **TOMMY LEE EDWARDS**

COLLECTION EDITORS: **JUSTIN EISINGER** AND **ALONZO SIMON**

COLLECTION DESIGNER: **NEIL UYETAKE**

Special thanks to Hasbro's Aaron Archer, Derryl DePriest, Joe Del Regno, Ed Lane, Joe Furfaro, Jos Huxley, Heather Hopkins, and Michael Kelly for their invaluable assistance.

IDW founded by Ted Adams, Alex Garner, Kris Oprisko, and Robbie Robbins |

ISBN: 978-1-61377-511-0

15 14 13 12   1 2 3 4

Licensed By:

Ted Adams, CEO & Publisher
Greg Goldstein, President & COO
Robbie Robbins, EVP/Sr. Graphic Artist
Chris Ryall, Chief Creative Officer/Editor-in-Chief
Matthew Ruzicka, CPA, Chief Financial Officer
Alan Payne, VP of Sales
Dirk Wood, VP of Marketing
Lorelei Bunjes, VP of Digital Services

Become our fan on Facebook **facebook.com/idwpublishing**
Follow us on Twitter **@idwpublishing**
Check us out on YouTube **youtube.com/idwpublishing**
www.IDWPUBLISHING.com

After the new Cobra
Commander was elected,
Cobra launched a full-fledged assault
on a Southeast Asian country that forced the
population to flee, demolished its drug
trade, and then nuked its empty cities. G.I.
JOE fought valiantly but was only able to
hold back Cobra in a limited capacity. The
consequences for G.I. JOE's failure have been
grave: General Hawk was stripped of command
and Duke was appointed leader of the JOEs,
but only after their operating budget was
markedly decreased. On top of that, Cobra
held a press conference where they revealed
the existence of this covert American unit
to the public at large...

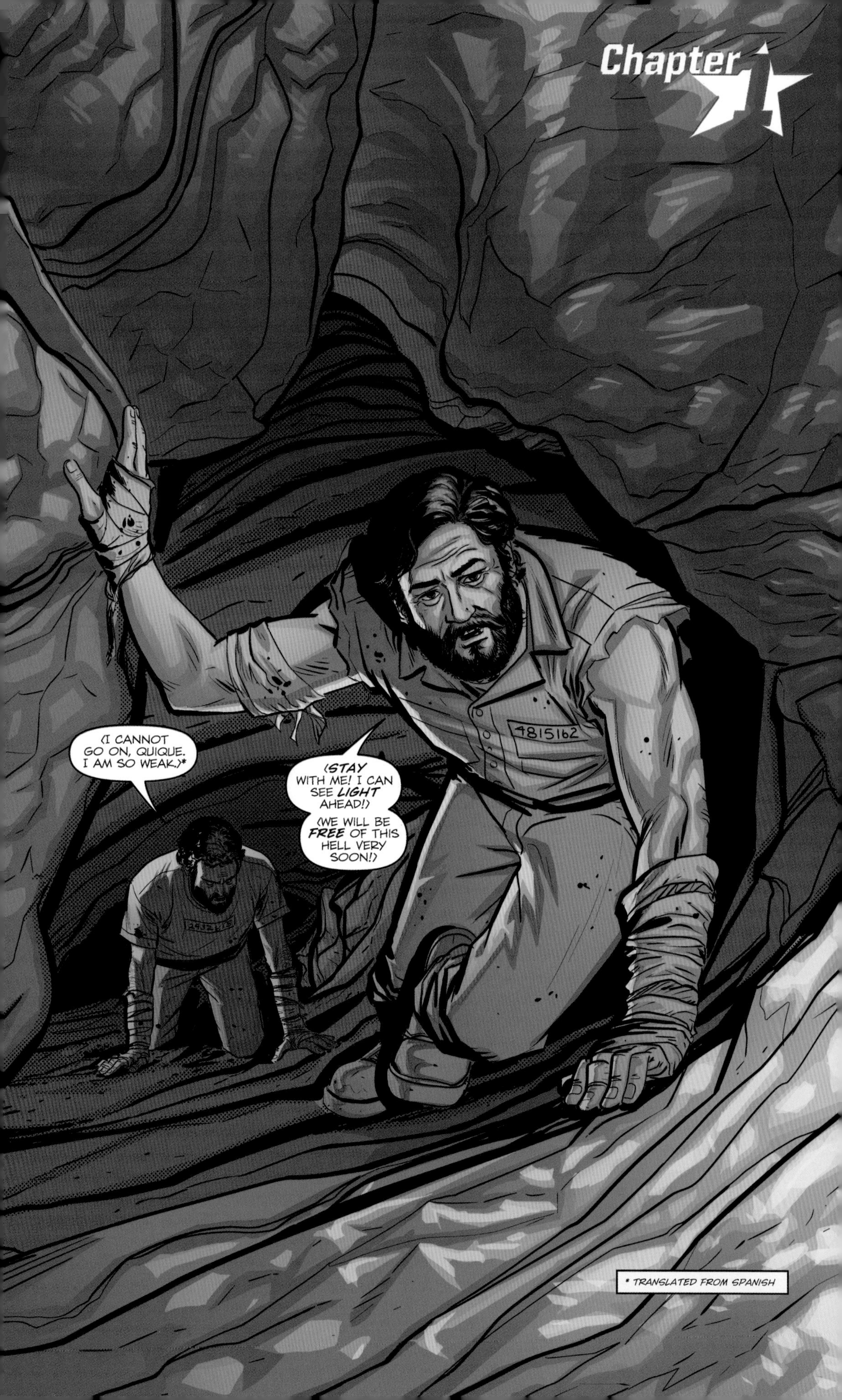
Chapter
‹I CANNOT GO ON, QUIQUE. I AM SO WEAK.›*
‹STAY WITH ME! I CAN SEE LIGHT AHEAD!›
‹WE WILL BE FREE OF THIS HELL VERY SOON!›
4815162
* TRANSLATED FROM SPANISH

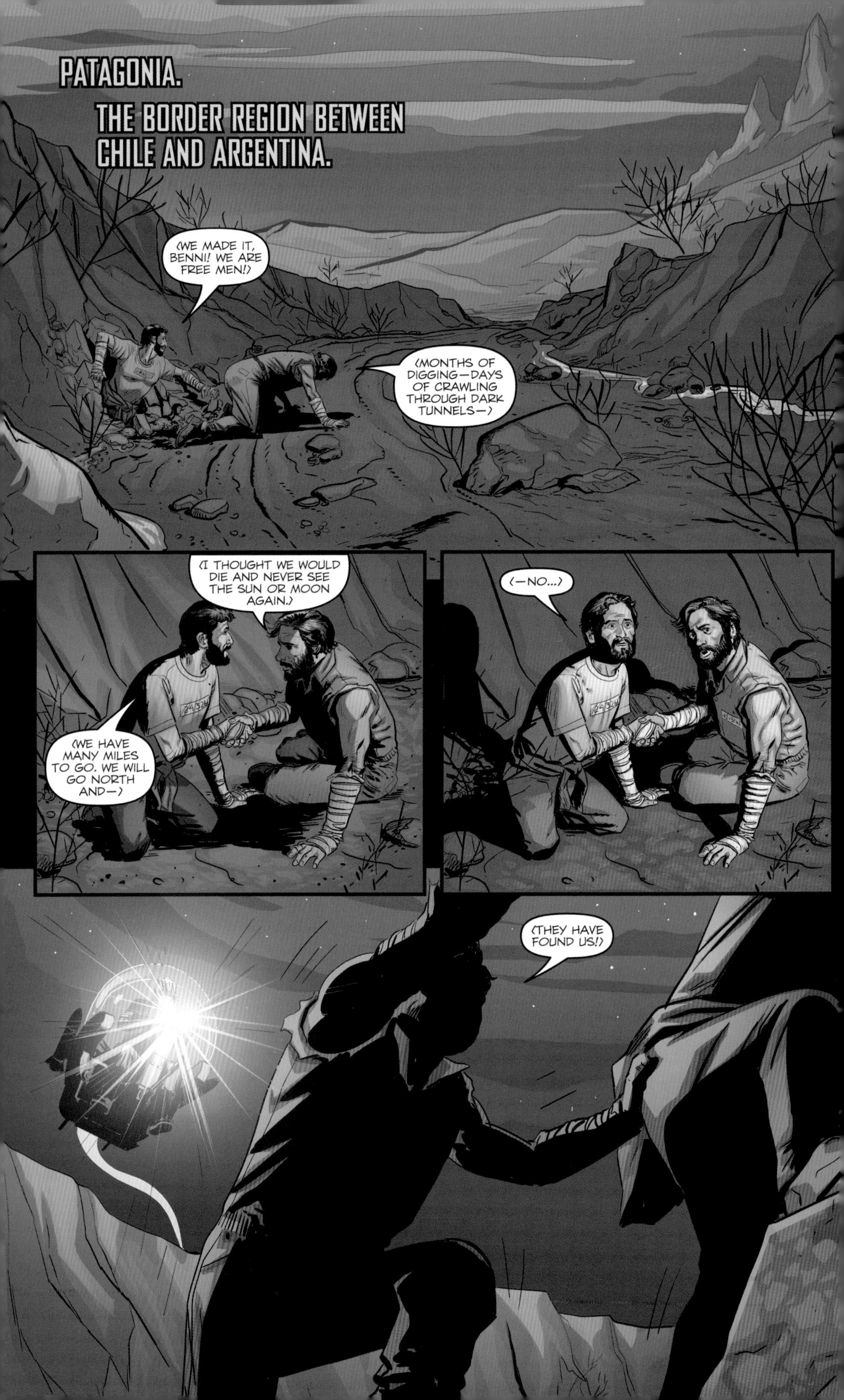
PATAGONIA.
THE BORDER REGION BETWEEN CHILE AND ARGENTINA.
(WE MADE IT, BENNI! WE ARE FREE MEN!)
(MONTHS OF DIGGING—DAYS OF CRAWLING THROUGH DARK TUNNELS—)
(I THOUGHT WE WOULD DIE AND NEVER SEE THE SUN OR MOON AGAIN.)
(WE HAVE MANY MILES TO GO. WE WILL GO NORTH AND—)
(—NO...)
(THEY HAVE FOUND US!)

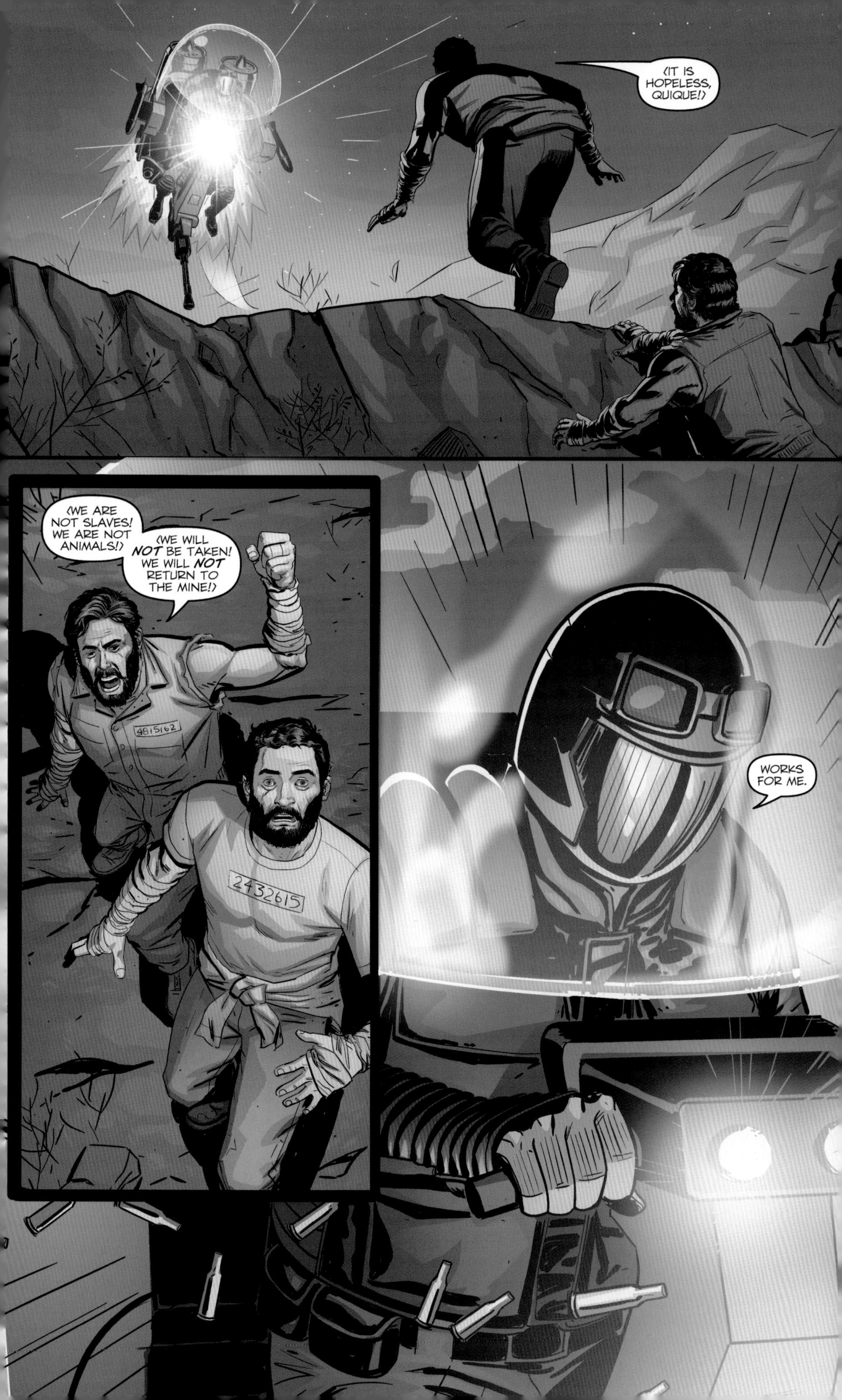
‹IT IS HOPELESS, QUIQUE!›
‹WE ARE NOT SLAVES! WE ARE NOT ANIMALS!›
‹WE WILL **NOT** BE TAKEN! WE WILL **NOT** RETURN TO THE MINE!›
4815162
2432615
WORKS FOR ME.

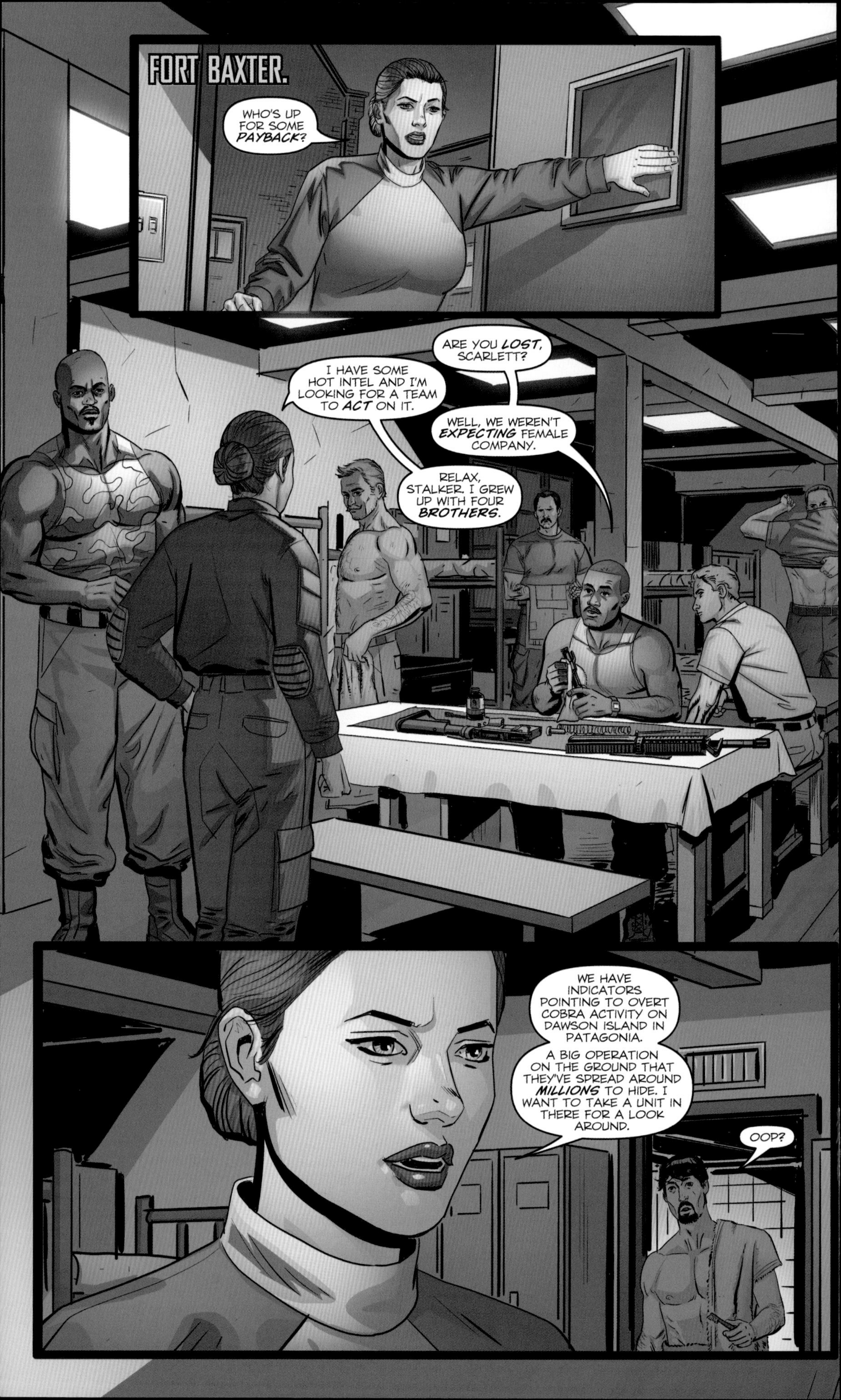
FORT BAXTER.
WHO'S UP FOR SOME PAYBACK?
ARE YOU LOST, SCARLETT?
I HAVE SOME HOT INTEL AND I'M LOOKING FOR A TEAM TO ACT ON IT.
WELL, WE WEREN'T EXPECTING FEMALE COMPANY.
RELAX, STALKER. I GREW UP WITH FOUR BROTHERS.
WE HAVE INDICATORS POINTING TO OVERT COBRA ACTIVITY ON DAWSON ISLAND IN PATAGONIA.
A BIG OPERATION ON THE GROUND THAT THEY'VE SPREAD AROUND MILLIONS TO HIDE. I WANT TO TAKE A UNIT IN THERE FOR A LOOK AROUND.
OOP?

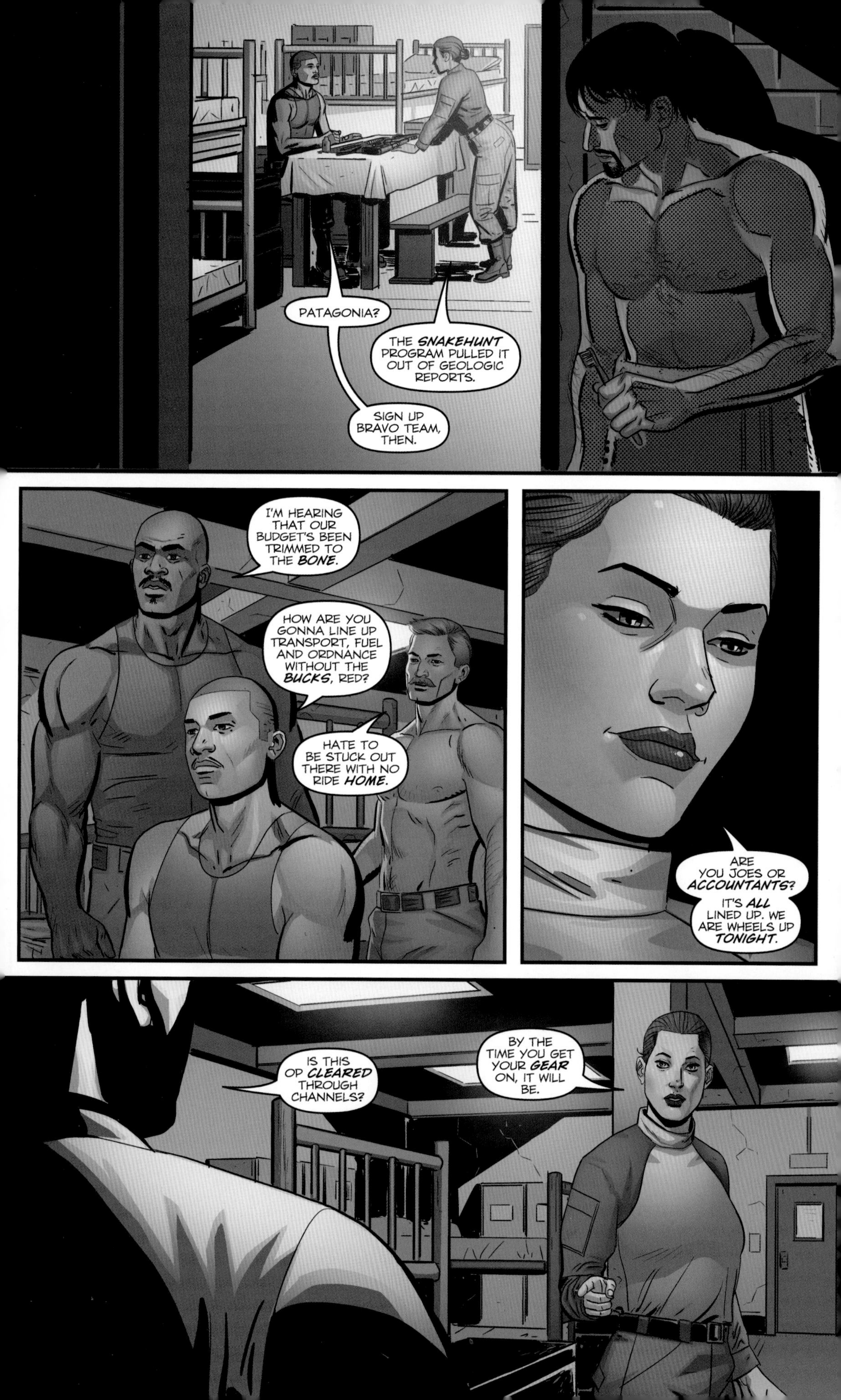
PATAGONIA?
THE SNAKEHUNT PROGRAM PULLED IT OUT OF GEOLOGIC REPORTS.
SIGN UP BRAVO TEAM, THEN.
I'M HEARING THAT OUR BUDGET'S BEEN TRIMMED TO THE BONE.
HOW ARE YOU GONNA LINE UP TRANSPORT, FUEL AND ORDNANCE WITHOUT THE BUCKS, RED?
HATE TO BE STUCK OUT THERE WITH NO RIDE HOME.
ARE YOU JOES OR ACCOUNTANTS?
IT'S ALL LINED UP. WE ARE WHEELS UP TONIGHT.
IS THIS OP CLEARED THROUGH CHANNELS?
BY THE TIME YOU GET YOUR GEAR ON, IT WILL BE.

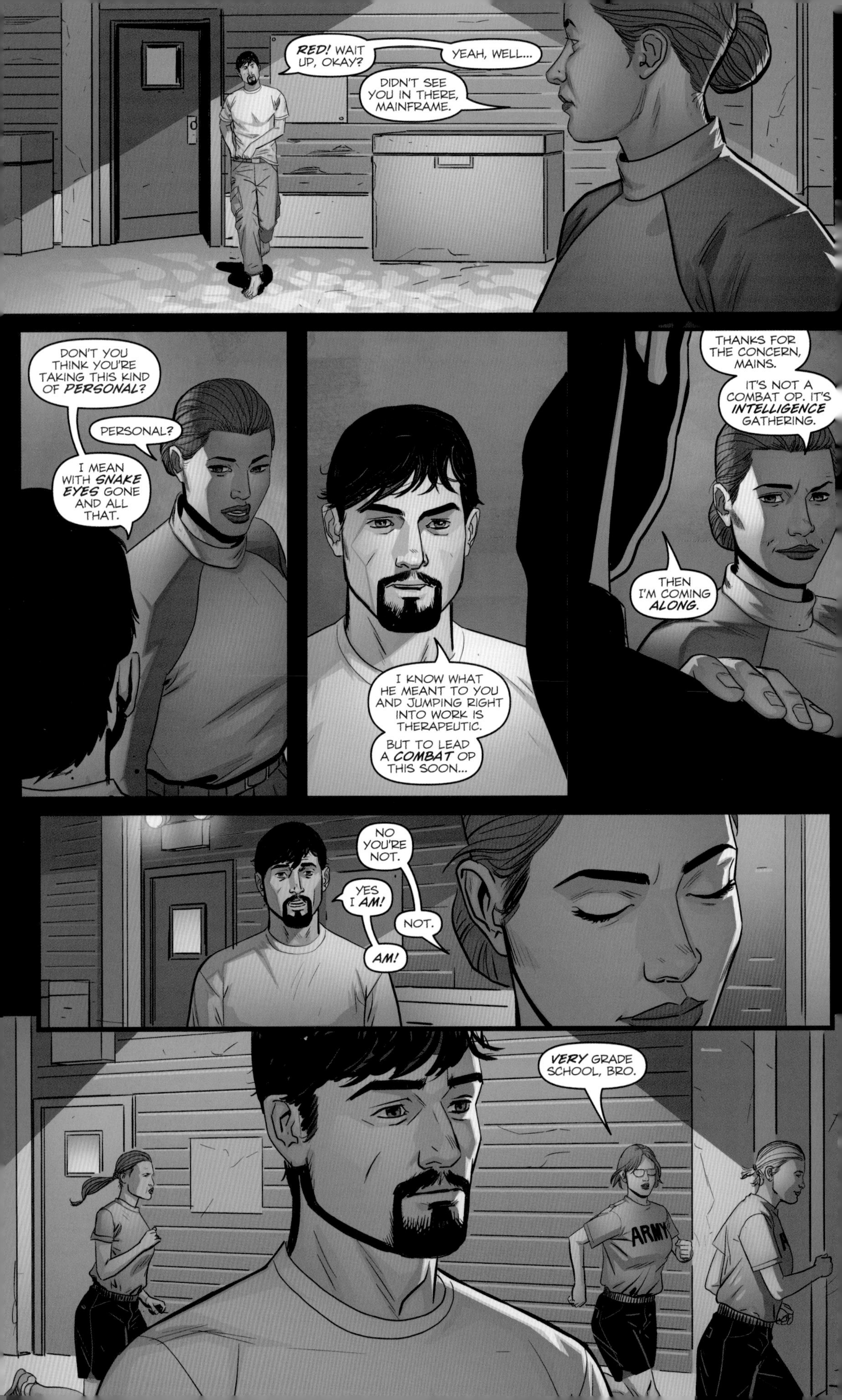
RED! WAIT UP, OKAY?
YEAH, WELL...
DIDN'T SEE YOU IN THERE, MAINFRAME.
DON'T YOU THINK YOU'RE TAKING THIS KIND OF PERSONAL?
PERSONAL?
I MEAN WITH SNAKE EYES GONE AND ALL THAT.
I KNOW WHAT HE MEANT TO YOU AND JUMPING RIGHT INTO WORK IS THERAPEUTIC.
BUT TO LEAD A COMBAT OP THIS SOON...
THANKS FOR THE CONCERN, MAINS.
IT'S NOT A COMBAT OP. IT'S INTELLIGENCE GATHERING.
THEN I'M COMING ALONG.
NO YOU'RE NOT.
YES I AM!
NOT.
AM!
VERY GRADE SCHOOL, BRO.
ARMY

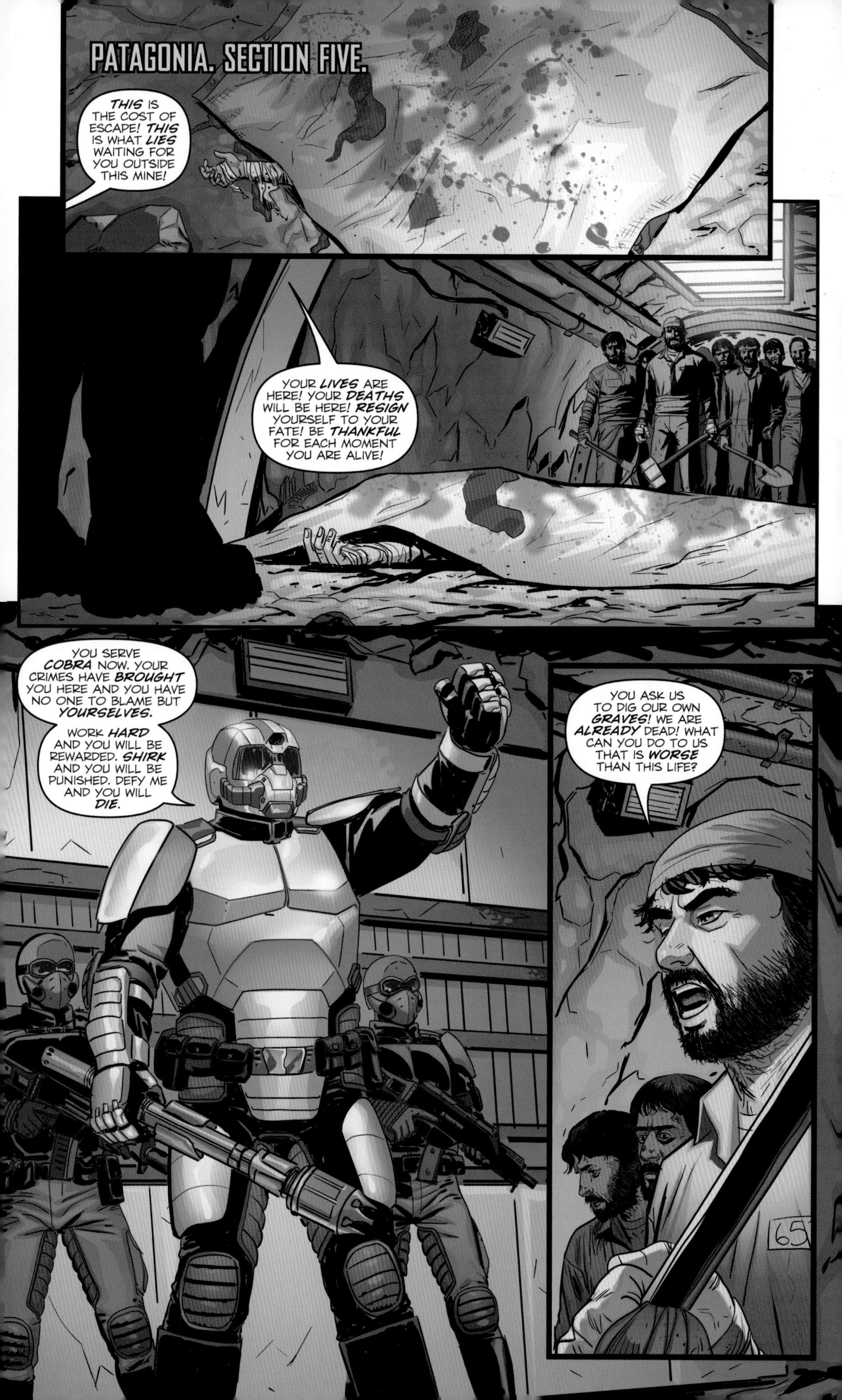
PATAGONIA. SECTION FIVE.
THIS IS THE COST OF ESCAPE! THIS IS WHAT LIES WAITING FOR YOU OUTSIDE THIS MINE!
YOUR LIVES ARE HERE! YOUR DEATHS WILL BE HERE! RESIGN YOURSELF TO YOUR FATE! BE THANKFUL FOR EACH MOMENT YOU ARE ALIVE!
YOU SERVE COBRA NOW. YOUR CRIMES HAVE BROUGHT YOU HERE AND YOU HAVE NO ONE TO BLAME BUT YOURSELVES.
WORK HARD AND YOU WILL BE REWARDED. SHIRK AND YOU WILL BE PUNISHED. DEFY ME AND YOU WILL DIE.
YOU ASK US TO DIG OUR OWN GRAVES! WE ARE ALREADY DEAD! WHAT CAN YOU DO TO US THAT IS WORSE THAN THIS LIFE?
65

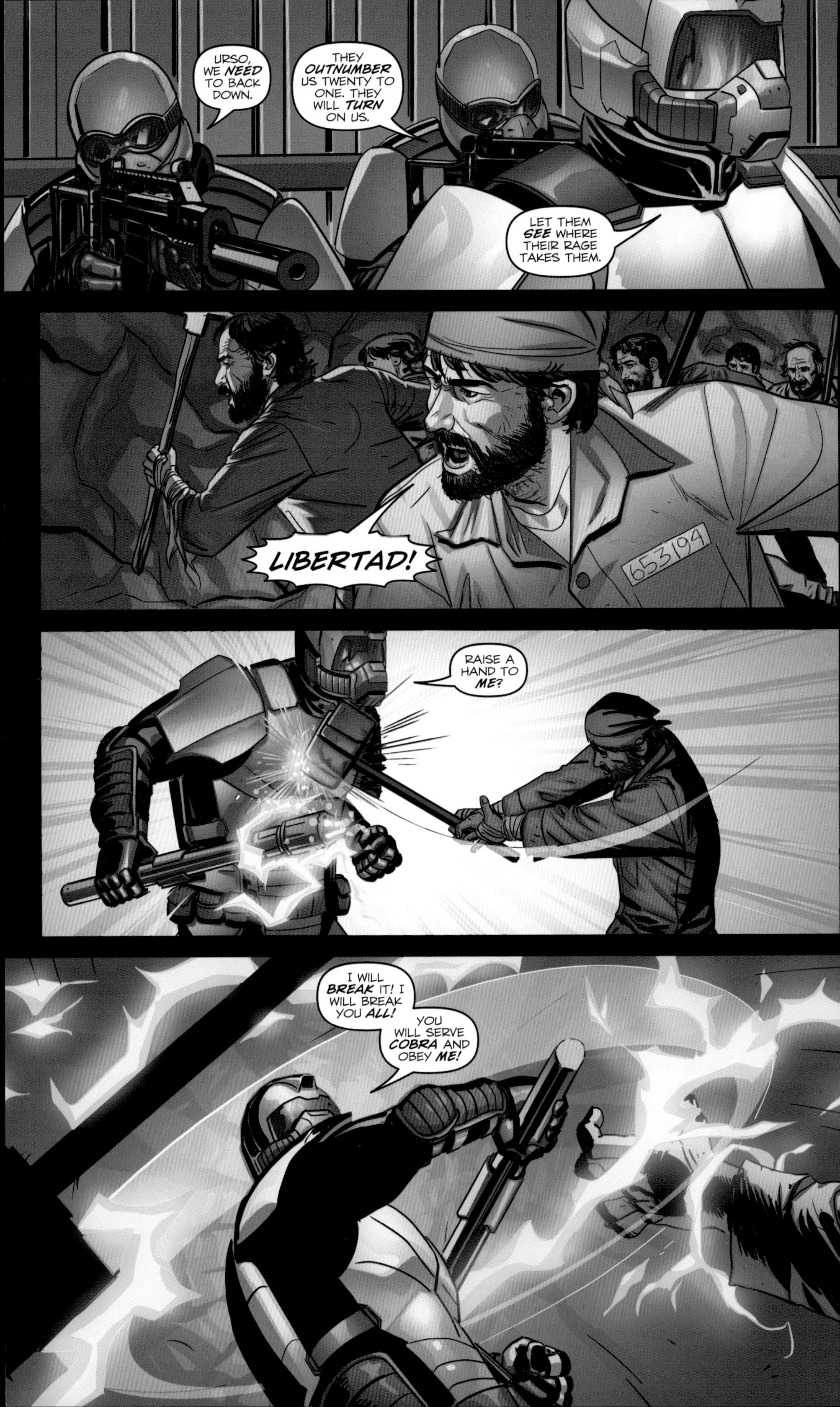
URSO, WE NEED TO BACK DOWN.
THEY OUTNUMBER US TWENTY TO ONE. THEY WILL TURN ON US.
LET THEM SEE WHERE THEIR RAGE TAKES THEM.
LIBERTAD!
653194
RAISE A HAND TO ME?
I WILL BREAK IT! I WILL BREAK YOU ALL!
YOU WILL SERVE COBRA AND OBEY ME!

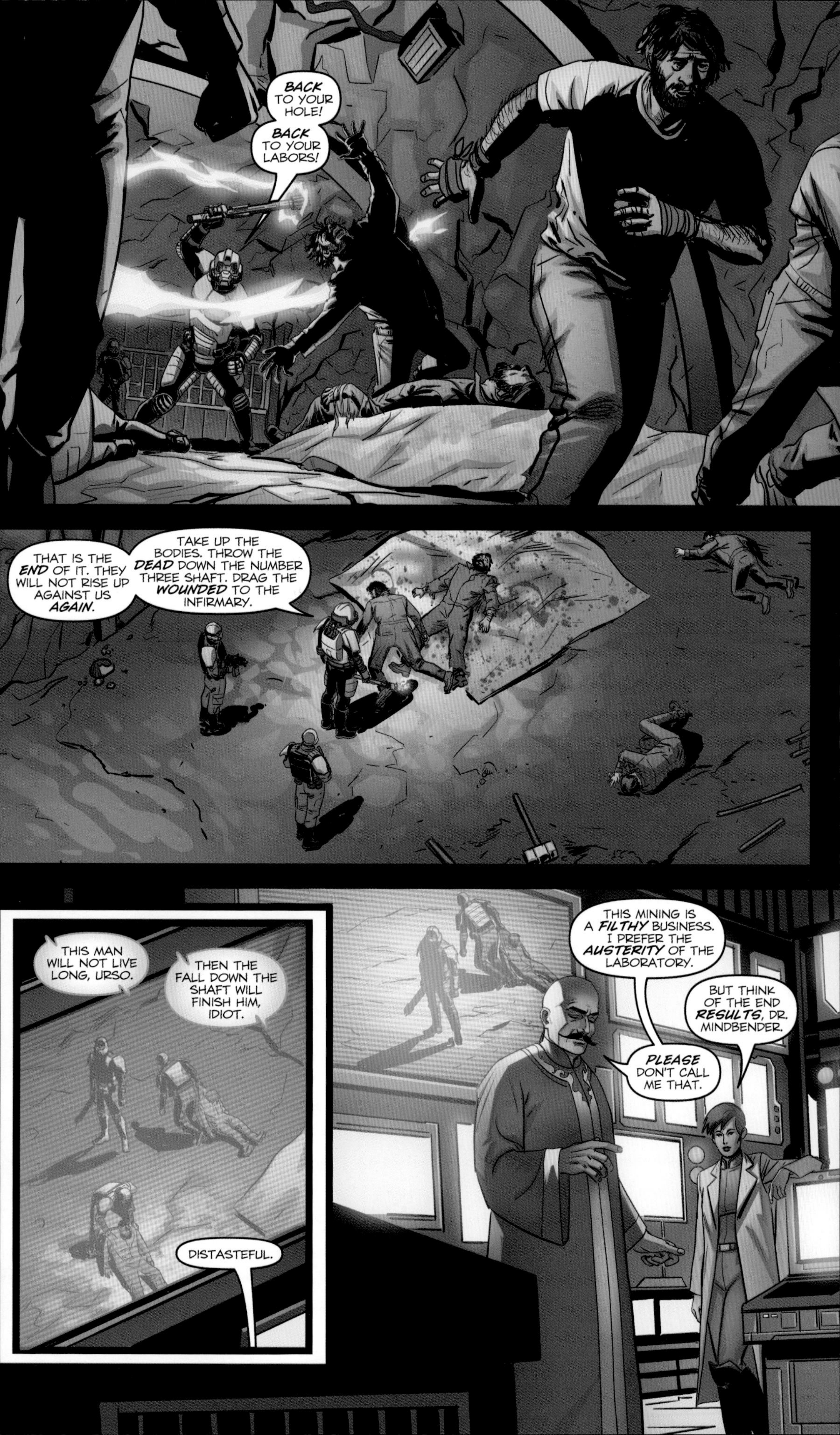
BACK TO YOUR HOLE!
BACK TO YOUR LABORS!
THAT IS THE END OF IT. THEY WILL NOT RISE UP AGAINST US AGAIN.
TAKE UP THE BODIES. THROW THE DEAD DOWN THE NUMBER THREE SHAFT. DRAG THE WOUNDED TO THE INFIRMARY.
THIS MAN WILL NOT LIVE LONG, URSO.
THEN THE FALL DOWN THE SHAFT WILL FINISH HIM, IDIOT.
DISTASTEFUL.
THIS MINING IS A FILTHY BUSINESS. I PREFER THE AUSTERITY OF THE LABORATORY.
BUT THINK OF THE END RESULTS, DR. MINDBENDER.
PLEASE DON'T CALL ME THAT.

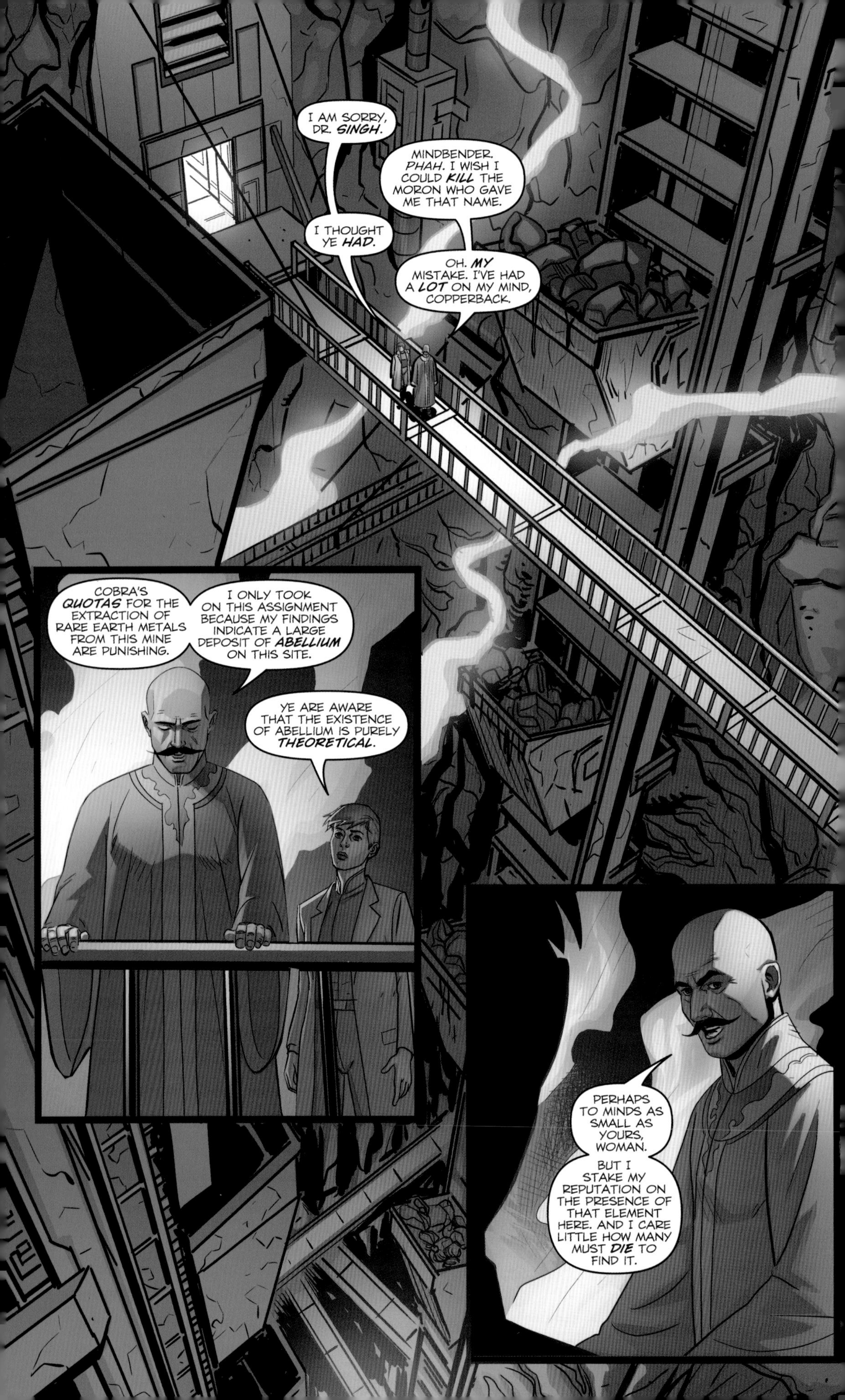
I AM SORRY, DR. SINGH.
MINDBENDER. PHAH. I WISH I COULD KILL THE MORON WHO GAVE ME THAT NAME.
I THOUGHT YE HAD.
OH. MY MISTAKE. I'VE HAD A LOT ON MY MIND, COPPERBACK.
COBRA'S QUOTAS FOR THE EXTRACTION OF RARE EARTH METALS FROM THIS MINE ARE PUNISHING.
I ONLY TOOK ON THIS ASSIGNMENT BECAUSE MY FINDINGS INDICATE A LARGE DEPOSIT OF ABELLIUM ON THIS SITE.
YE ARE AWARE THAT THE EXISTENCE OF ABELLIUM IS PURELY THEORETICAL.
PERHAPS TO MINDS AS SMALL AS YOURS, WOMAN.
BUT I STAKE MY REPUTATION ON THE PRESENCE OF THAT ELEMENT HERE. AND I CARE LITTLE HOW MANY MUST DIE TO FIND IT.

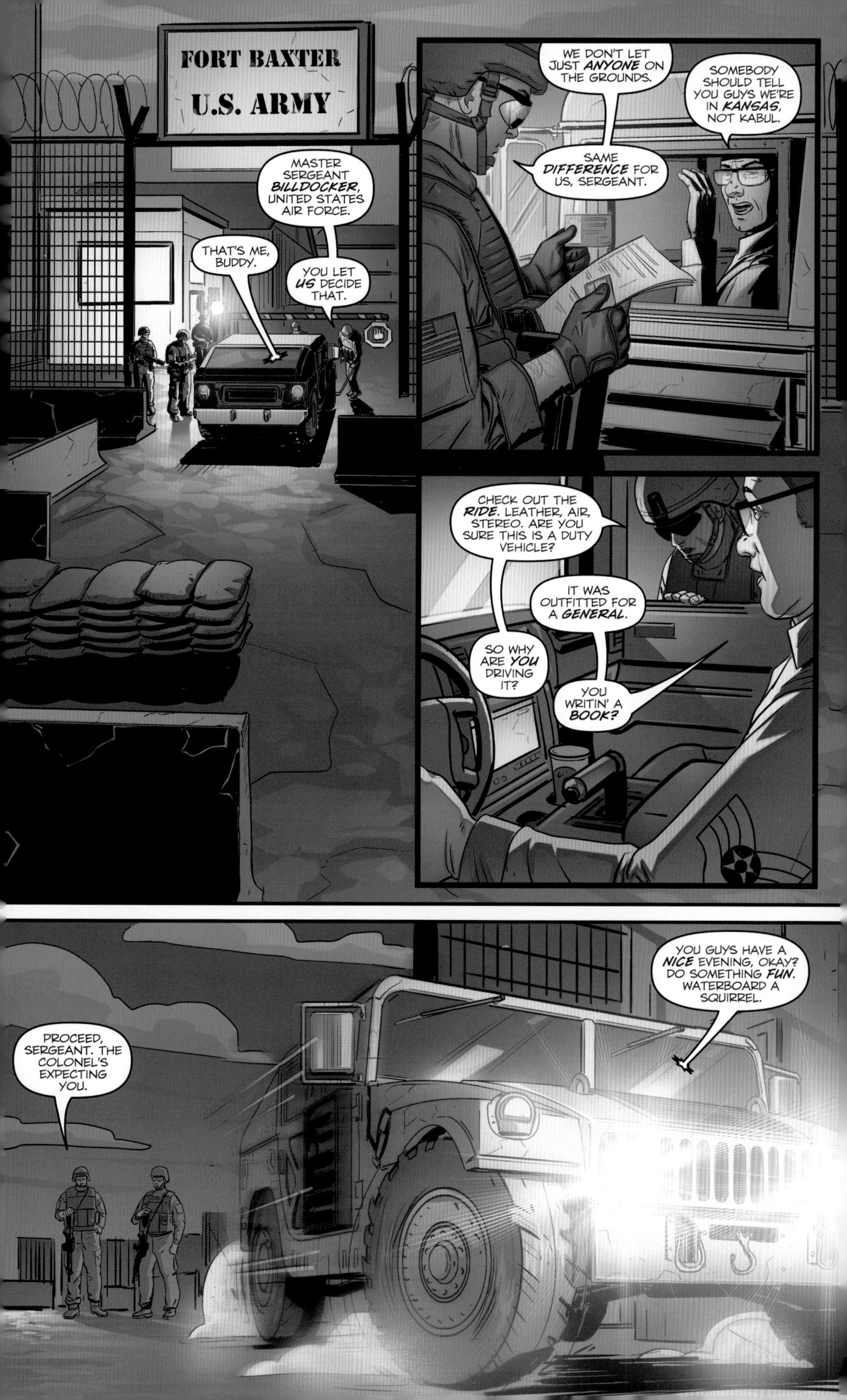
FORT BAXTER
U.S. ARMY
MASTER SERGEANT BILLDOCKER, UNITED STATES AIR FORCE.
THAT'S ME, BUDDY.
YOU LET US DECIDE THAT.
WE DON'T LET JUST ANYONE ON THE GROUNDS.
SOMEBODY SHOULD TELL YOU GUYS WE'RE IN KANSAS, NOT KABUL.
SAME DIFFERENCE FOR US, SERGEANT.
CHECK OUT THE RIDE. LEATHER, AIR, STEREO. ARE YOU SURE THIS IS A DUTY VEHICLE?
IT WAS OUTFITTED FOR A GENERAL.
SO WHY ARE YOU DRIVING IT?
YOU WRITIN' A BOOK?
PROCEED, SERGEANT. THE COLONEL'S EXPECTING YOU.
YOU GUYS HAVE A NICE EVENING, OKAY? DO SOMETHING FUN. WATERBOARD A SQUIRREL.

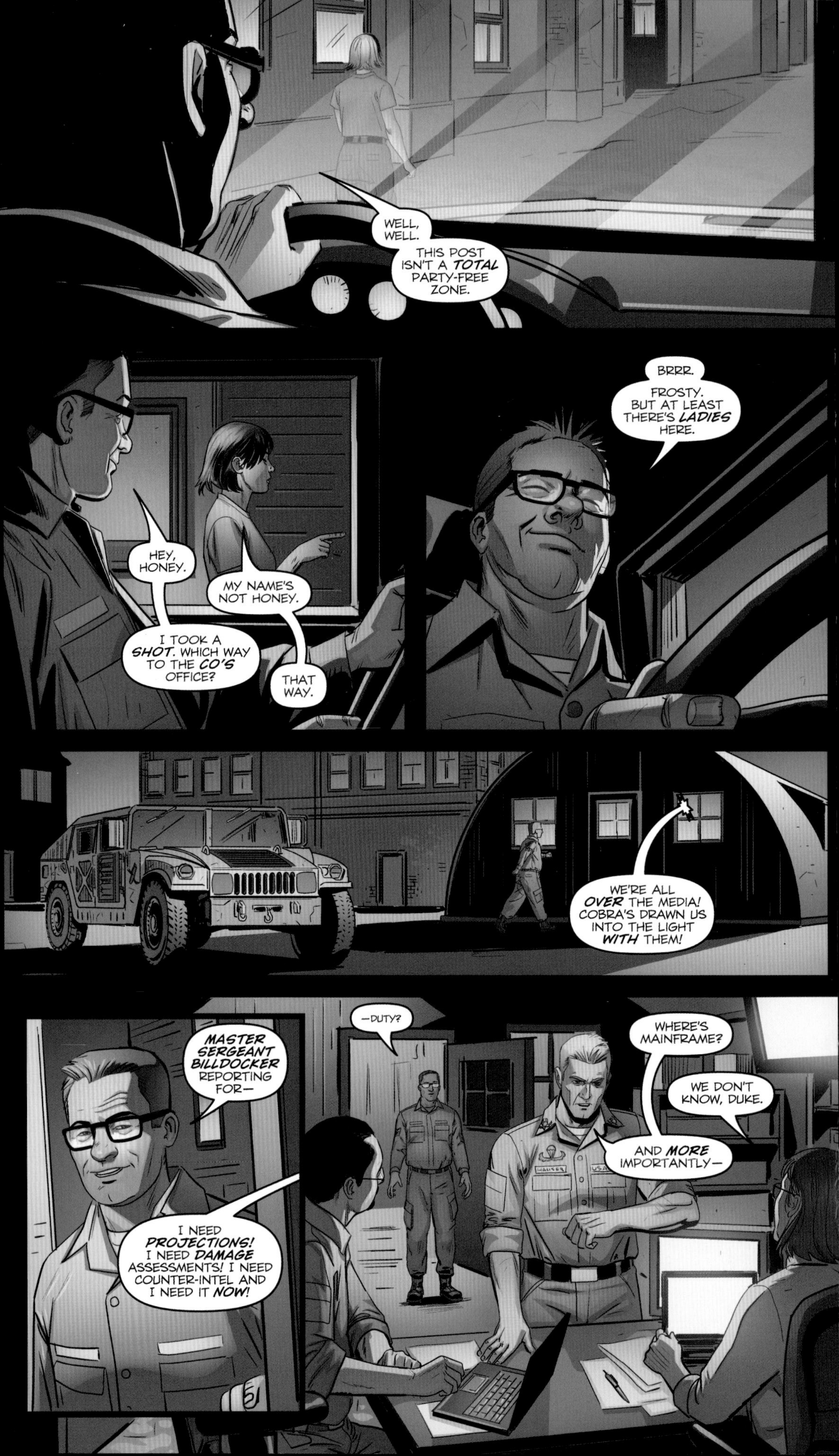
WELL, WELL.
THIS POST ISN'T A TOTAL PARTY-FREE ZONE.
HEY, HONEY.
MY NAME'S NOT HONEY.
I TOOK A SHOT. WHICH WAY TO THE CO'S OFFICE?
THAT WAY.
BRRR.
FROSTY. BUT AT LEAST THERE'S LADIES HERE.
WE'RE ALL OVER THE MEDIA! COBRA'S DRAWN US INTO THE LIGHT WITH THEM!
MASTER SERGEANT BILLDOCKER REPORTING FOR—
—DUTY?
I NEED PROJECTIONS! I NEED DAMAGE ASSESSMENTS! I NEED COUNTER-INTEL AND I NEED IT NOW!
WHERE'S MAINFRAME?
WE DON'T KNOW, DUKE.
AND MORE IMPORTANTLY—

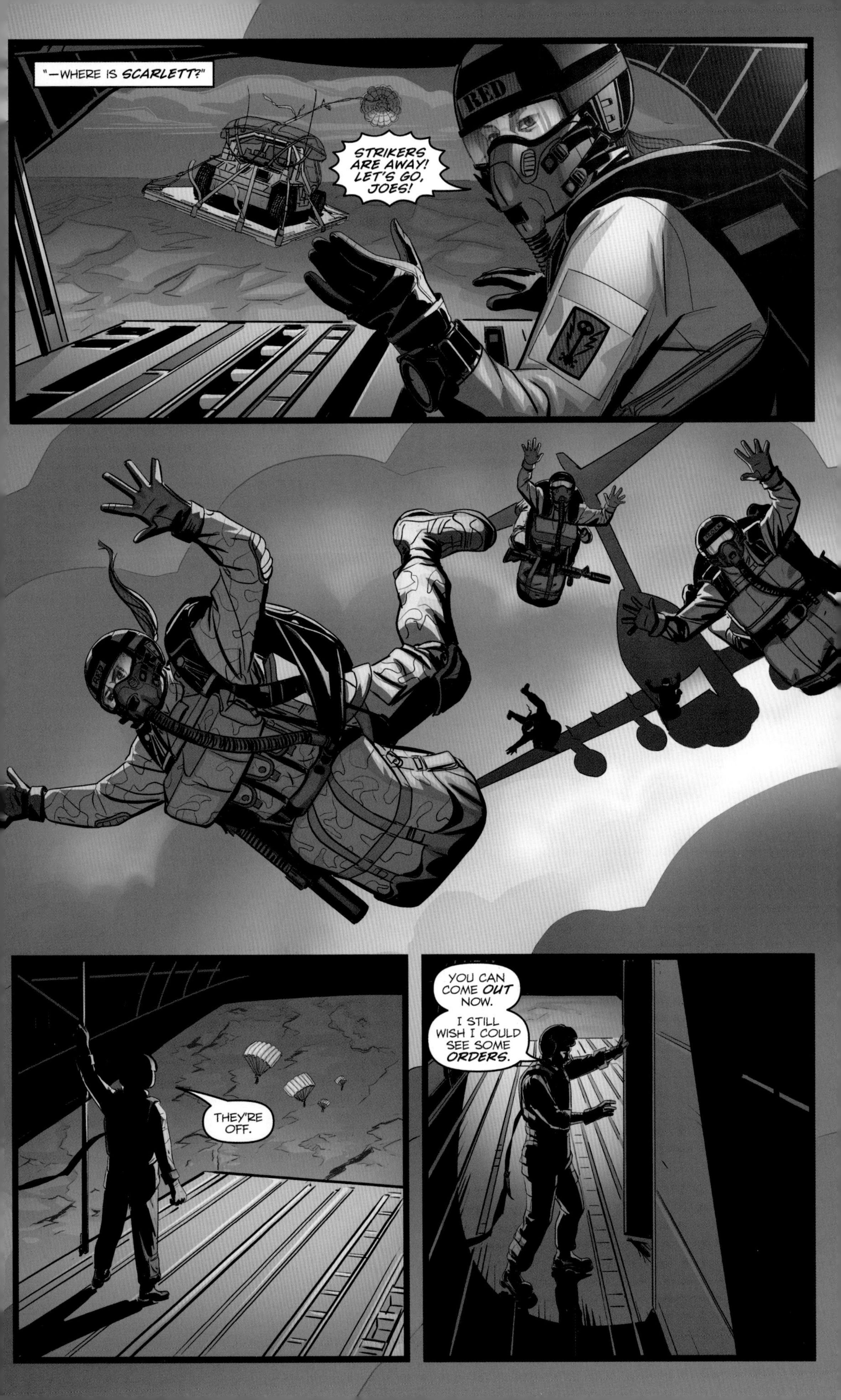
"—WHERE IS SCARLETT?"
STRIKERS ARE AWAY! LET'S GO, JOES!
RED
THEY'RE OFF.
YOU CAN COME OUT NOW.
I STILL WISH I COULD SEE SOME ORDERS.

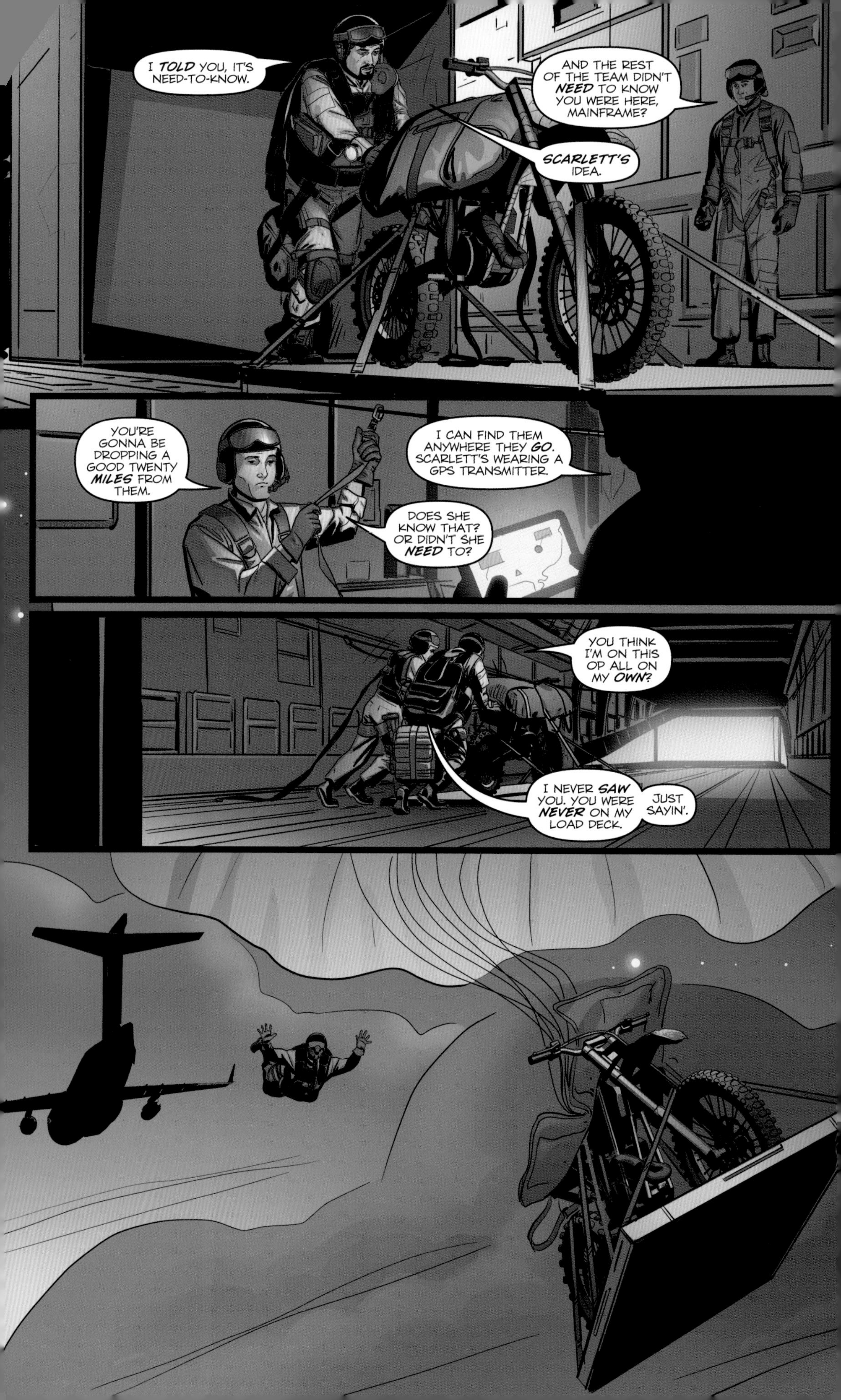
I TOLD YOU, IT'S NEED-TO-KNOW.
AND THE REST OF THE TEAM DIDN'T NEED TO KNOW YOU WERE HERE, MAINFRAME?
SCARLETT'S IDEA.
YOU'RE GONNA BE DROPPING A GOOD TWENTY MILES FROM THEM.
I CAN FIND THEM ANYWHERE THEY GO. SCARLETT'S WEARING A GPS TRANSMITTER.
DOES SHE KNOW THAT? OR DIDN'T SHE NEED TO?
YOU THINK I'M ON THIS OP ALL ON MY OWN?
I NEVER SAW YOU. YOU WERE NEVER ON MY LOAD DECK.
JUST SAYIN'.

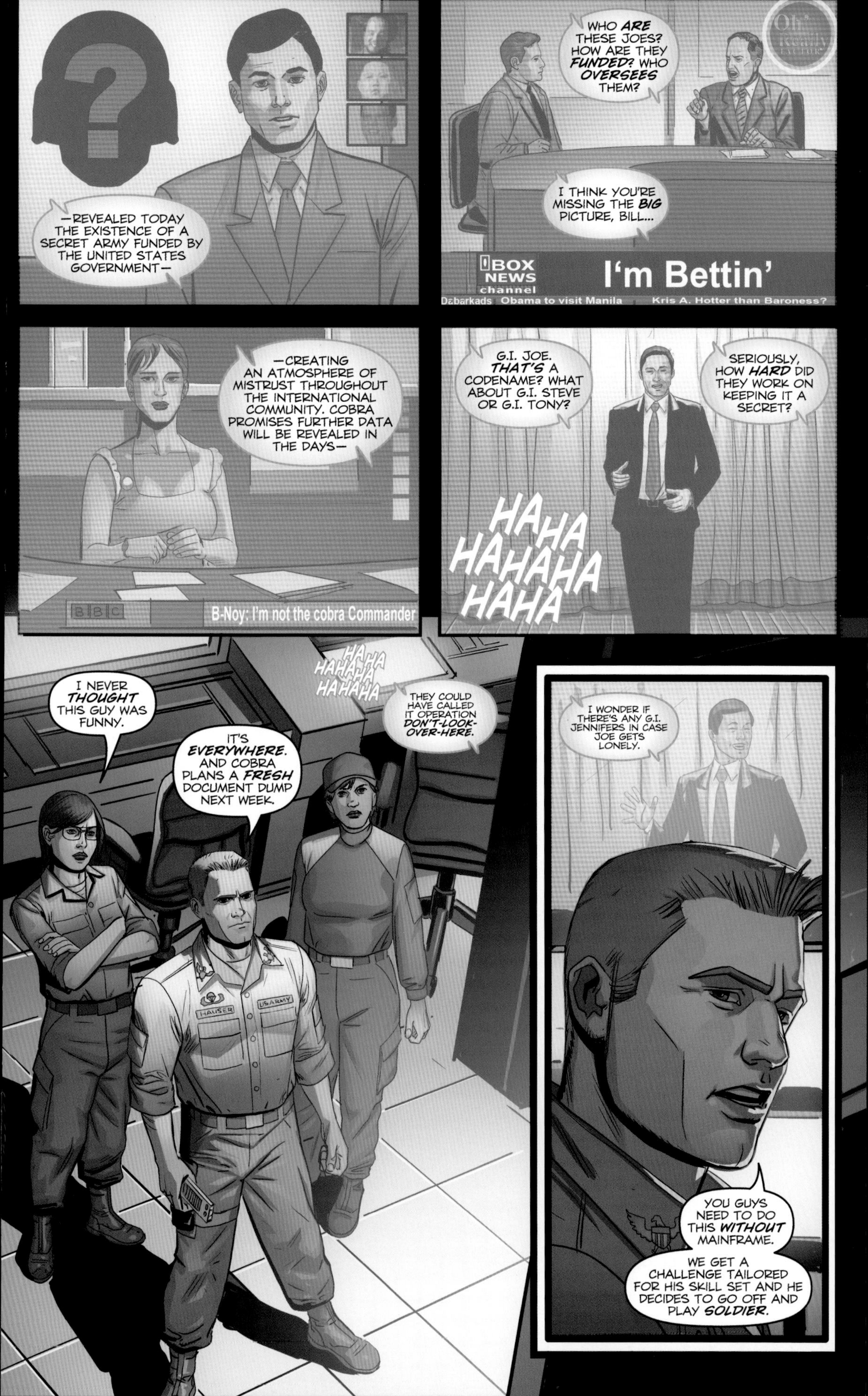
—REVEALED TODAY THE EXISTENCE OF A SECRET ARMY FUNDED BY THE UNITED STATES GOVERNMENT—
WHO ARE THESE JOES? HOW ARE THEY FUNDED? WHO OVERSEES THEM?
I THINK YOU'RE MISSING THE BIG PICTURE, BILL...
BOX NEWS channel
I'm Bettin'
Obama to visit Manila
Kris A. Hotter than Baroness?
—CREATING AN ATMOSPHERE OF MISTRUST THROUGHOUT THE INTERNATIONAL COMMUNITY. COBRA PROMISES FURTHER DATA WILL BE REVEALED IN THE DAYS—
BBC
B-Noy: I'm not the cobra Commander
G.I. JOE. THAT'S A CODENAME? WHAT ABOUT G.I. STEVE OR G.I. TONY?
SERIOUSLY, HOW HARD DID THEY WORK ON KEEPING IT A SECRET?
HAHA HAHAHA HAHA
HAHA HAHAHA HAHAHA
I NEVER THOUGHT THIS GUY WAS FUNNY.
IT'S EVERYWHERE. AND COBRA PLANS A FRESH DOCUMENT DUMP NEXT WEEK.
THEY COULD HAVE CALLED IT OPERATION DON'T-LOOK-OVER-HERE.
HAUSER
US ARMY
I WONDER IF THERE'S ANY G.I. JENNIFERS IN CASE JOE GETS LONELY.
YOU GUYS NEED TO DO THIS WITHOUT MAINFRAME.
WE GET A CHALLENGE TAILORED FOR HIS SKILL SET AND HE DECIDES TO GO OFF AND PLAY SOLDIER.

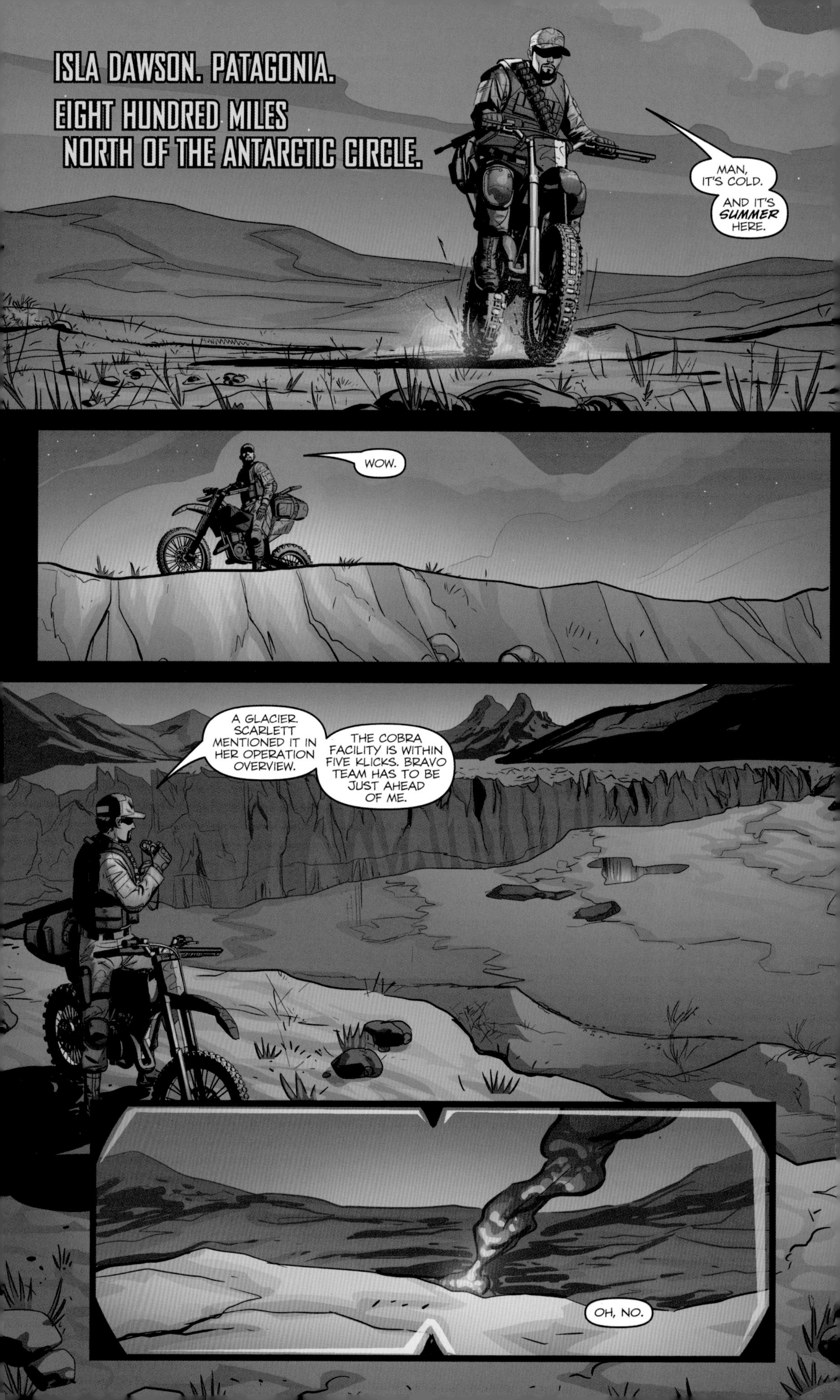
ISLA DAWSON. PATAGONIA.
EIGHT HUNDRED MILES NORTH OF THE ANTARCTIC CIRCLE.
MAN, IT'S COLD.
AND IT'S SUMMER HERE.
WOW.
A GLACIER. SCARLETT MENTIONED IT IN HER OPERATION OVERVIEW.
THE COBRA FACILITY IS WITHIN FIVE KLICKS. BRAVO TEAM HAS TO BE JUST AHEAD OF ME.
OH, NO.

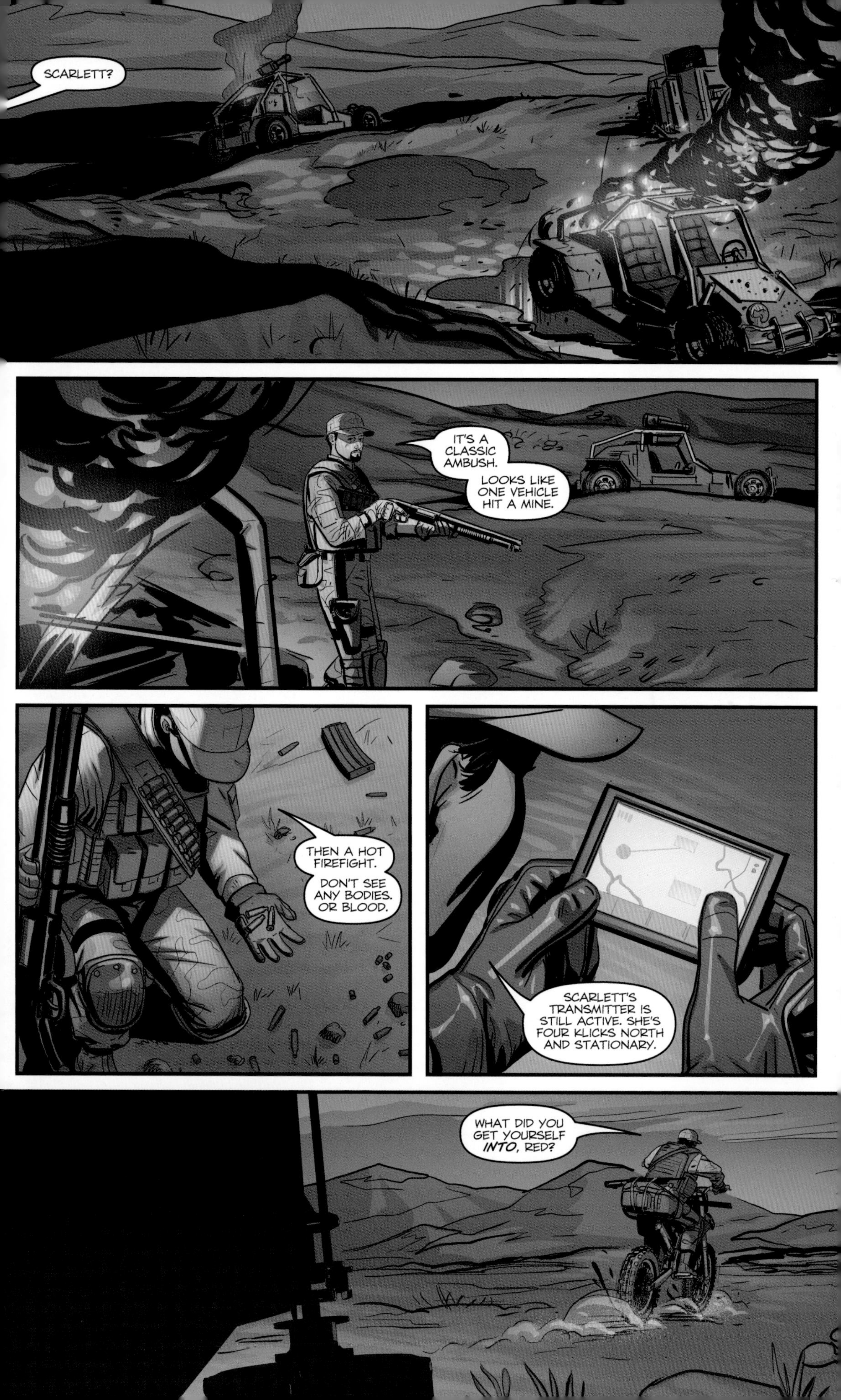
SCARLETT?
IT'S A CLASSIC AMBUSH.
LOOKS LIKE ONE VEHICLE HIT A MINE.
THEN A HOT FIREFIGHT.
DON'T SEE ANY BODIES. OR BLOOD.
SCARLETT'S TRANSMITTER IS STILL ACTIVE. SHE'S FOUR KLICKS NORTH AND STATIONARY.
WHAT DID YOU GET YOURSELF *INTO*, RED?

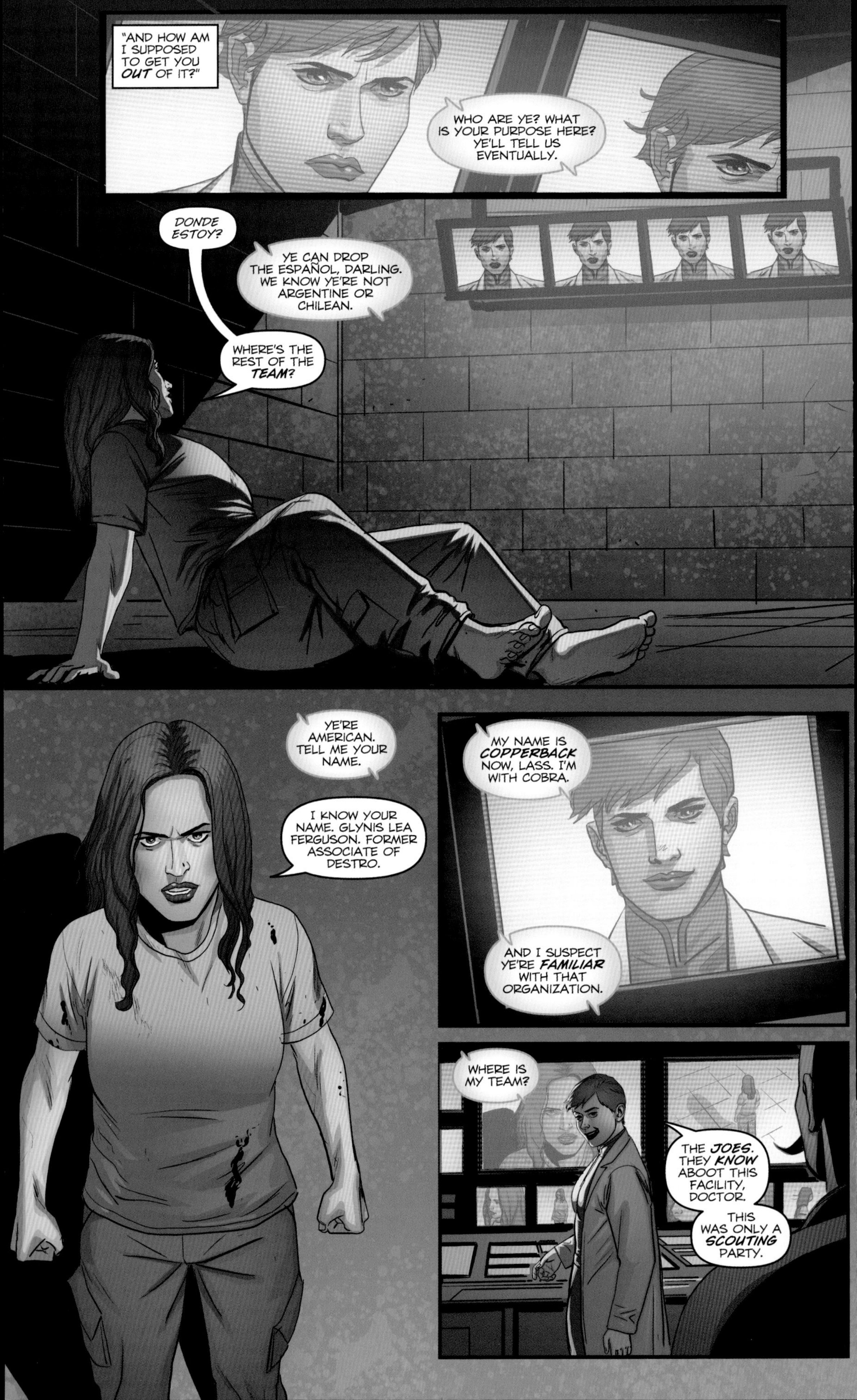
"AND HOW AM I SUPPOSED TO GET YOU *OUT* OF IT?"
WHO ARE YE? WHAT IS YOUR PURPOSE HERE? YE'LL TELL US EVENTUALLY.
DONDE ESTOY?
YE CAN DROP THE ESPAÑOL, DARLING. WE KNOW YE'RE NOT ARGENTINE OR CHILEAN.
WHERE'S THE REST OF THE ***TEAM***?
YE'RE AMERICAN. TELL ME YOUR NAME.
I KNOW YOUR NAME. GLYNIS LEA FERGUSON. FORMER ASSOCIATE OF DESTRO.
MY NAME IS ***COPPERBACK*** NOW, LASS. I'M WITH COBRA.
AND I SUSPECT YE'RE ***FAMILIAR*** WITH THAT ORGANIZATION.
WHERE IS MY TEAM?
THE ***JOES***. THEY ***KNOW*** ABOOT THIS FACILITY, DOCTOR.
THIS WAS ONLY A ***SCOUTING*** PARTY.

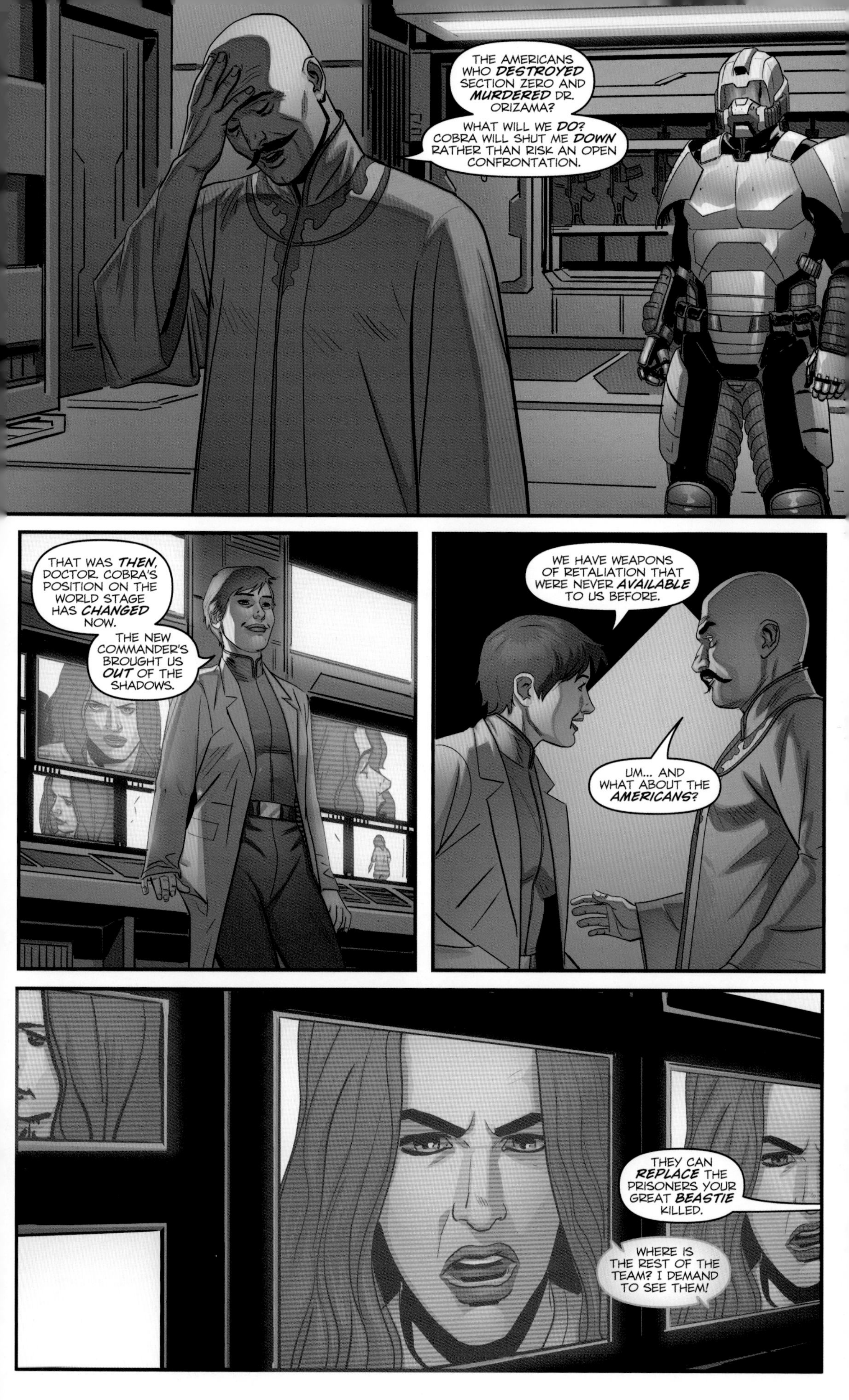
THE AMERICANS WHO DESTROYED SECTION ZERO AND MURDERED DR. ORIZAMA?
WHAT WILL WE DO? COBRA WILL SHUT ME DOWN RATHER THAN RISK AN OPEN CONFRONTATION.
THAT WAS THEN, DOCTOR. COBRA'S POSITION ON THE WORLD STAGE HAS CHANGED NOW.
THE NEW COMMANDER'S BROUGHT US OUT OF THE SHADOWS.
WE HAVE WEAPONS OF RETALIATION THAT WERE NEVER AVAILABLE TO US BEFORE.
UM... AND WHAT ABOUT THE AMERICANS?
THEY CAN REPLACE THE PRISONERS YOUR GREAT BEASTIE KILLED.
WHERE IS THE REST OF THE TEAM? I DEMAND TO SEE THEM!

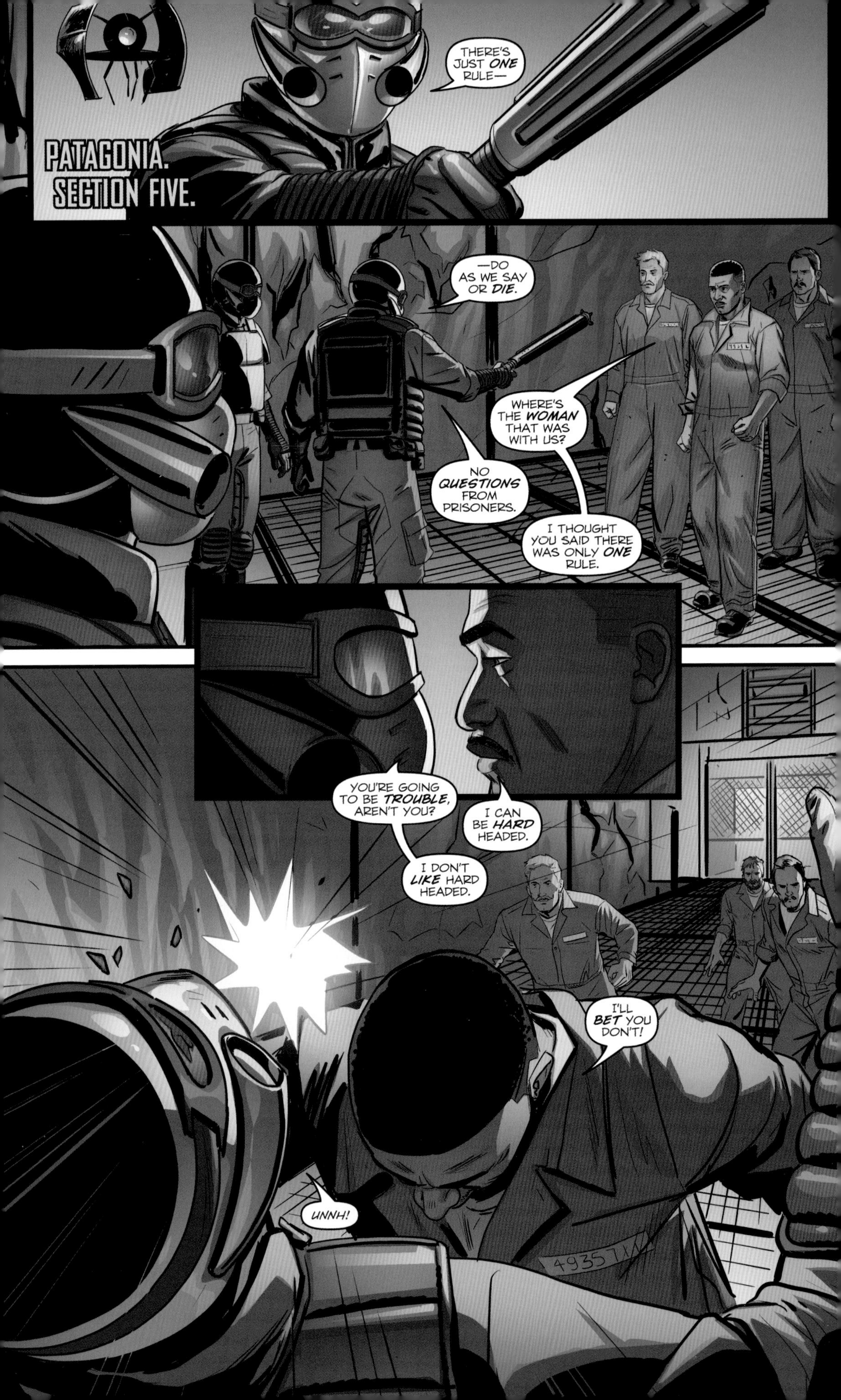
THERE'S JUST ONE RULE—
PATAGONIA. SECTION FIVE.
—DO AS WE SAY OR DIE.
WHERE'S THE WOMAN THAT WAS WITH US?
NO QUESTIONS FROM PRISONERS.
I THOUGHT YOU SAID THERE WAS ONLY ONE RULE.
YOU'RE GOING TO BE TROUBLE, AREN'T YOU?
I CAN BE HARD HEADED.
I DON'T LIKE HARD HEADED.
I'LL BET YOU DON'T!
UNNH!
4935

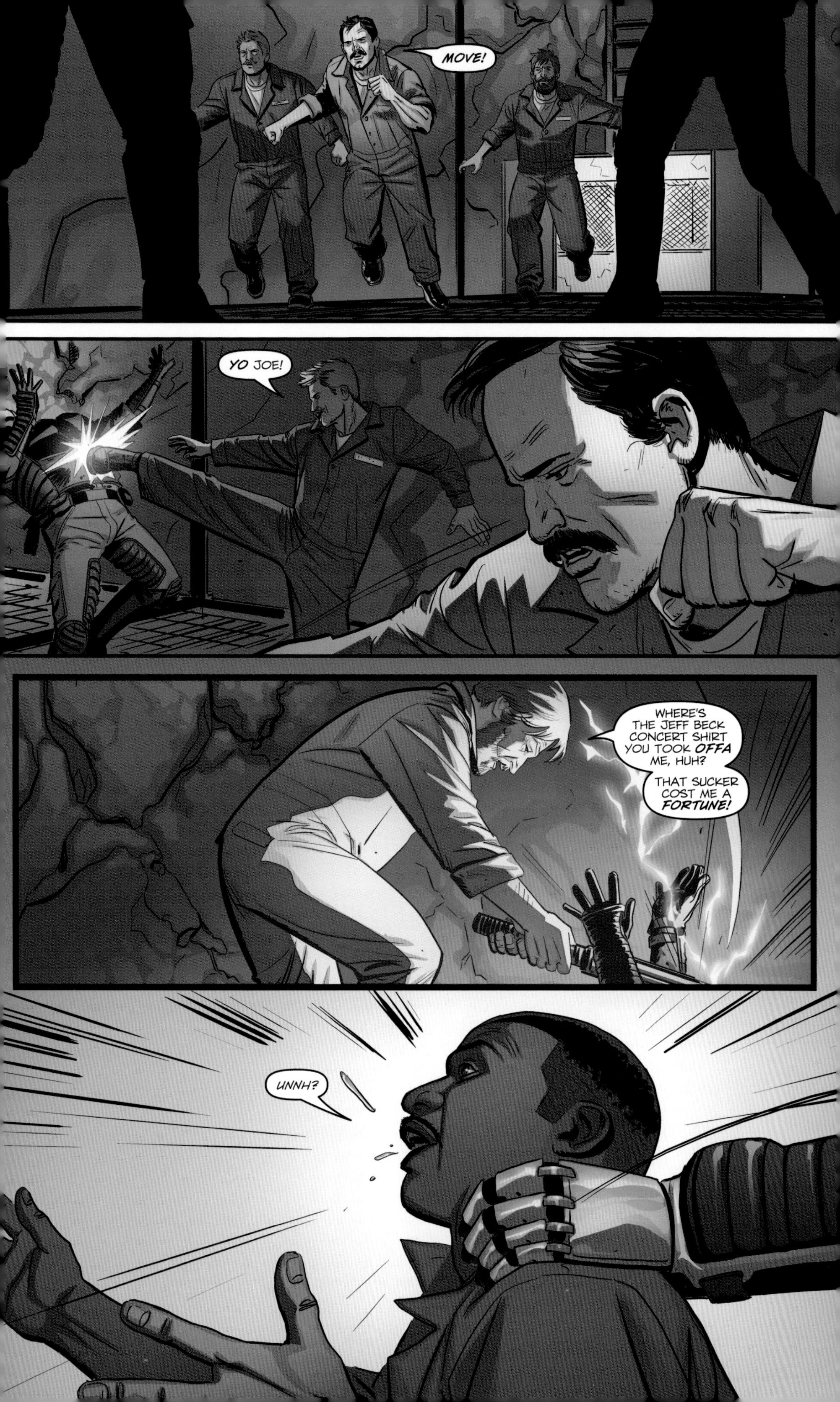
MOVE!
YO JOE!
WHERE'S THE JEFF BECK CONCERT SHIRT YOU TOOK OFFA ME, HUH?
THAT SUCKER COST ME A FORTUNE!
UNNH?

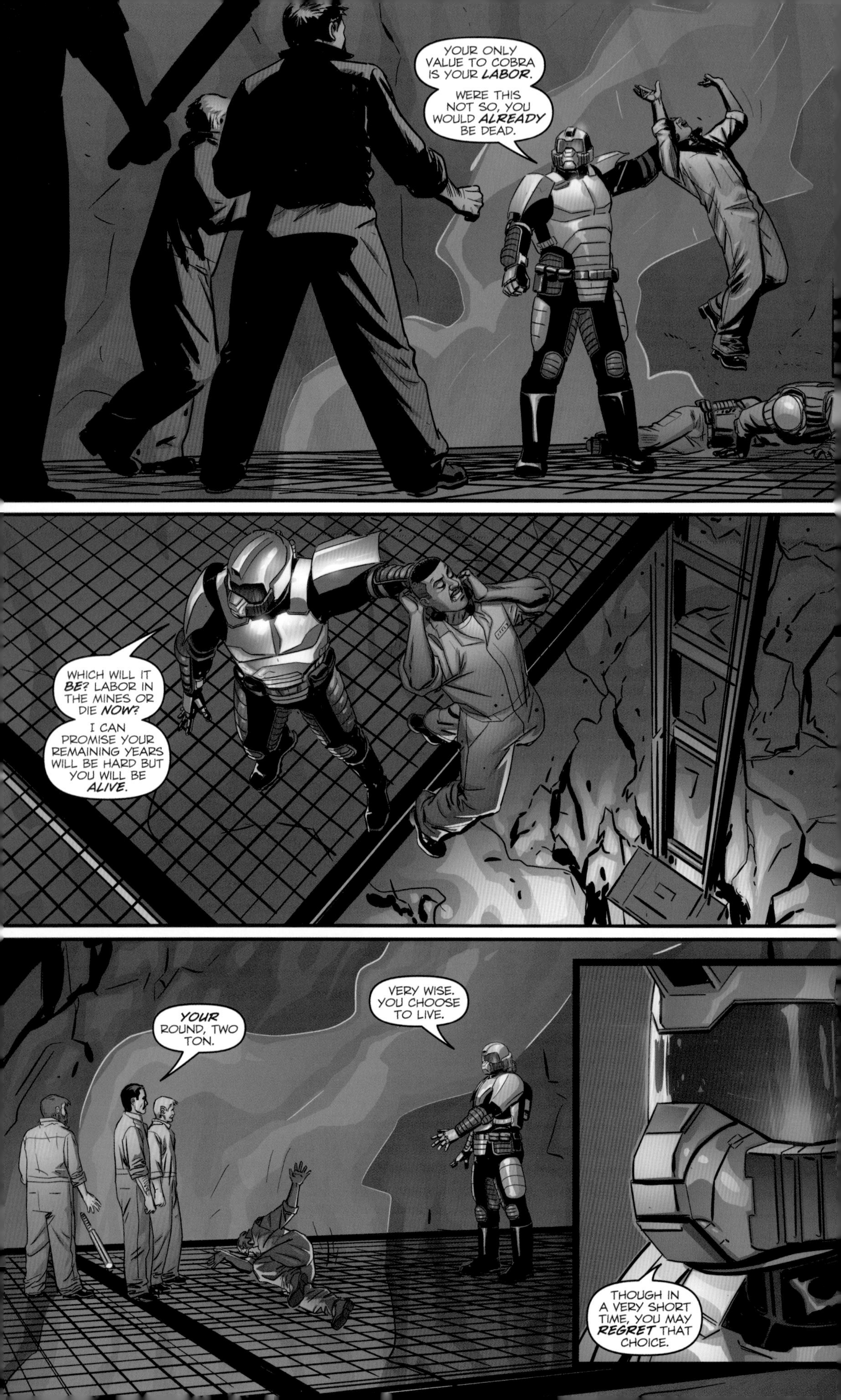
YOUR ONLY VALUE TO COBRA IS YOUR LABOR.
WERE THIS NOT SO, YOU WOULD ALREADY BE DEAD.
WHICH WILL IT BE? LABOR IN THE MINES OR DIE NOW?
I CAN PROMISE YOUR REMAINING YEARS WILL BE HARD BUT YOU WILL BE ALIVE.
YOUR ROUND, TWO TON.
VERY WISE. YOU CHOOSE TO LIVE.
THOUGH IN A VERY SHORT TIME, YOU MAY REGRET THAT CHOICE.

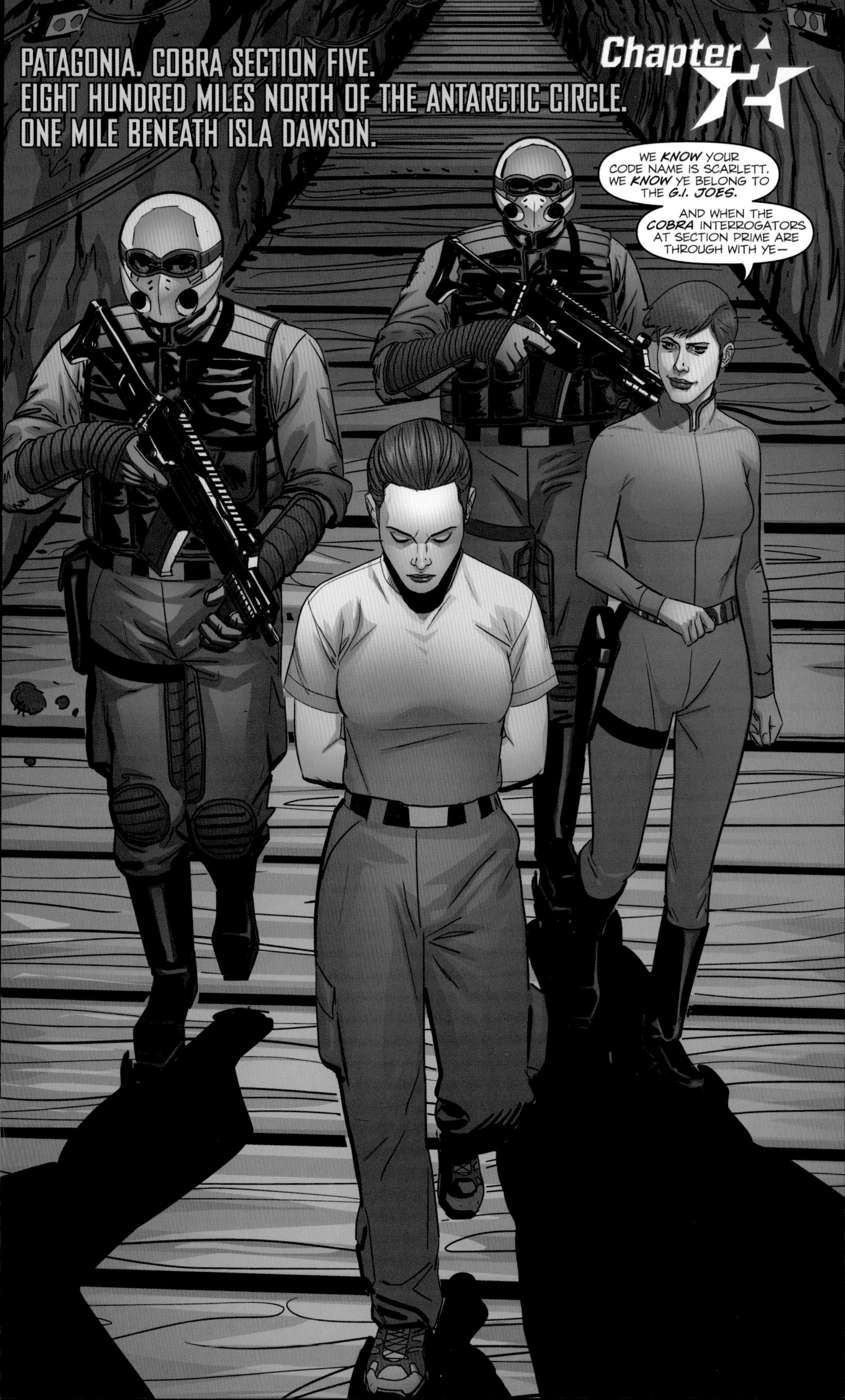
PATAGONIA. COBRA SECTION FIVE.
EIGHT HUNDRED MILES NORTH OF THE ANTARCTIC CIRCLE.
ONE MILE BENEATH ISLA DAWSON.
Chapter
WE KNOW YOUR CODE NAME IS SCARLETT. WE KNOW YE BELONG TO THE G.I. JOES.
AND WHEN THE COBRA INTERROGATORS AT SECTION PRIME ARE THROUGH WITH YE—

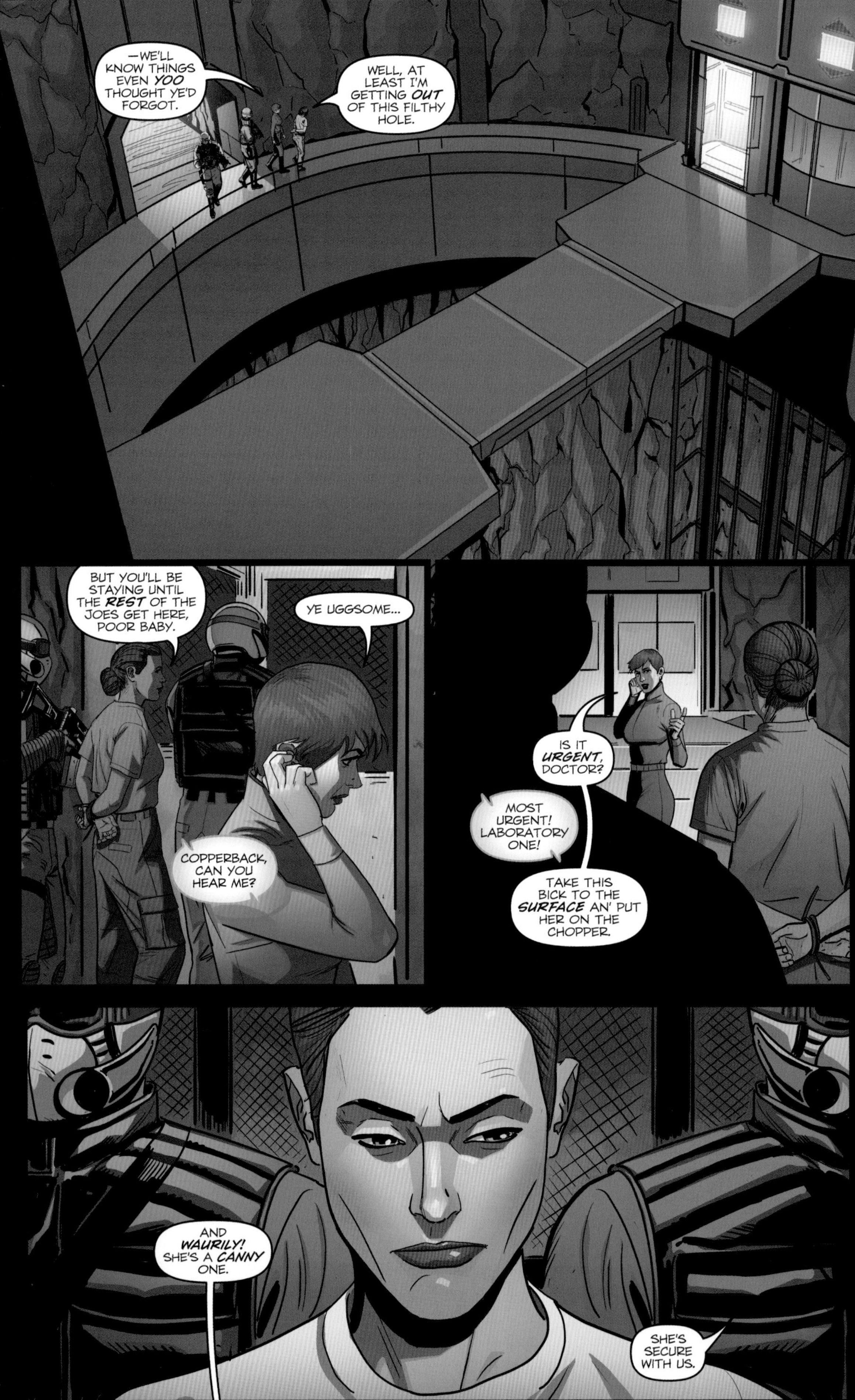
—WE'LL KNOW THINGS EVEN YOO THOUGHT YE'D FORGOT.
WELL, AT LEAST I'M GETTING OUT OF THIS FILTHY HOLE.
BUT YOU'LL BE STAYING UNTIL THE REST OF THE JOES GET HERE, POOR BABY.
YE UGGSOME...
COPPERBACK, CAN YOU HEAR ME?
IS IT URGENT, DOCTOR?
MOST URGENT! LABORATORY ONE!
TAKE THIS BICK TO THE SURFACE AN' PUT HER ON THE CHOPPER.
AND WAURILY! SHE'S A CANNY ONE.
SHE'S SECURE WITH US.

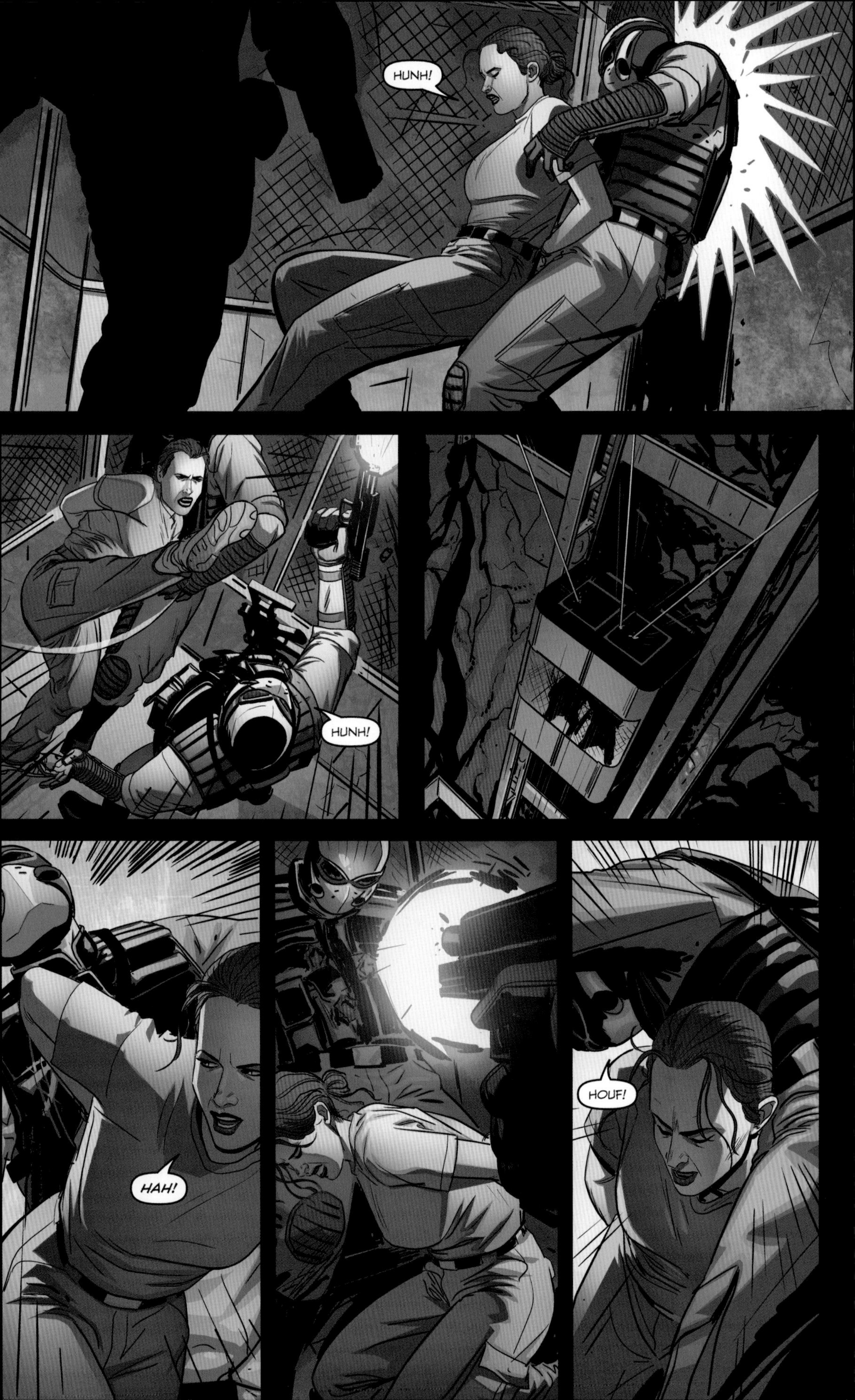
HUNH!
HUNH!
HAH!
HOUF!

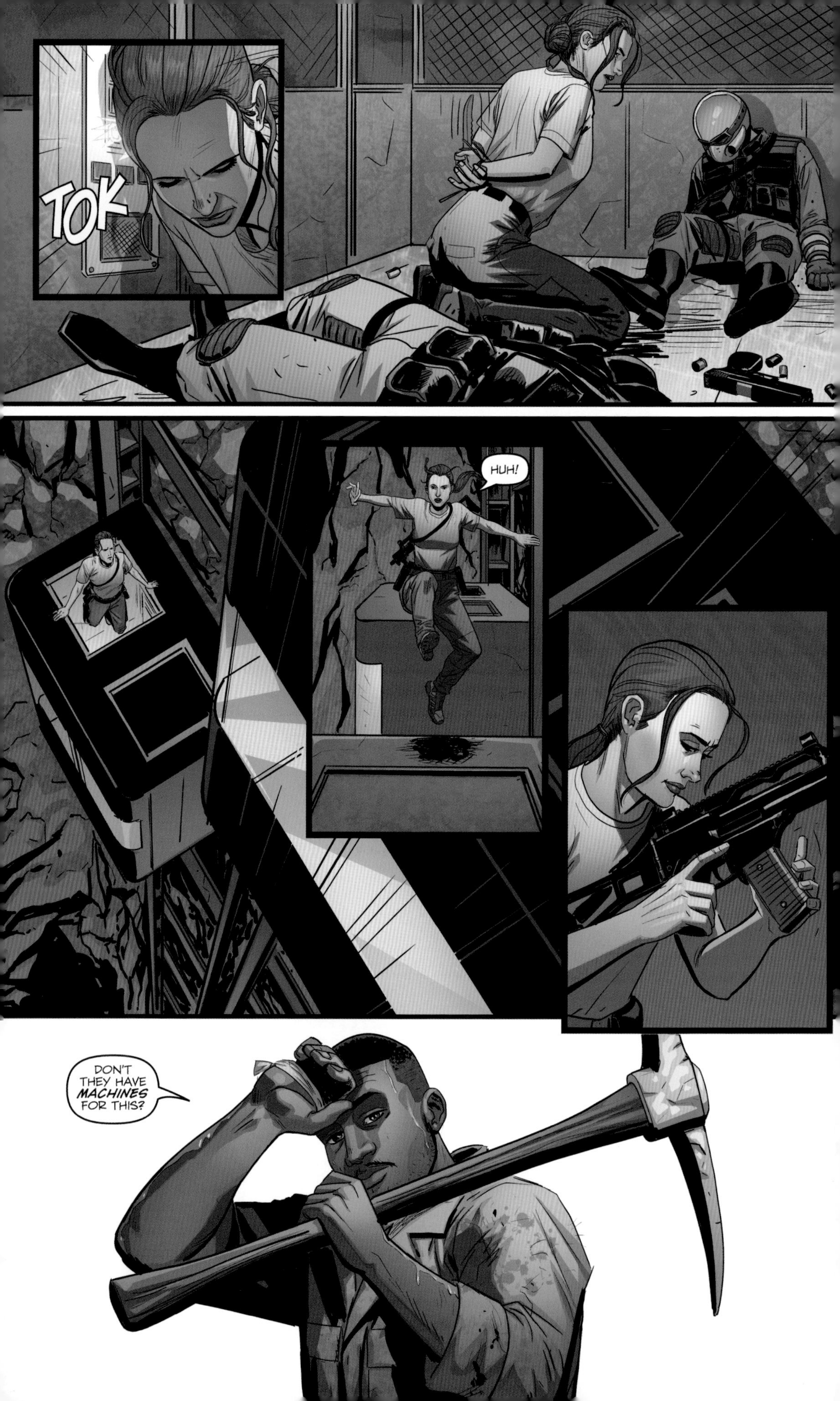
TOK
HUH!
DON'T THEY HAVE MACHINES FOR THIS?

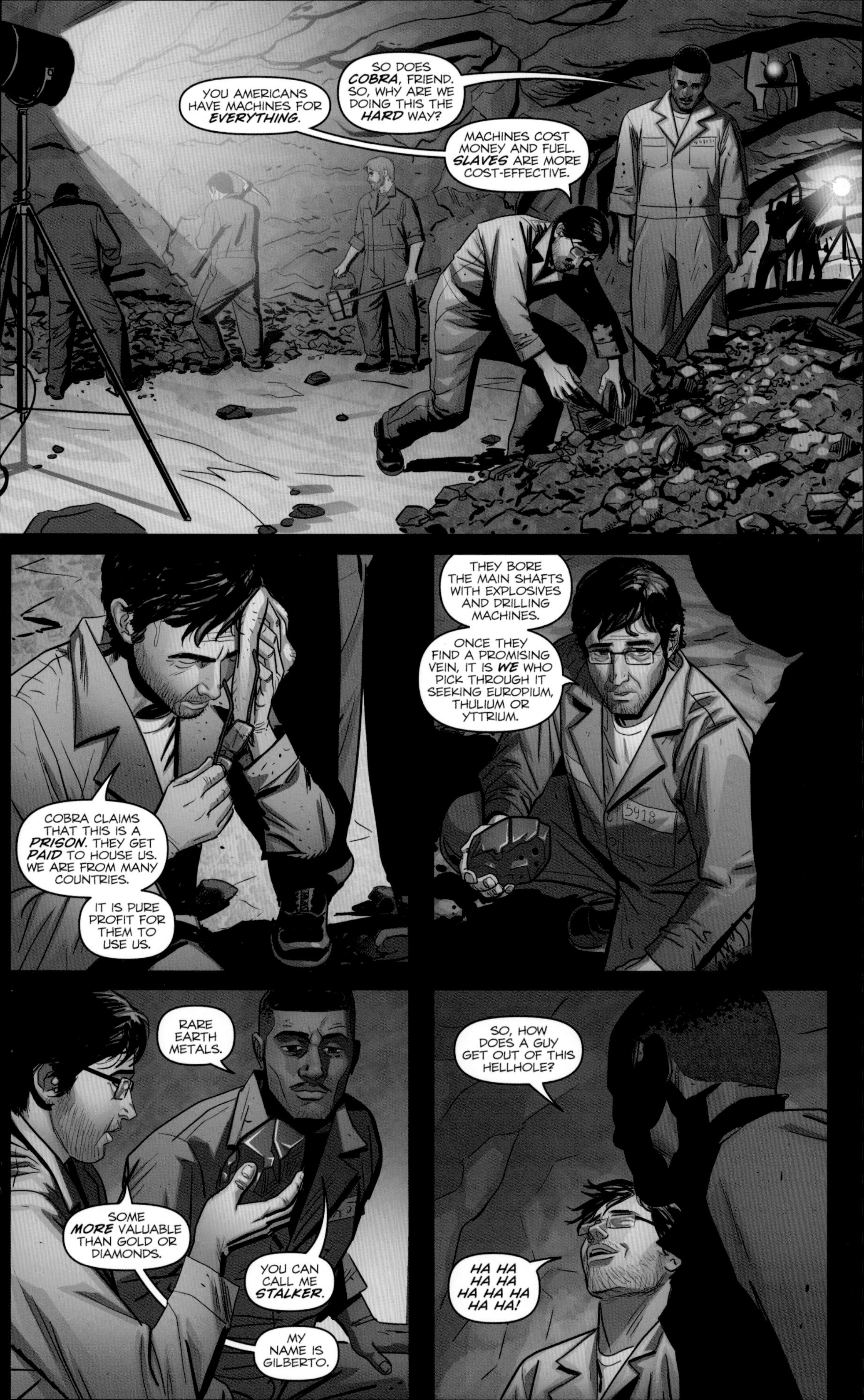

YOU AMERICANS HAVE MACHINES FOR EVERYTHING.
SO DOES COBRA, FRIEND. SO, WHY ARE WE DOING THIS THE HARD WAY?
MACHINES COST MONEY AND FUEL. SLAVES ARE MORE COST-EFFECTIVE.
COBRA CLAIMS THAT THIS IS A PRISON. THEY GET PAID TO HOUSE US. WE ARE FROM MANY COUNTRIES.
IT IS PURE PROFIT FOR THEM TO USE US.
THEY BORE THE MAIN SHAFTS WITH EXPLOSIVES AND DRILLING MACHINES.
ONCE THEY FIND A PROMISING VEIN, IT IS WE WHO PICK THROUGH IT SEEKING EUROPIUM, THULIUM OR YTTRIUM.
5918
RARE EARTH METALS.
SOME MORE VALUABLE THAN GOLD OR DIAMONDS.
YOU CAN CALL ME STALKER.
MY NAME IS GILBERTO.
SO, HOW DOES A GUY GET OUT OF THIS HELLHOLE?
HA HA HA HA HA HA HA HA HA!

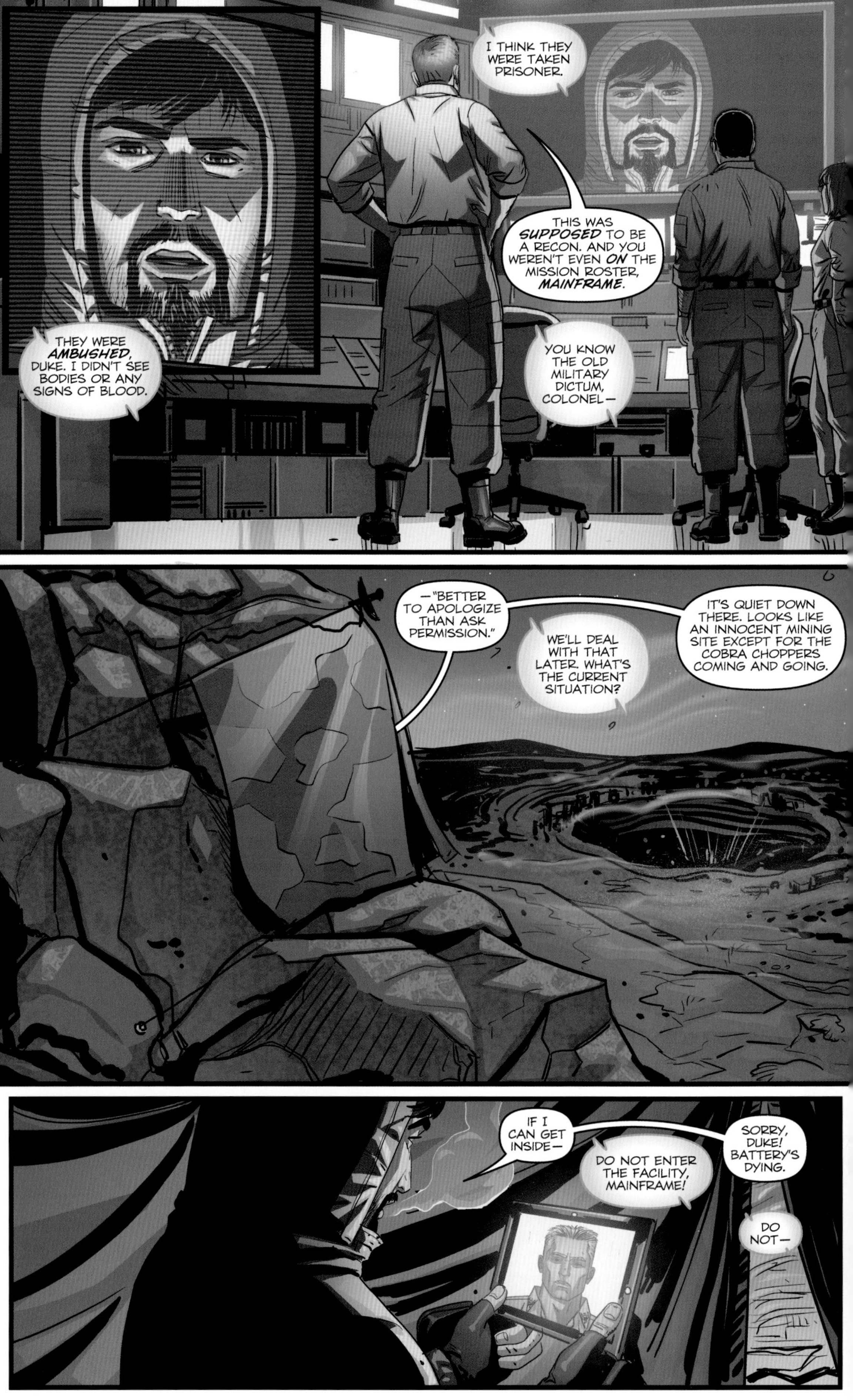
I THINK THEY WERE TAKEN PRISONER.
THEY WERE AMBUSHED, DUKE. I DIDN'T SEE BODIES OR ANY SIGNS OF BLOOD.
THIS WAS SUPPOSED TO BE A RECON. AND YOU WEREN'T EVEN ON THE MISSION ROSTER, MAINFRAME.
YOU KNOW THE OLD MILITARY DICTUM, COLONEL—
—"BETTER TO APOLOGIZE THAN ASK PERMISSION."
WE'LL DEAL WITH THAT LATER. WHAT'S THE CURRENT SITUATION?
IT'S QUIET DOWN THERE. LOOKS LIKE AN INNOCENT MINING SITE EXCEPT FOR THE COBRA CHOPPERS COMING AND GOING.
IF I CAN GET INSIDE—
DO NOT ENTER THE FACILITY, MAINFRAME!
SORRY, DUKE! BATTERY'S DYING.
DO NOT—

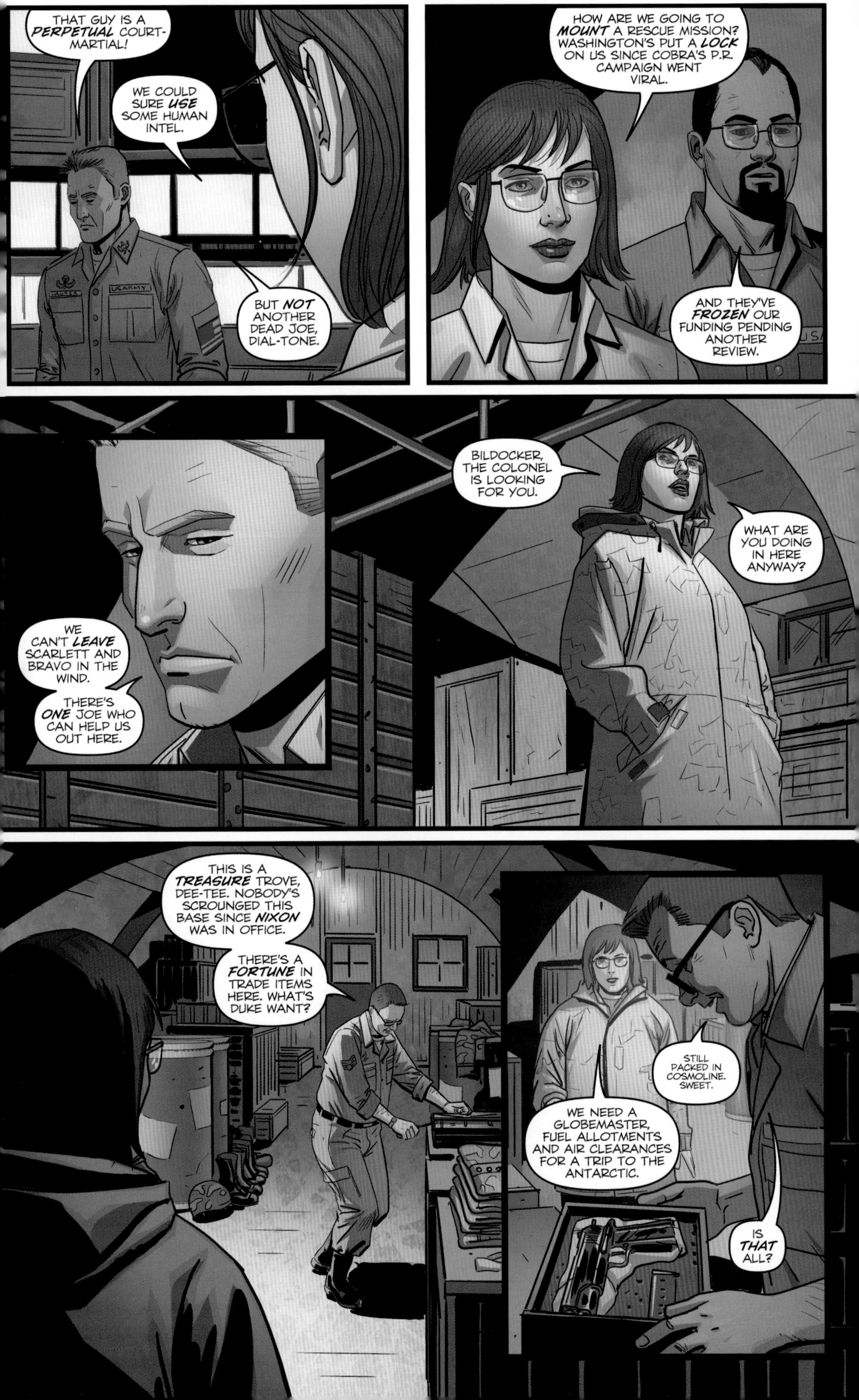

THAT GUY IS A *PERPETUAL* COURT-MARTIAL!
WE COULD SURE *USE* SOME HUMAN INTEL.
BUT *NOT* ANOTHER DEAD JOE, DIAL-TONE.
HOW ARE WE GOING TO *MOUNT* A RESCUE MISSION? WASHINGTON'S PUT A *LOCK* ON US SINCE COBRA'S P.R. CAMPAIGN WENT VIRAL.
AND THEY'VE *FROZEN* OUR FUNDING PENDING ANOTHER REVIEW.
WE CAN'T *LEAVE* SCARLETT AND BRAVO IN THE WIND.
THERE'S *ONE* JOE WHO CAN HELP US OUT HERE.
BILDOCKER, THE COLONEL IS LOOKING FOR YOU.
WHAT ARE YOU DOING IN HERE ANYWAY?
THIS IS A *TREASURE* TROVE, DEE-TEE. NOBODY'S SCROUNGED THIS BASE SINCE *NIXON* WAS IN OFFICE.
THERE'S A *FORTUNE* IN TRADE ITEMS HERE. WHAT'S DUKE WANT?
STILL PACKED IN COSMOLINE. SWEET.
WE NEED A GLOBEMASTER, FUEL ALLOTMENTS AND AIR CLEARANCES FOR A TRIP TO THE ANTARCTIC.
IS *THAT* ALL?

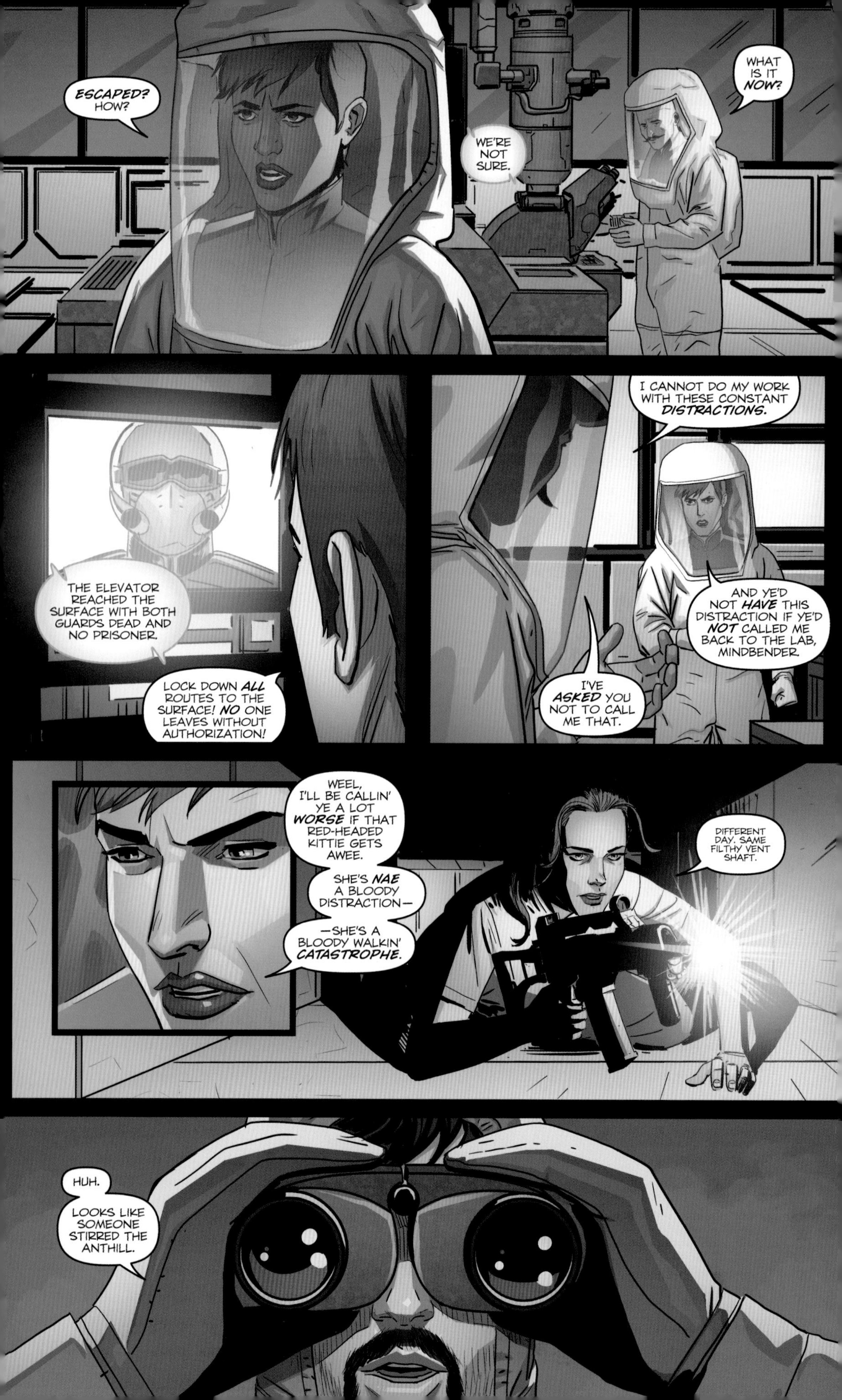

ESCAPED? HOW?
WE'RE NOT SURE.
WHAT IS IT NOW?
THE ELEVATOR REACHED THE SURFACE WITH BOTH GUARDS DEAD AND NO PRISONER.
LOCK DOWN ALL ROUTES TO THE SURFACE! NO ONE LEAVES WITHOUT AUTHORIZATION!
I CANNOT DO MY WORK WITH THESE CONSTANT DISTRACTIONS.
AND YE'D NOT HAVE THIS DISTRACTION IF YE'D NOT CALLED ME BACK TO THE LAB, MINDBENDER.
I'VE ASKED YOU NOT TO CALL ME THAT.
WEEL, I'LL BE CALLIN' YE A LOT WORSE IF THAT RED-HEADED KITTIE GETS AWEE.
SHE'S NAE A BLOODY DISTRACTION—
—SHE'S A BLOODY WALKIN' CATASTROPHE.
DIFFERENT DAY. SAME FILTHY VENT SHAFT.
HUH.
LOOKS LIKE SOMEONE STIRRED THE ANTHILL.

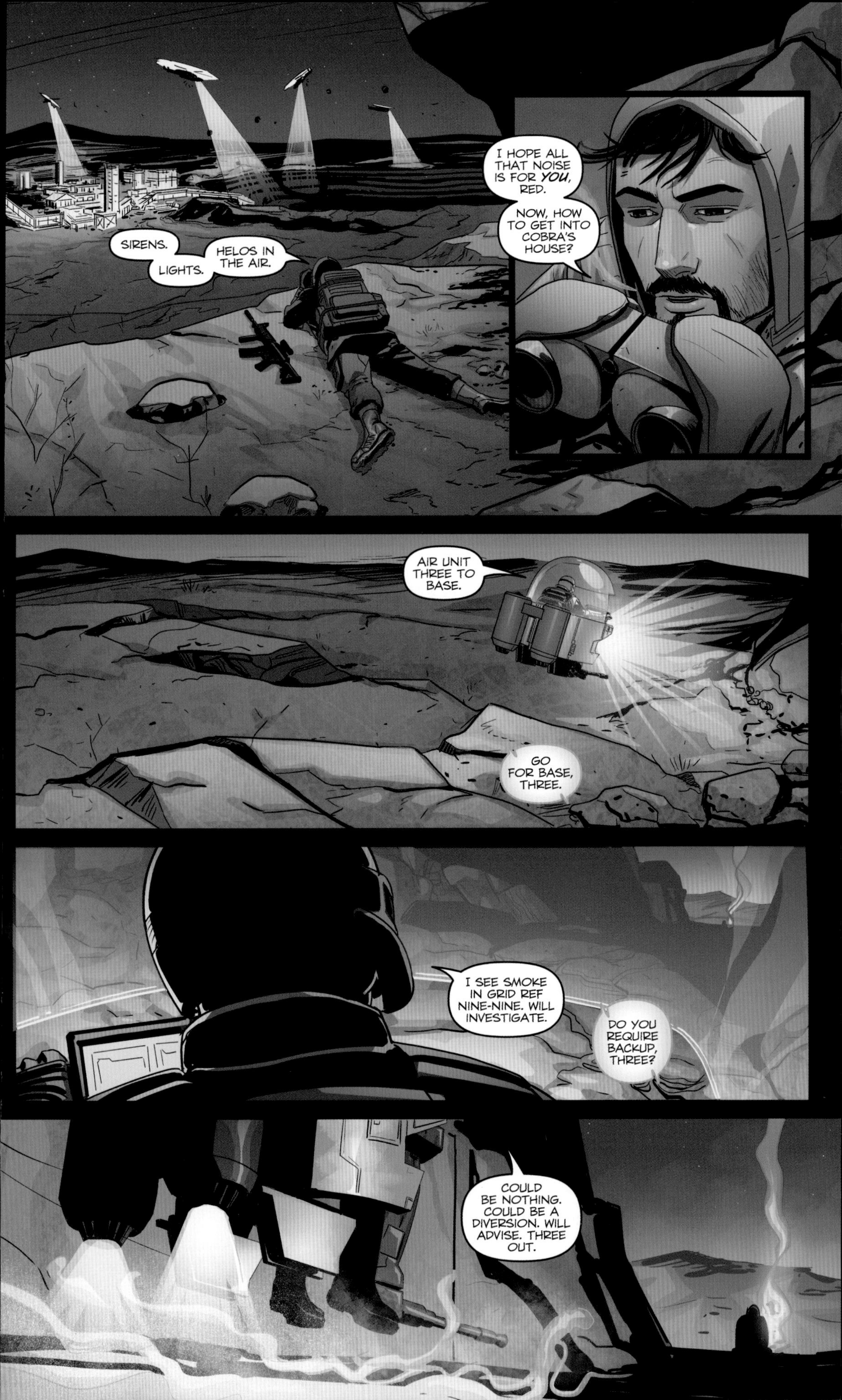
SIRENS.
LIGHTS.
HELOS IN THE AIR.
I HOPE ALL THAT NOISE IS FOR *YOU*, RED.
NOW, HOW TO GET INTO COBRA'S HOUSE?
AIR UNIT THREE TO BASE.
GO FOR BASE, THREE.
I SEE SMOKE IN GRID REF NINE-NINE. WILL INVESTIGATE.
DO YOU REQUIRE BACKUP, THREE?
COULD BE NOTHING. COULD BE A DIVERSION. WILL ADVISE. THREE OUT.

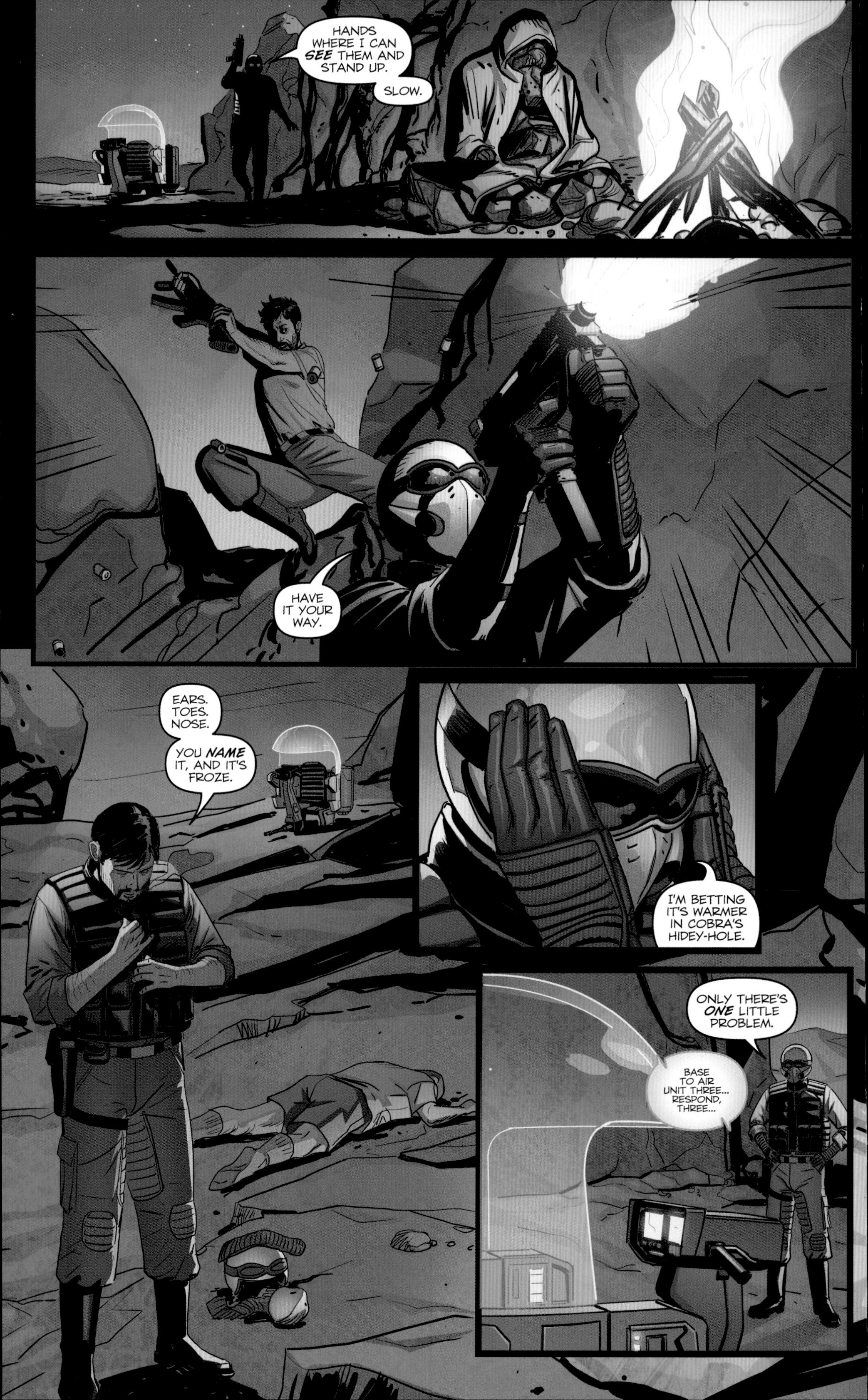
HANDS WHERE I CAN SEE THEM AND STAND UP.
SLOW.
HAVE IT YOUR WAY.
EARS. TOES. NOSE.
YOU NAME IT, AND IT'S FROZE.
I'M BETTING IT'S WARMER IN COBRA'S HIDEY-HOLE.
ONLY THERE'S ONE LITTLE PROBLEM.
BASE TO AIR UNIT THREE... RESPOND, THREE...

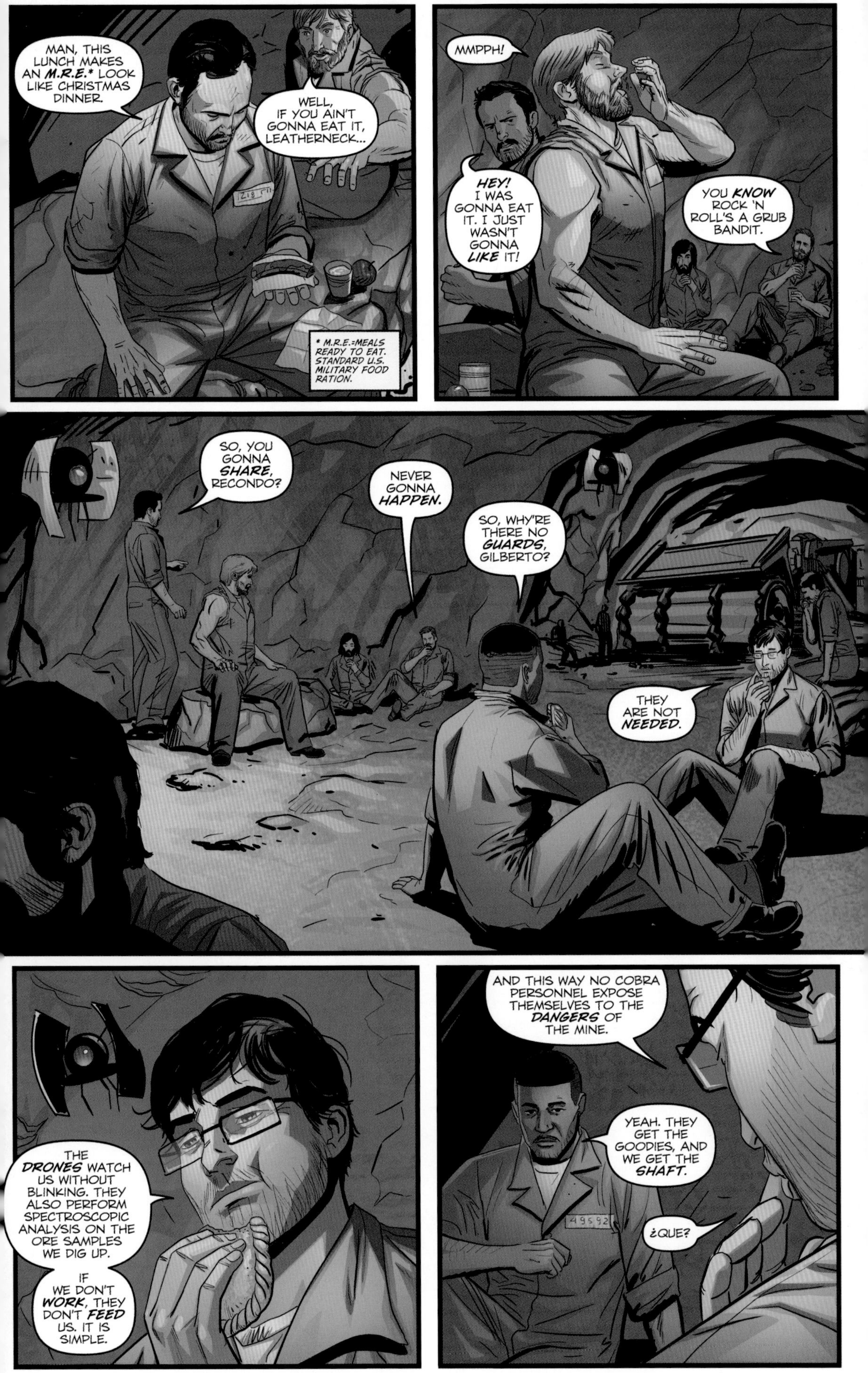
MAN, THIS LUNCH MAKES AN M.R.E.* LOOK LIKE CHRISTMAS DINNER.
WELL, IF YOU AIN'T GONNA EAT IT, LEATHERNECK...
* M.R.E.=MEALS READY TO EAT. STANDARD U.S. MILITARY FOOD RATION.
MMPPH!
HEY! I WAS GONNA EAT IT. I JUST WASN'T GONNA LIKE IT!
YOU KNOW ROCK 'N ROLL'S A GRUB BANDIT.
SO, YOU GONNA SHARE, RECONDO?
NEVER GONNA HAPPEN.
SO, WHY'RE THERE NO GUARDS, GILBERTO?
THEY ARE NOT NEEDED.
THE DRONES WATCH US WITHOUT BLINKING. THEY ALSO PERFORM SPECTROSCOPIC ANALYSIS ON THE ORE SAMPLES WE DIG UP.
IF WE DON'T WORK, THEY DON'T FEED US. IT IS SIMPLE.
AND THIS WAY NO COBRA PERSONNEL EXPOSE THEMSELVES TO THE DANGERS OF THE MINE.
YEAH. THEY GET THE GOODIES, AND WE GET THE SHAFT.
¿QUE?

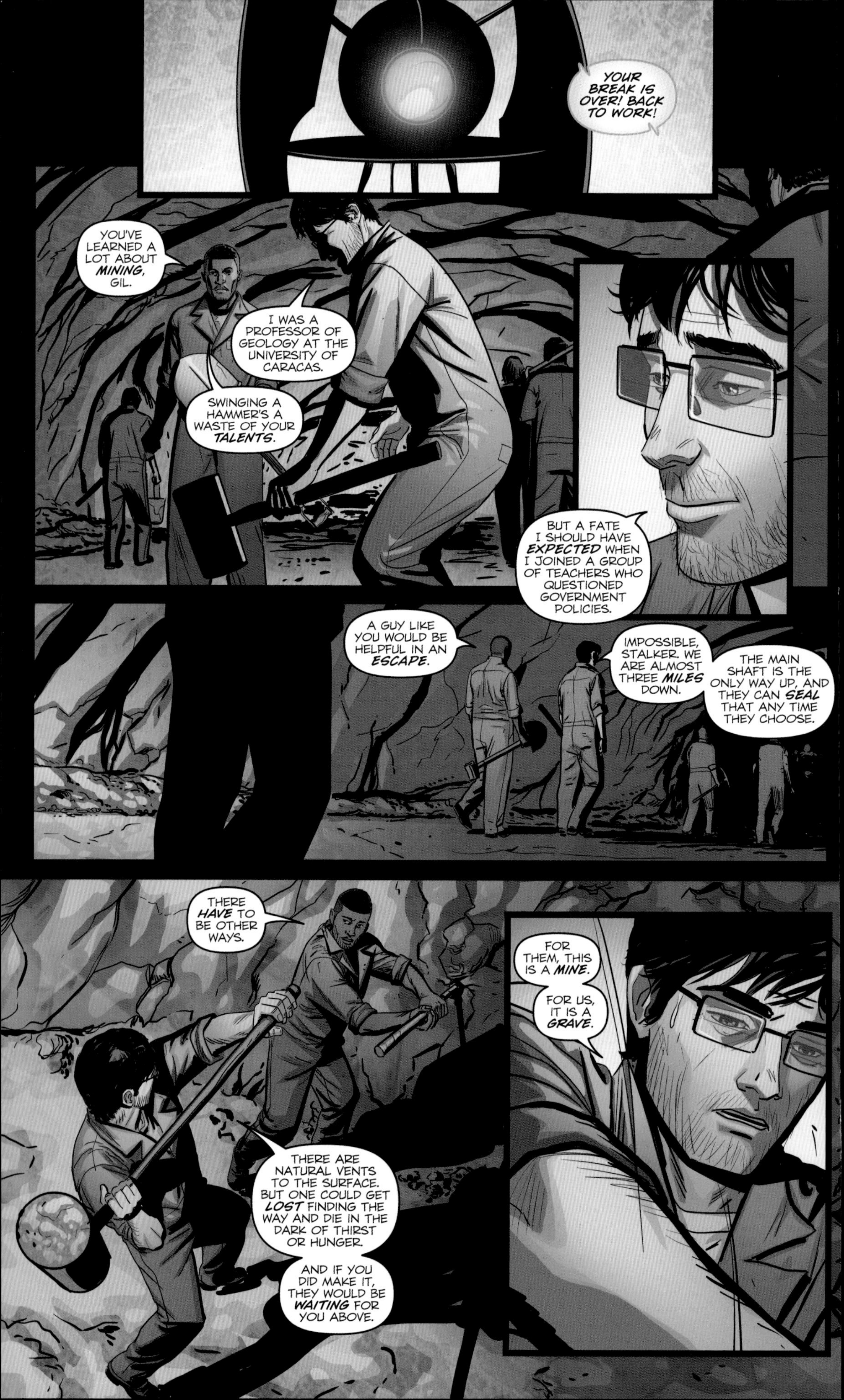
YOUR BREAK IS OVER! BACK TO WORK!
YOU'VE LEARNED A LOT ABOUT MINING, GIL.
I WAS A PROFESSOR OF GEOLOGY AT THE UNIVERSITY OF CARACAS.
SWINGING A HAMMER'S A WASTE OF YOUR TALENTS.
BUT A FATE I SHOULD HAVE EXPECTED WHEN I JOINED A GROUP OF TEACHERS WHO QUESTIONED GOVERNMENT POLICIES.
A GUY LIKE YOU WOULD BE HELPFUL IN AN ESCAPE.
IMPOSSIBLE, STALKER. WE ARE ALMOST THREE MILES DOWN.
THE MAIN SHAFT IS THE ONLY WAY UP, AND THEY CAN SEAL THAT ANY TIME THEY CHOOSE.
THERE HAVE TO BE OTHER WAYS.
THERE ARE NATURAL VENTS TO THE SURFACE. BUT ONE COULD GET LOST FINDING THE WAY AND DIE IN THE DARK OF THIRST OR HUNGER.
AND IF YOU DID MAKE IT, THEY WOULD BE WAITING FOR YOU ABOVE.
FOR THEM, THIS IS A MINE.
FOR US, IT IS A GRAVE.

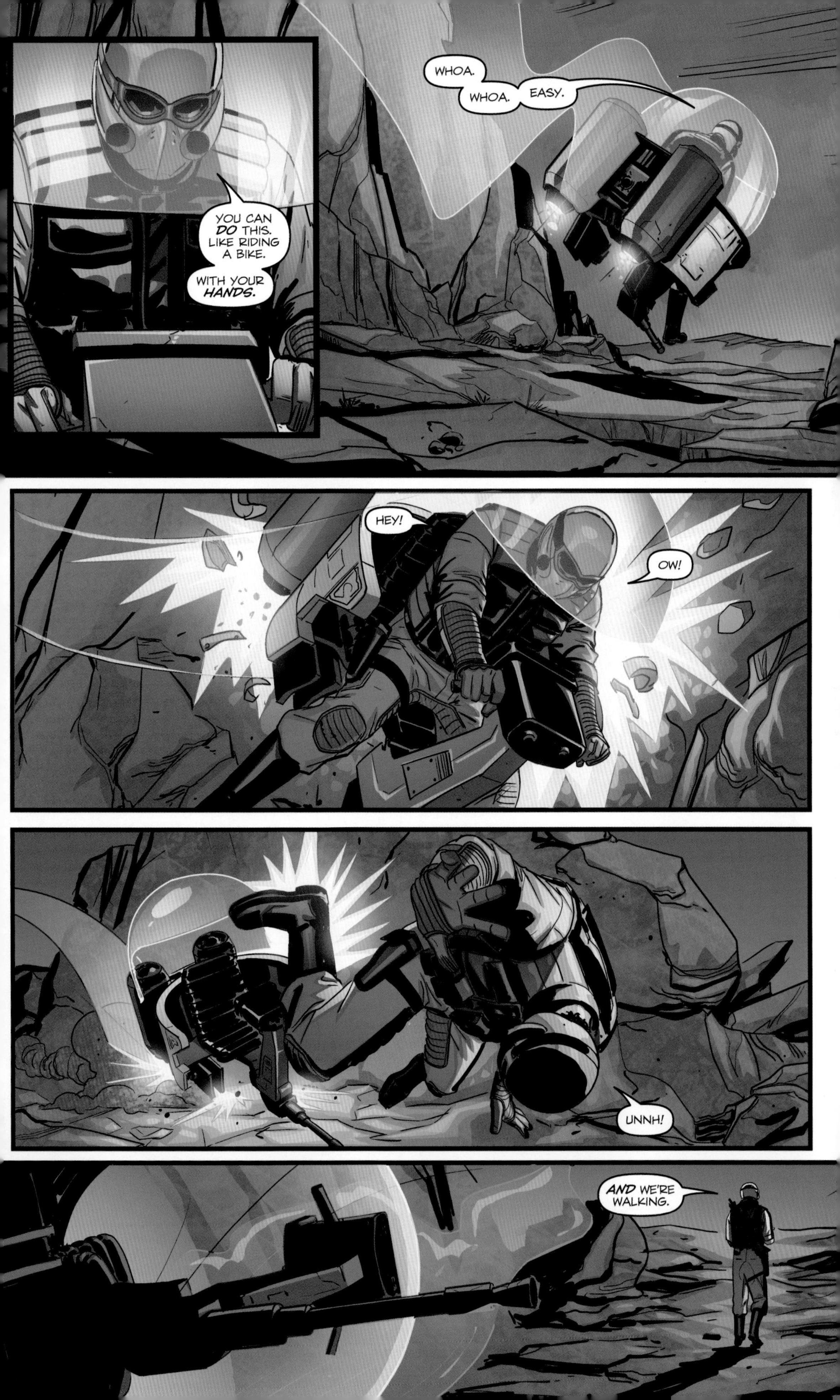
YOU CAN DO THIS. LIKE RIDING A BIKE.
WITH YOUR HANDS.
WHOA.
WHOA. EASY.
HEY!
OW!
UNNH!
AND WE'RE WALKING.

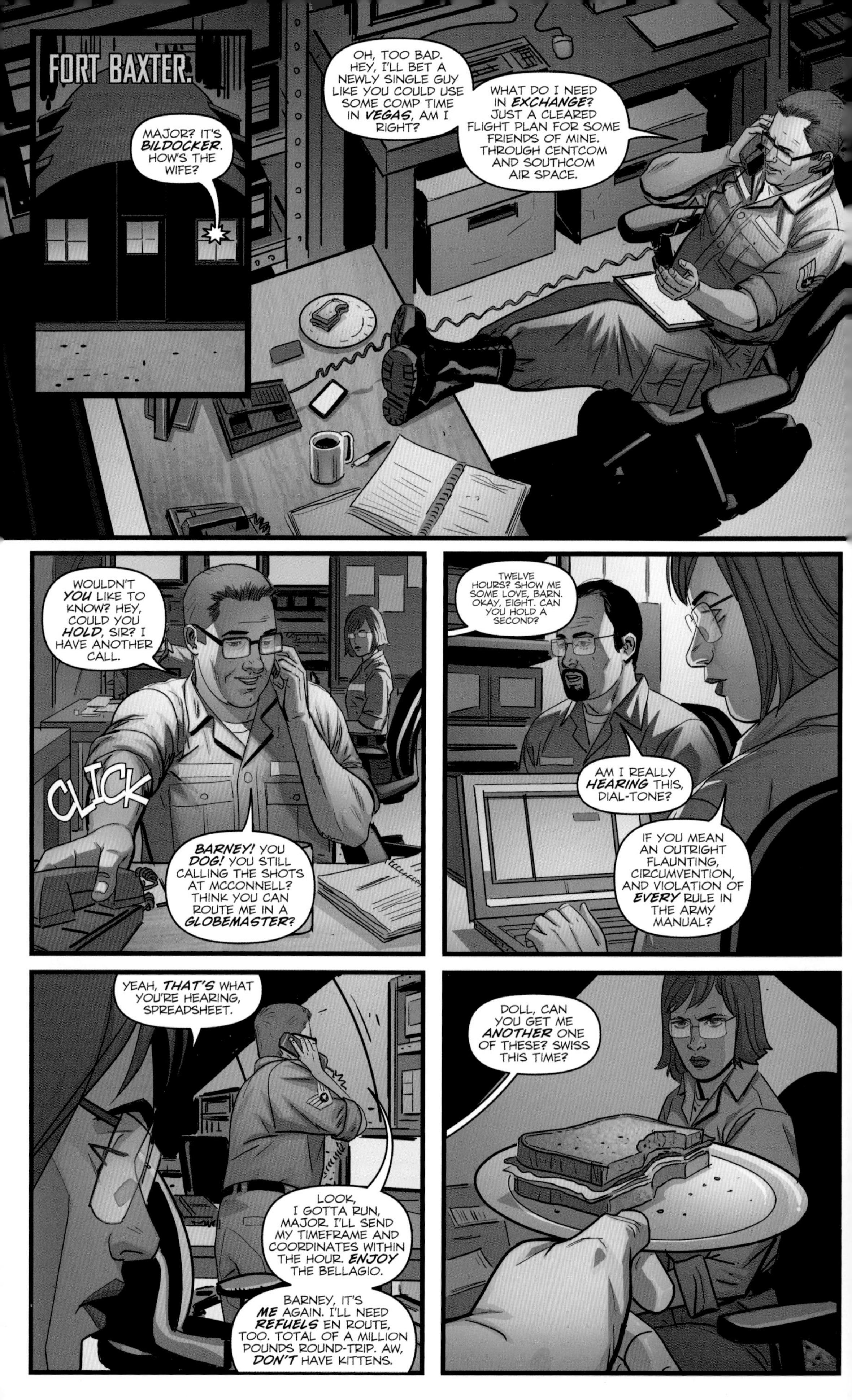
FORT BAXTER.
MAJOR? IT'S BILDOCKER. HOW'S THE WIFE?
OH, TOO BAD. HEY, I'LL BET A NEWLY SINGLE GUY LIKE YOU COULD USE SOME COMP TIME IN VEGAS, AM I RIGHT?
WHAT DO I NEED IN EXCHANGE? JUST A CLEARED FLIGHT PLAN FOR SOME FRIENDS OF MINE. THROUGH CENTCOM AND SOUTHCOM AIR SPACE.
WOULDN'T YOU LIKE TO KNOW? HEY, COULD YOU HOLD, SIR? I HAVE ANOTHER CALL.
CLICK
BARNEY! YOU DOG! YOU STILL CALLING THE SHOTS AT MCCONNELL? THINK YOU CAN ROUTE ME IN A GLOBEMASTER?
TWELVE HOURS? SHOW ME SOME LOVE, BARN. OKAY, EIGHT. CAN YOU HOLD A SECOND?
AM I REALLY HEARING THIS, DIAL-TONE?
IF YOU MEAN AN OUTRIGHT FLAUNTING, CIRCUMVENTION, AND VIOLATION OF EVERY RULE IN THE ARMY MANUAL?
YEAH, THAT'S WHAT YOU'RE HEARING, SPREADSHEET.
LOOK, I GOTTA RUN, MAJOR. I'LL SEND MY TIMEFRAME AND COORDINATES WITHIN THE HOUR. ENJOY THE BELLAGIO.
BARNEY, IT'S ME AGAIN. I'LL NEED REFUELS EN ROUTE, TOO. TOTAL OF A MILLION POUNDS ROUND-TRIP. AW, DON'T HAVE KITTENS.
DOLL, CAN YOU GET ME ANOTHER ONE OF THESE? SWISS THIS TIME?

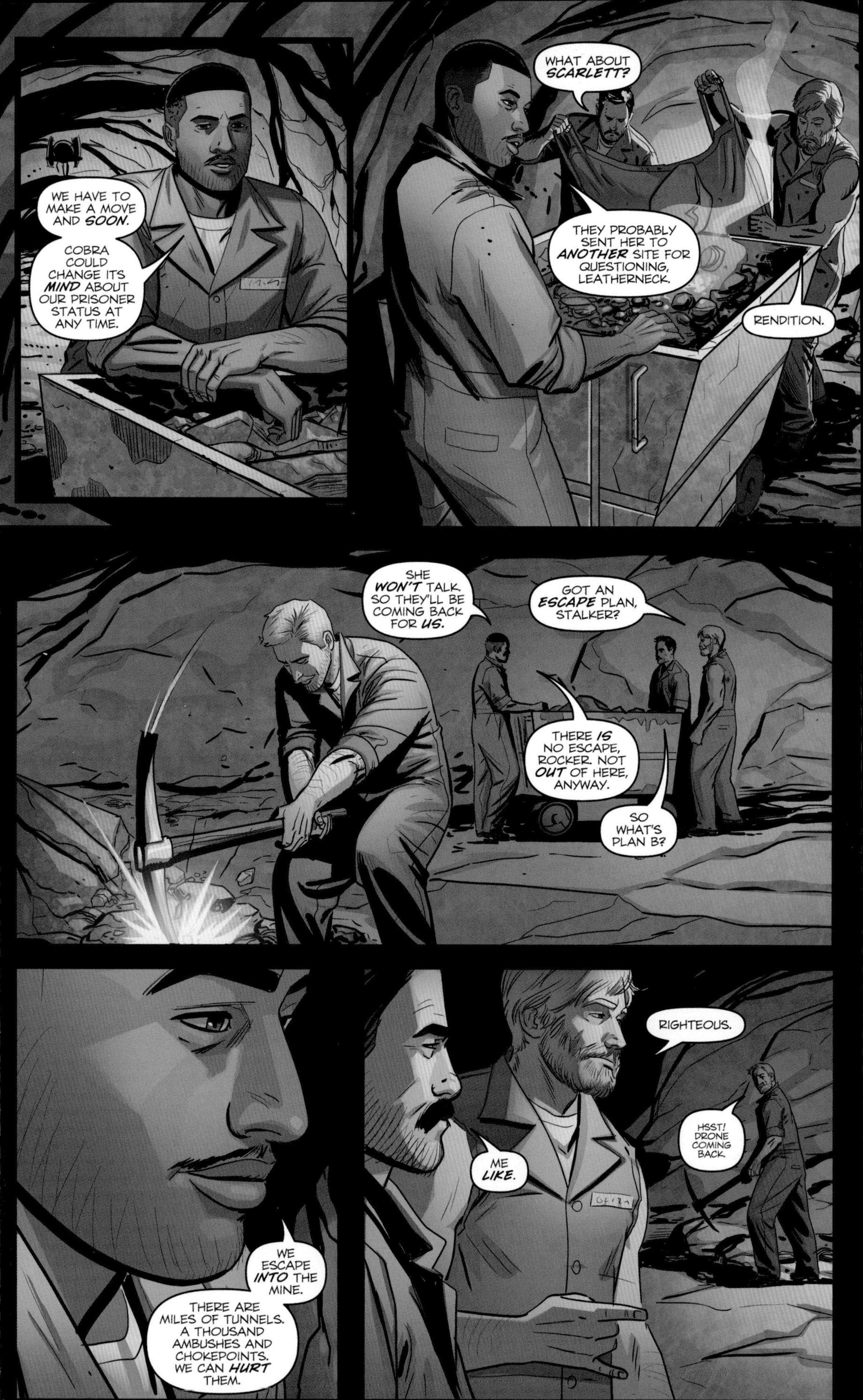
WE HAVE TO MAKE A MOVE AND *SOON*.
COBRA COULD CHANGE ITS *MIND* ABOUT OUR PRISONER STATUS AT ANY TIME.
WHAT ABOUT *SCARLETT?*
THEY PROBABLY SENT HER TO *ANOTHER* SITE FOR QUESTIONING, LEATHERNECK.
RENDITION.
SHE *WON'T* TALK. SO THEY'LL BE COMING BACK FOR *US*.
GOT AN *ESCAPE* PLAN, STALKER?
THERE *IS* NO ESCAPE, ROCKER. NOT *OUT* OF HERE, ANYWAY.
SO WHAT'S PLAN B?
WE ESCAPE *INTO* THE MINE.
THERE ARE MILES OF TUNNELS. A THOUSAND AMBUSHES AND CHOKEPOINTS. WE CAN *HURT* THEM.
RIGHTEOUS.
ME *LIKE*.
HSST! DRONE COMING BACK.

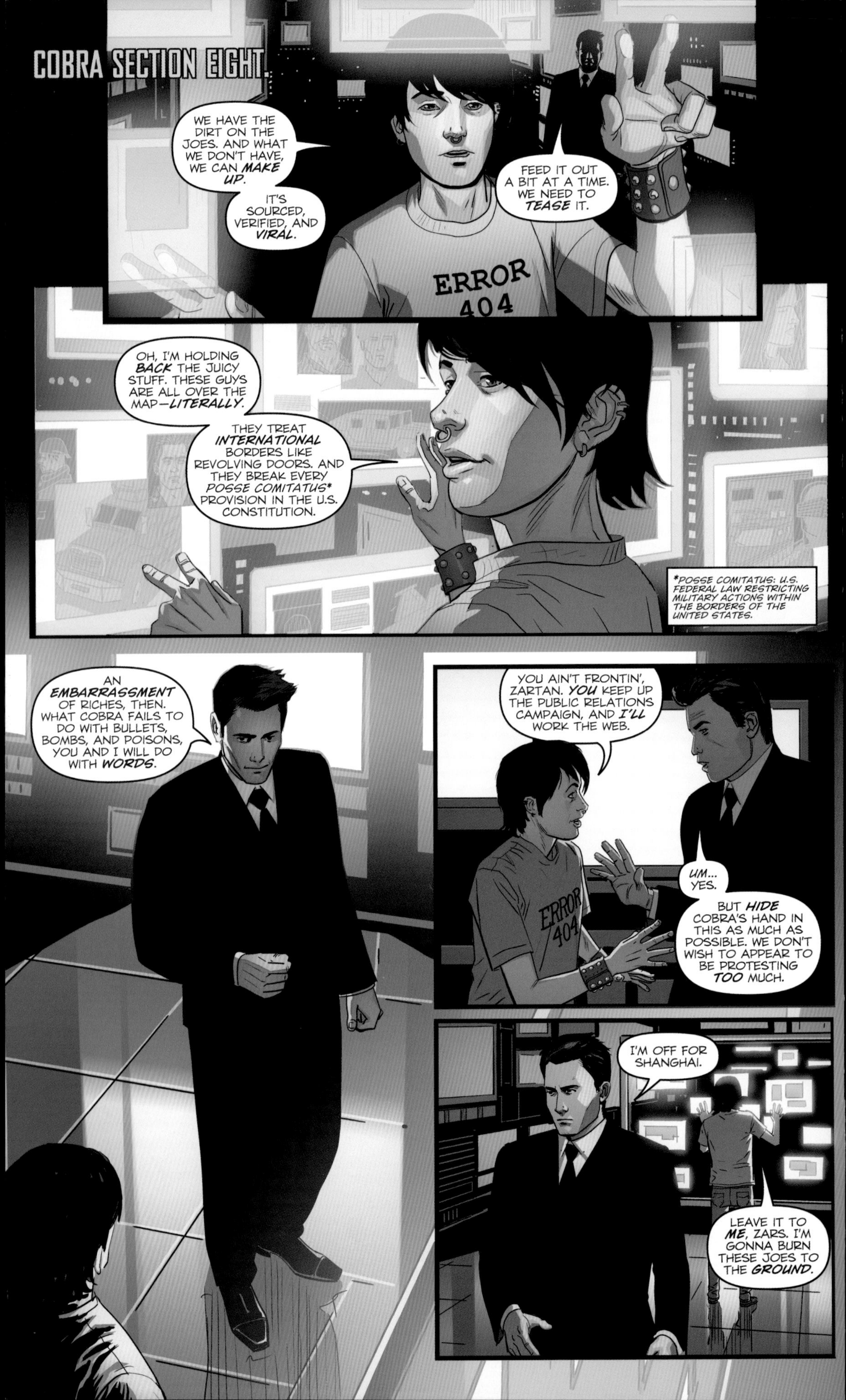
COBRA SECTION EIGHT.
WE HAVE THE DIRT ON THE JOES. AND WHAT WE DON'T HAVE, WE CAN MAKE UP.
IT'S SOURCED, VERIFIED, AND VIRAL.
FEED IT OUT A BIT AT A TIME. WE NEED TO TEASE IT.
ERROR 404
OH, I'M HOLDING BACK THE JUICY STUFF. THESE GUYS ARE ALL OVER THE MAP—LITERALLY.
THEY TREAT INTERNATIONAL BORDERS LIKE REVOLVING DOORS. AND THEY BREAK EVERY POSSE COMITATUS* PROVISION IN THE U.S. CONSTITUTION.
*POSSE COMITATUS: U.S. FEDERAL LAW RESTRICTING MILITARY ACTIONS WITHIN THE BORDERS OF THE UNITED STATES.
AN EMBARRASSMENT OF RICHES, THEN. WHAT COBRA FAILS TO DO WITH BULLETS, BOMBS, AND POISONS, YOU AND I WILL DO WITH WORDS.
YOU AIN'T FRONTIN', ZARTAN. YOU KEEP UP THE PUBLIC RELATIONS CAMPAIGN, AND I'LL WORK THE WEB.
UM... YES.
BUT HIDE COBRA'S HAND IN THIS AS MUCH AS POSSIBLE. WE DON'T WISH TO APPEAR TO BE PROTESTING TOO MUCH.
ERROR 404
I'M OFF FOR SHANGHAI.
LEAVE IT TO ME, ZARS. I'M GONNA BURN THESE JOES TO THE GROUND.

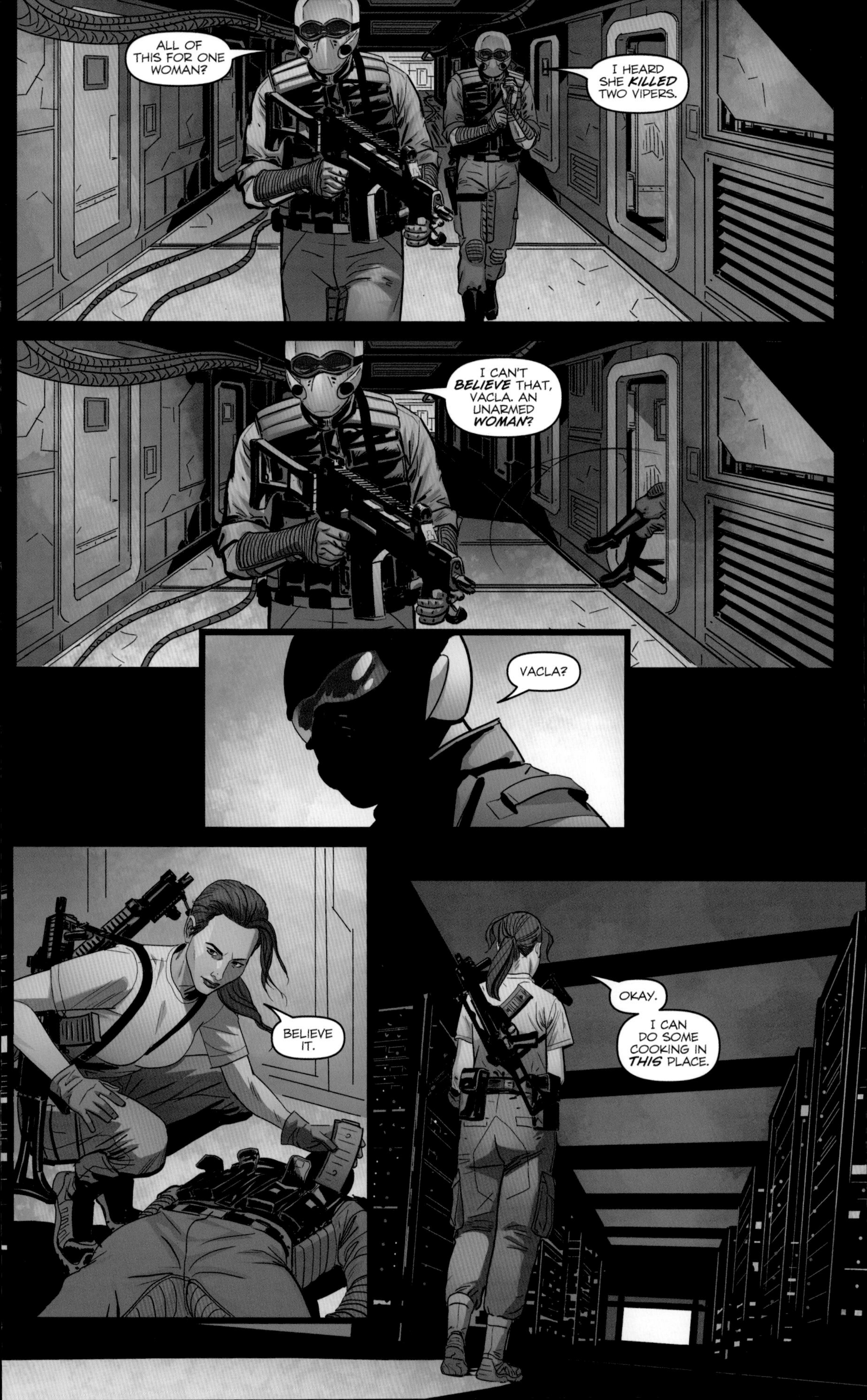
ALL OF THIS FOR ONE WOMAN?
I HEARD SHE KILLED TWO VIPERS.
I CAN'T BELIEVE THAT, VACLA. AN UNARMED WOMAN?
VACLA?
BELIEVE IT.
OKAY.
I CAN DO SOME COOKING IN THIS PLACE.

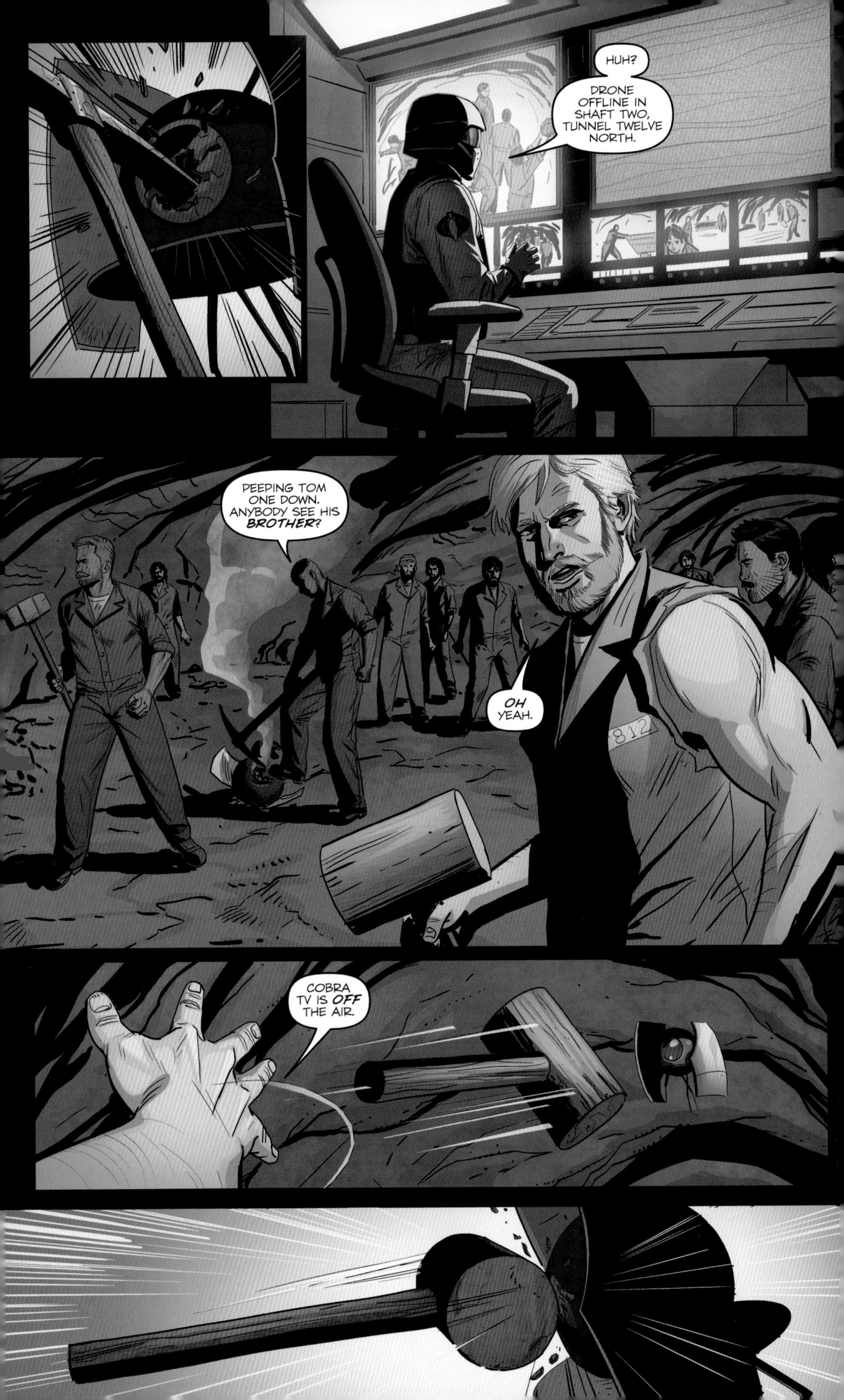

HUH?
DRONE OFFLINE IN SHAFT TWO, TUNNEL TWELVE NORTH.
PEEPING TOM ONE DOWN. ANYBODY SEE HIS *BROTHER*?
OH YEAH.
812
COBRA TV IS *OFF* THE AIR.

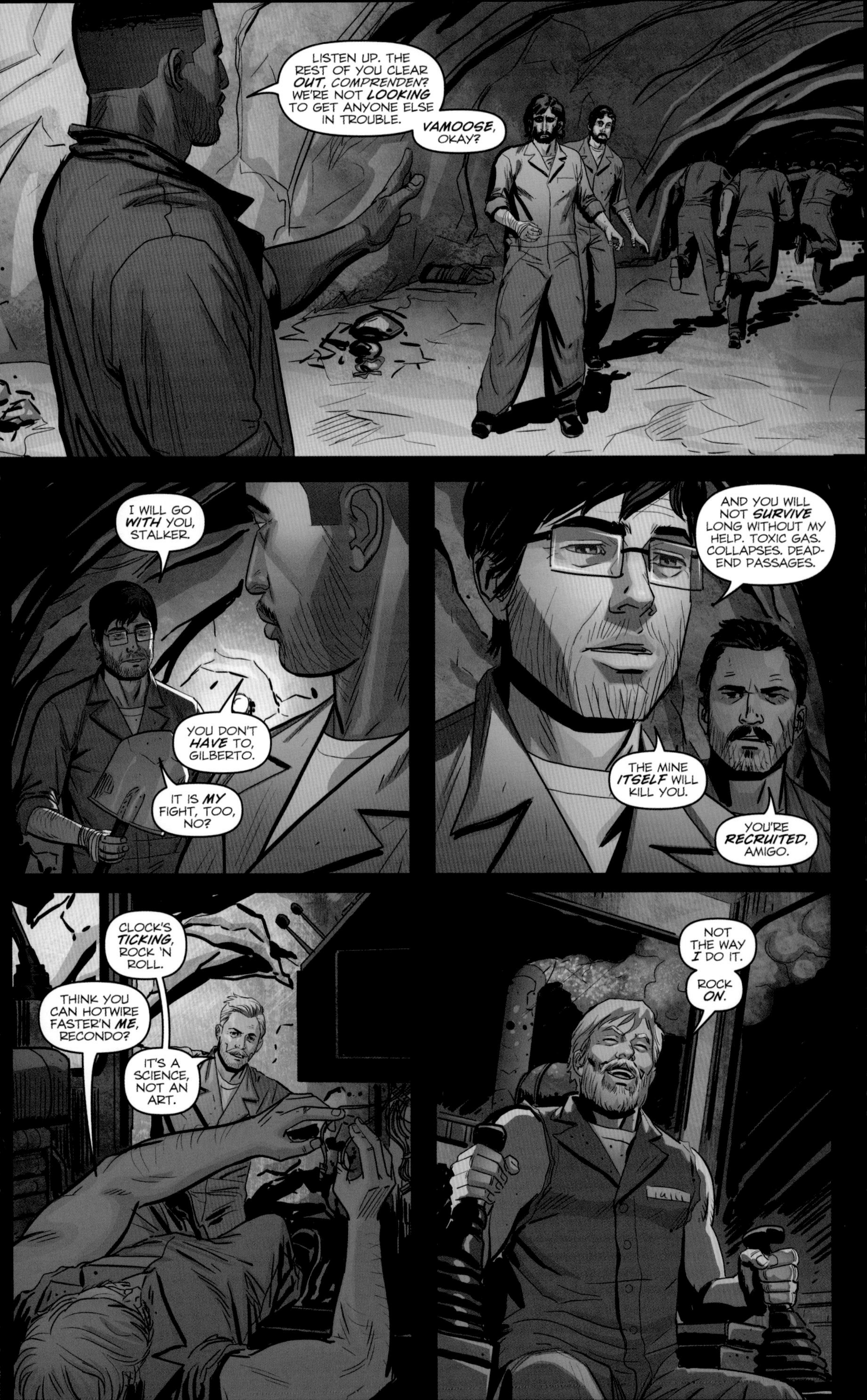
LISTEN UP. THE REST OF YOU CLEAR OUT, COMPRENDEN? WE'RE NOT LOOKING TO GET ANYONE ELSE IN TROUBLE.
VAMOOSE, OKAY?
I WILL GO WITH YOU, STALKER.
YOU DON'T HAVE TO, GILBERTO.
IT IS MY FIGHT, TOO, NO?
AND YOU WILL NOT SURVIVE LONG WITHOUT MY HELP. TOXIC GAS. COLLAPSES. DEAD-END PASSAGES.
THE MINE ITSELF WILL KILL YOU.
YOU'RE RECRUITED, AMIGO.
CLOCK'S TICKING, ROCK 'N ROLL.
THINK YOU CAN HOTWIRE FASTER'N ME, RECONDO?
IT'S A SCIENCE, NOT AN ART.
NOT THE WAY I DO IT.
ROCK ON.

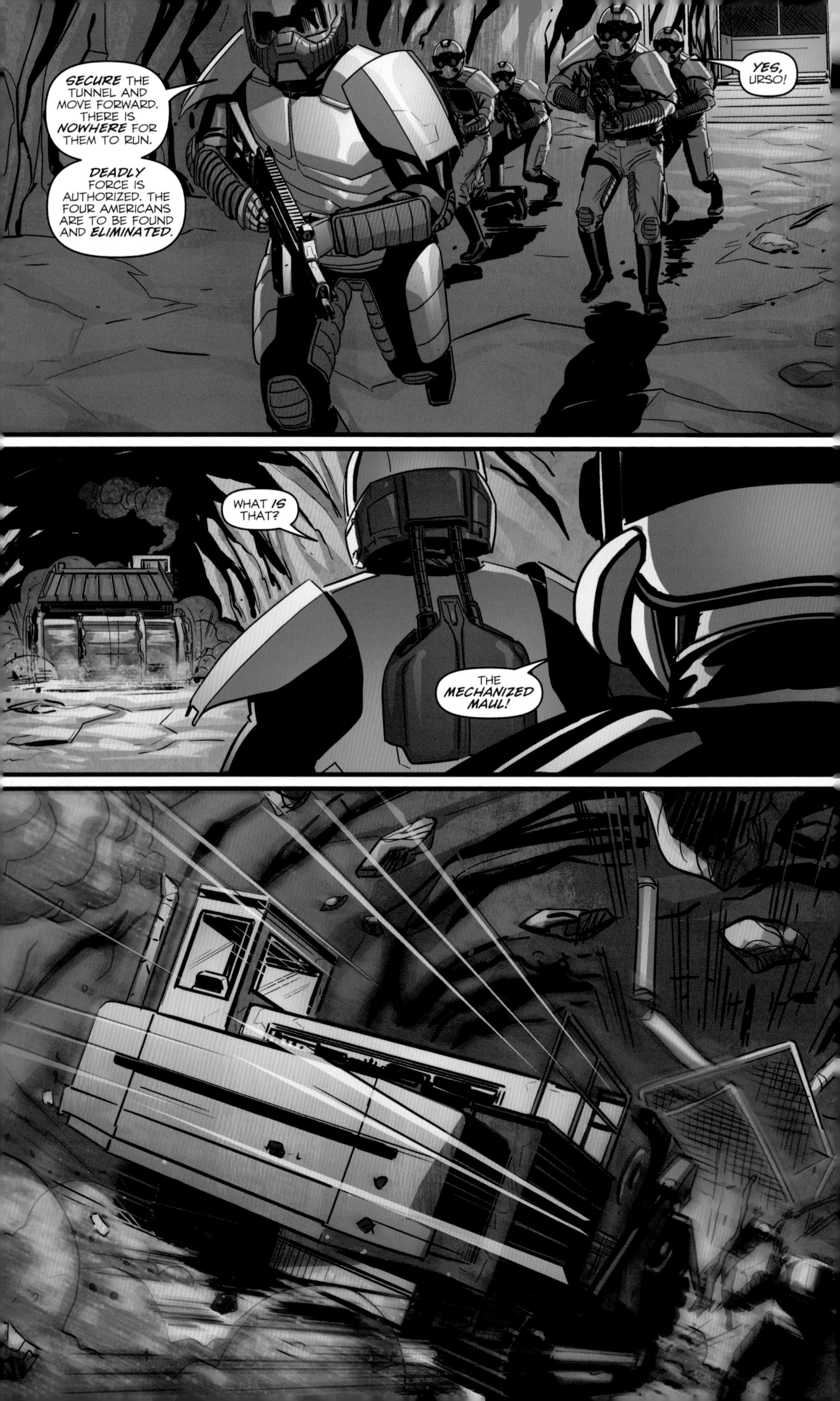
SECURE THE TUNNEL AND MOVE FORWARD. THERE IS NOWHERE FOR THEM TO RUN.
DEADLY FORCE IS AUTHORIZED. THE FOUR AMERICANS ARE TO BE FOUND AND ELIMINATED.
YES, URSO!
WHAT IS THAT?
THE MECHANIZED MAUL!

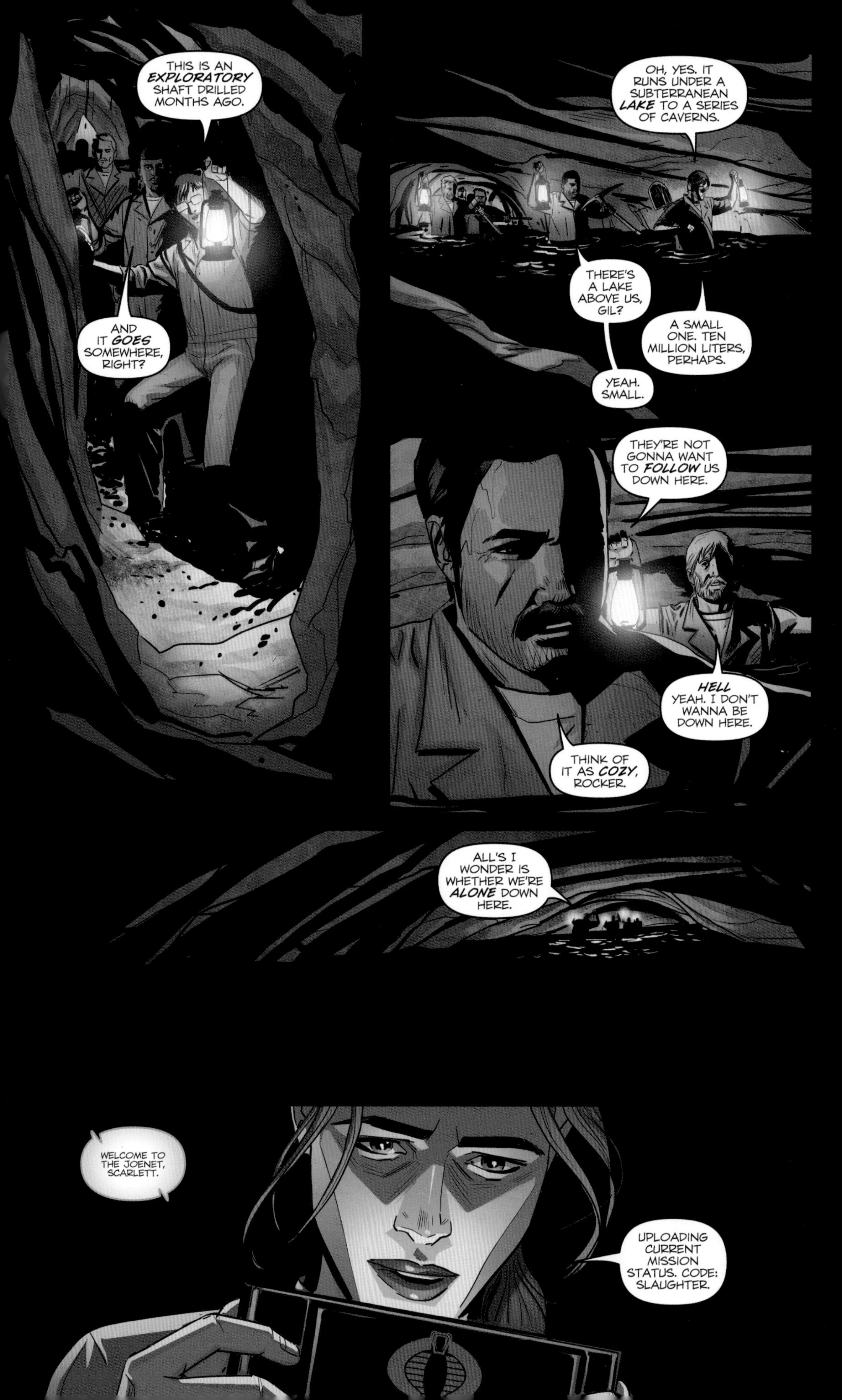
THIS IS AN EXPLORATORY SHAFT DRILLED MONTHS AGO.
AND IT GOES SOMEWHERE, RIGHT?
OH, YES. IT RUNS UNDER A SUBTERRANEAN LAKE TO A SERIES OF CAVERNS.
THERE'S A LAKE ABOVE US, GIL?
A SMALL ONE. TEN MILLION LITERS, PERHAPS.
YEAH. SMALL.
THEY'RE NOT GONNA WANT TO FOLLOW US DOWN HERE.
HELL YEAH. I DON'T WANNA BE DOWN HERE.
THINK OF IT AS COZY, ROCKER.
ALL'S I WONDER IS WHETHER WE'RE ALONE DOWN HERE.
WELCOME TO THE JOENET, SCARLETT.
UPLOADING CURRENT MISSION STATUS. CODE: SLAUGHTER.

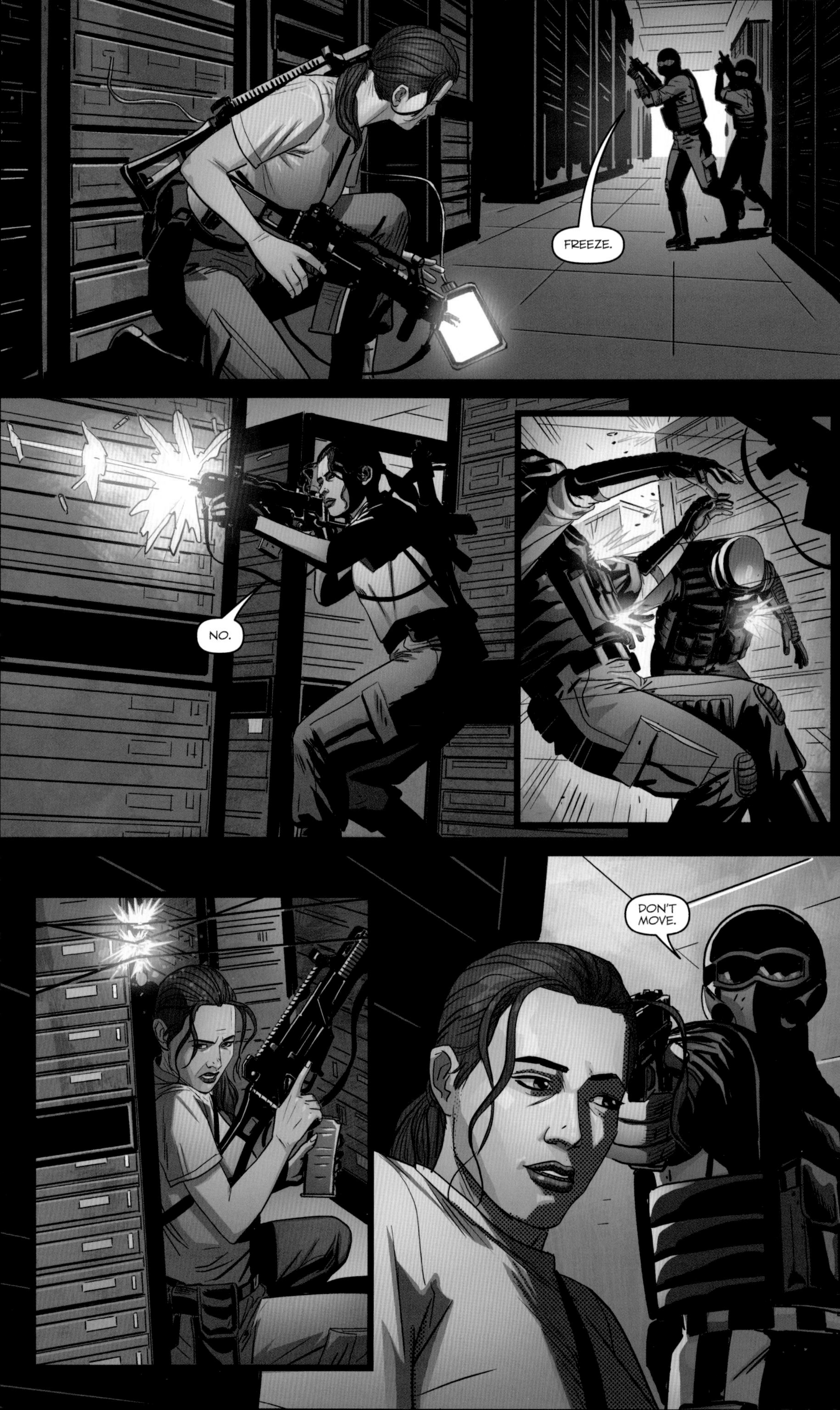
FREEZE.
NO.
DON'T MOVE.

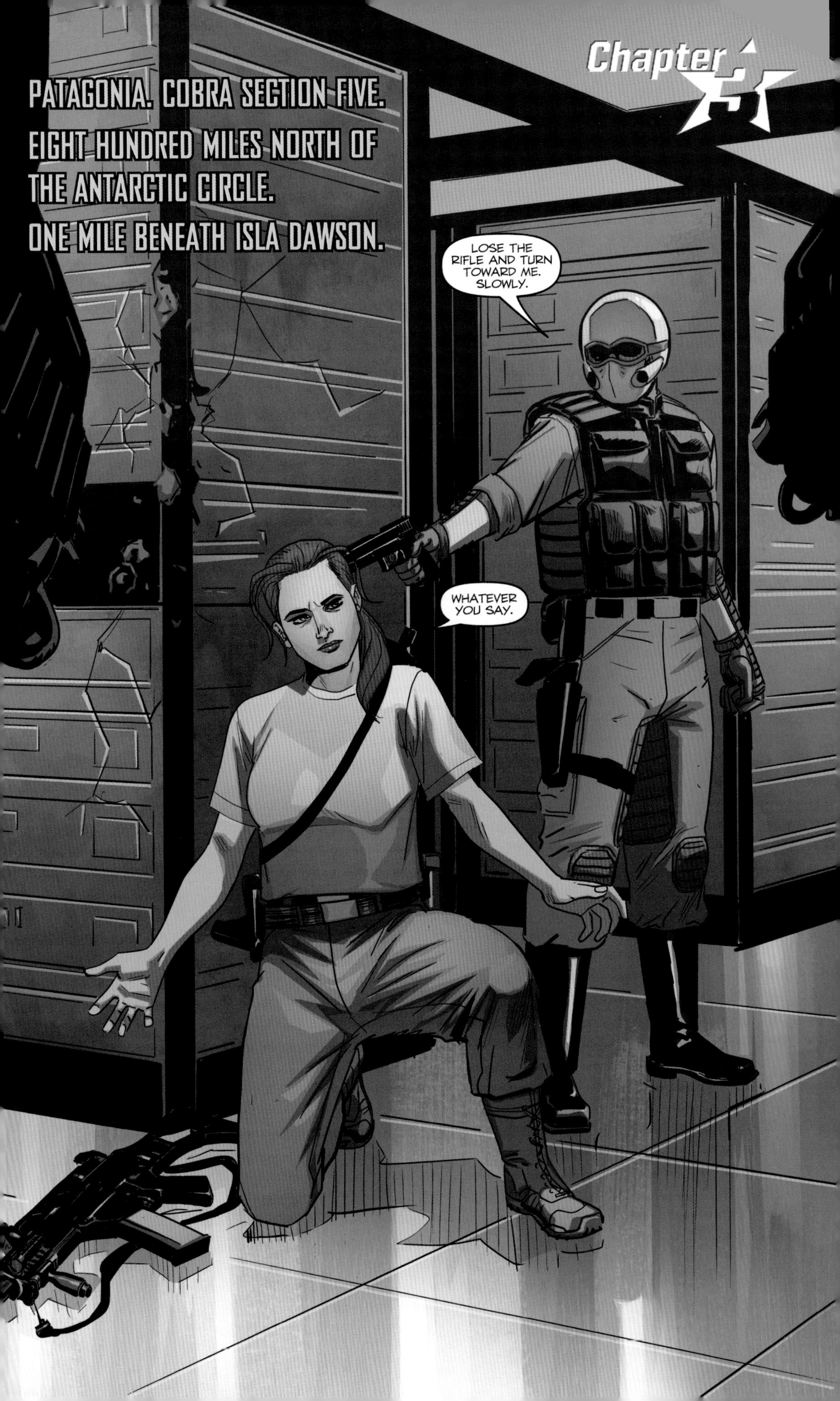
Chapter 5
PATAGONIA. COBRA SECTION FIVE.
EIGHT HUNDRED MILES NORTH OF THE ANTARCTIC CIRCLE.
ONE MILE BENEATH ISLA DAWSON.
LOSE THE RIFLE AND TURN TOWARD ME. SLOWLY.
WHATEVER YOU SAY.

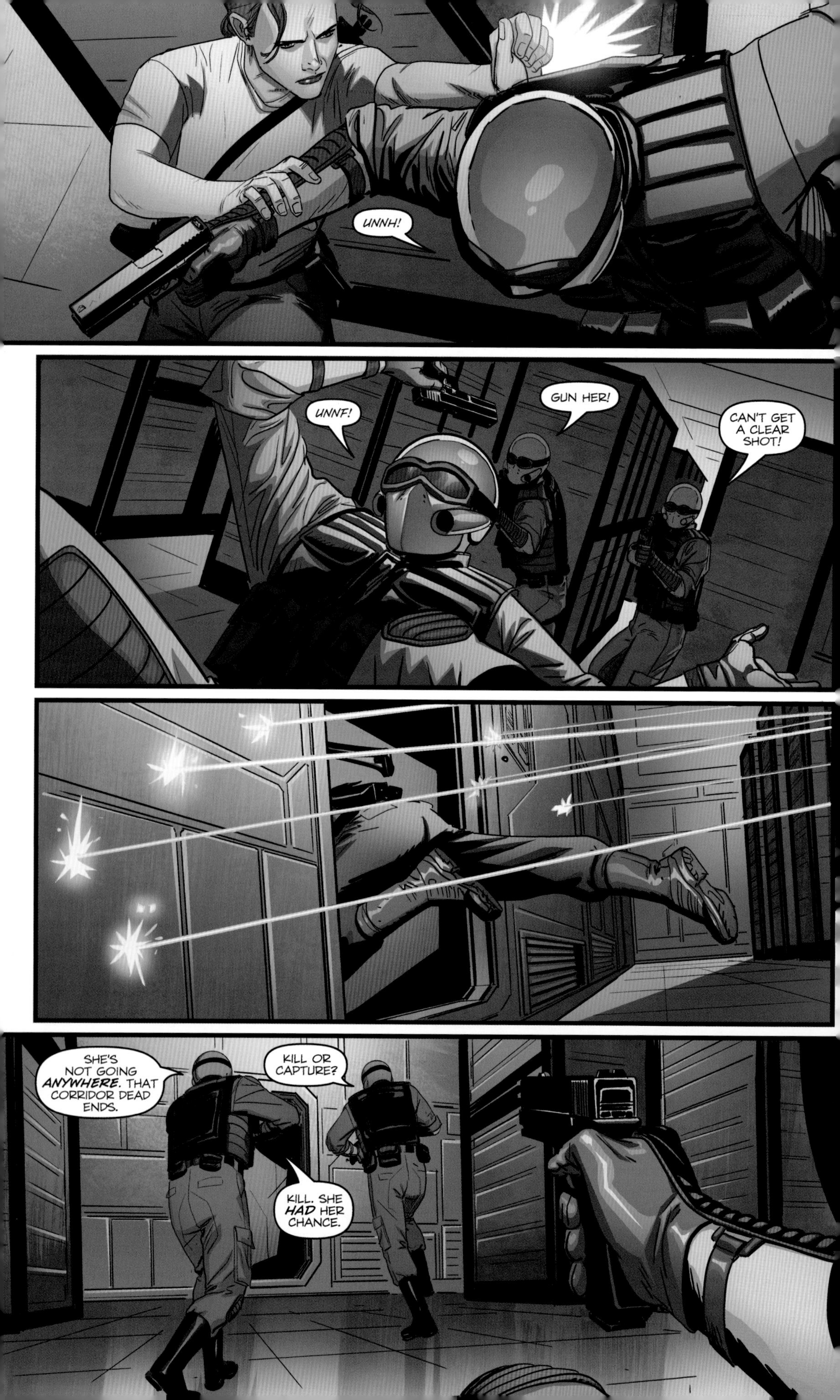
UNNH!
UNNF!
GUN HER!
CAN'T GET A CLEAR SHOT!
SHE'S NOT GOING ANYWHERE. THAT CORRIDOR DEAD ENDS.
KILL OR CAPTURE?
KILL. SHE HAD HER CHANCE.

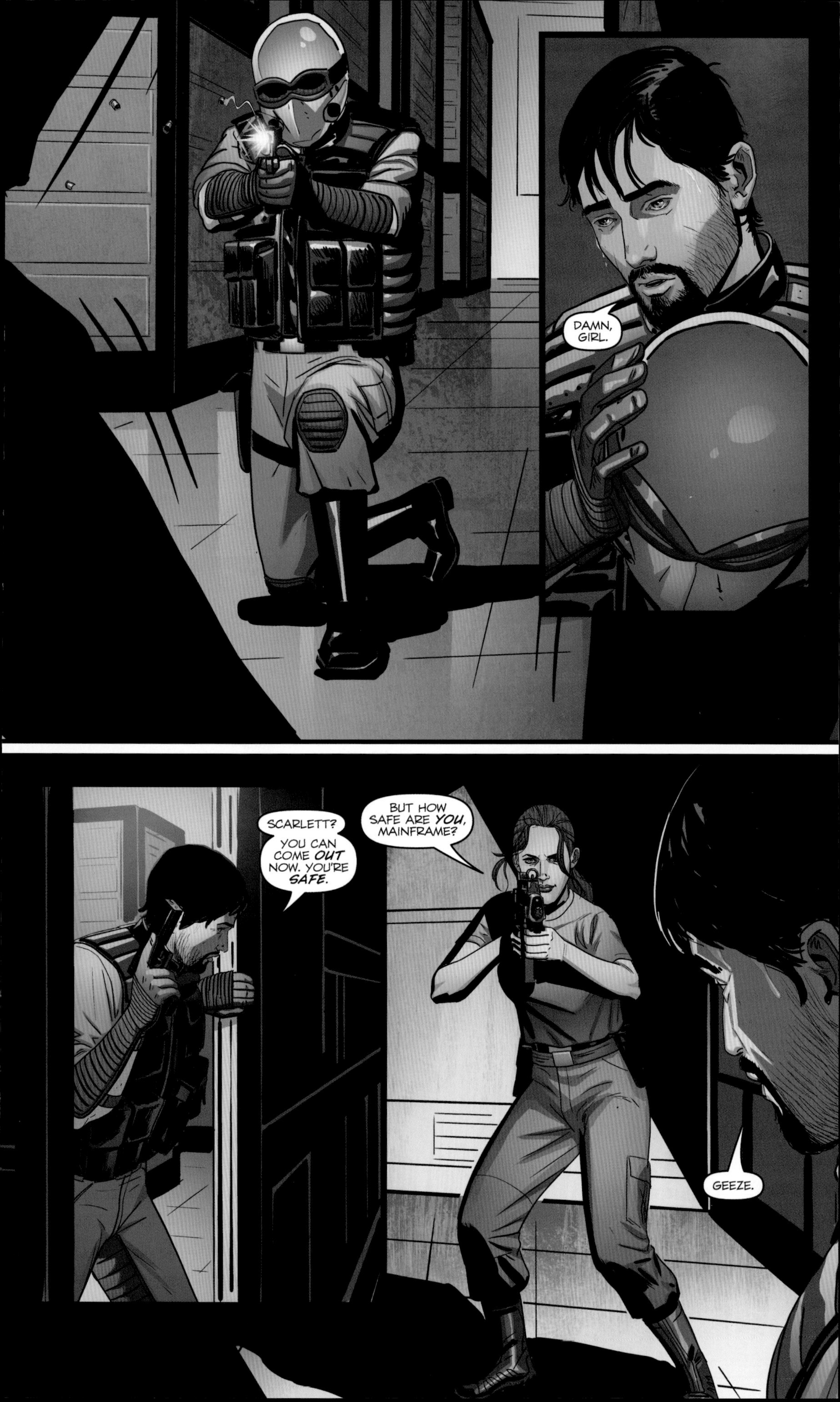
DAMN, GIRL.
SCARLETT? YOU CAN COME OUT NOW. YOU'RE SAFE.
BUT HOW SAFE ARE YOU, MAINFRAME?
GEEZE.

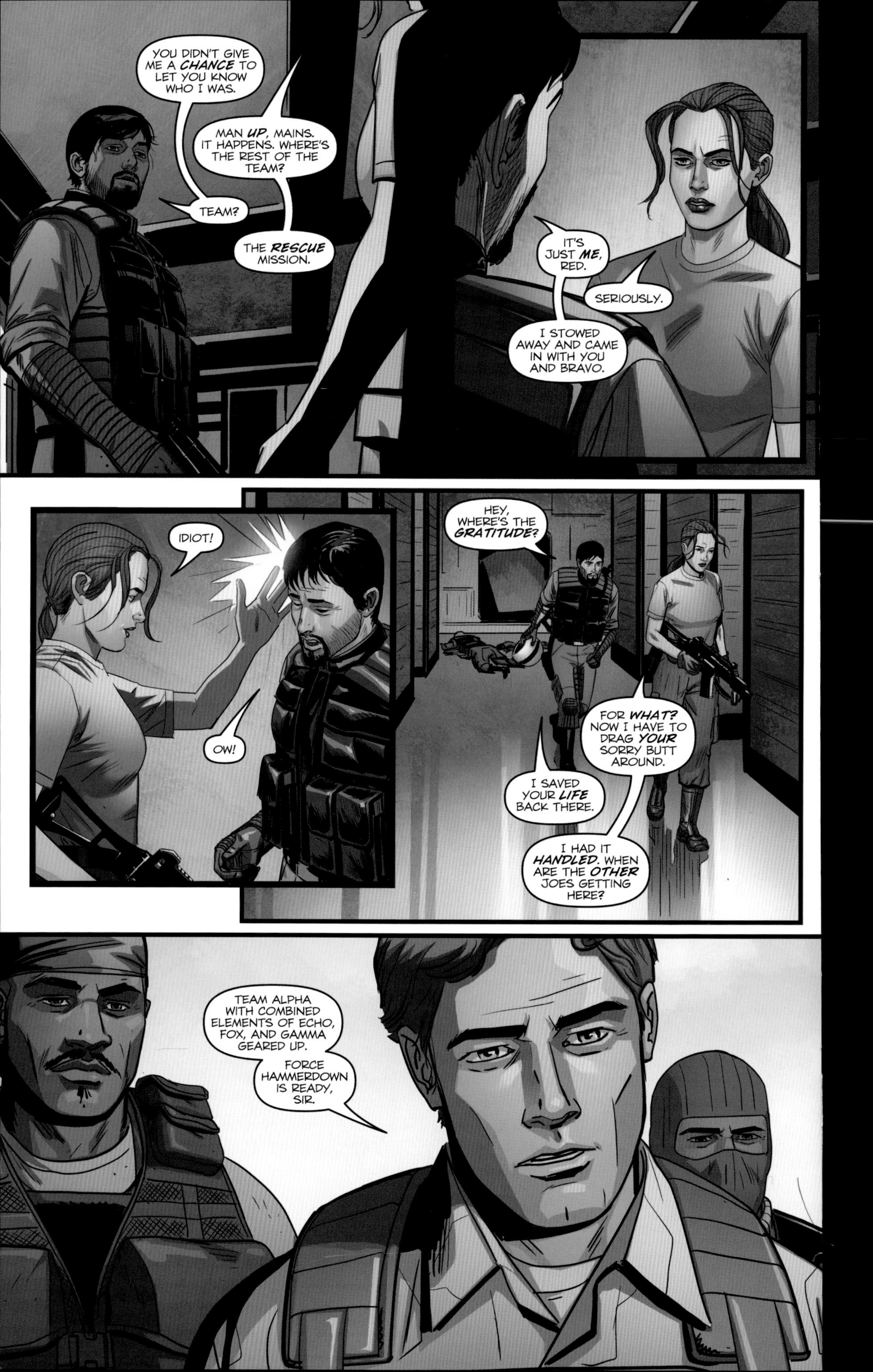

YOU DIDN'T GIVE ME A CHANCE TO LET YOU KNOW WHO I WAS.
MAN UP, MAINS. IT HAPPENS. WHERE'S THE REST OF THE TEAM?
TEAM?
THE RESCUE MISSION.
IT'S JUST ME, RED.
SERIOUSLY.
I STOWED AWAY AND CAME IN WITH YOU AND BRAVO.
IDIOT!
OW!
HEY, WHERE'S THE GRATITUDE?
I SAVED YOUR LIFE BACK THERE.
FOR WHAT? NOW I HAVE TO DRAG YOUR SORRY BUTT AROUND.
I HAD IT HANDLED. WHEN ARE THE OTHER JOES GETTING HERE?
TEAM ALPHA WITH COMBINED ELEMENTS OF ECHO, FOX, AND GAMMA GEARED UP.
FORCE HAMMERDOWN IS READY, SIR.

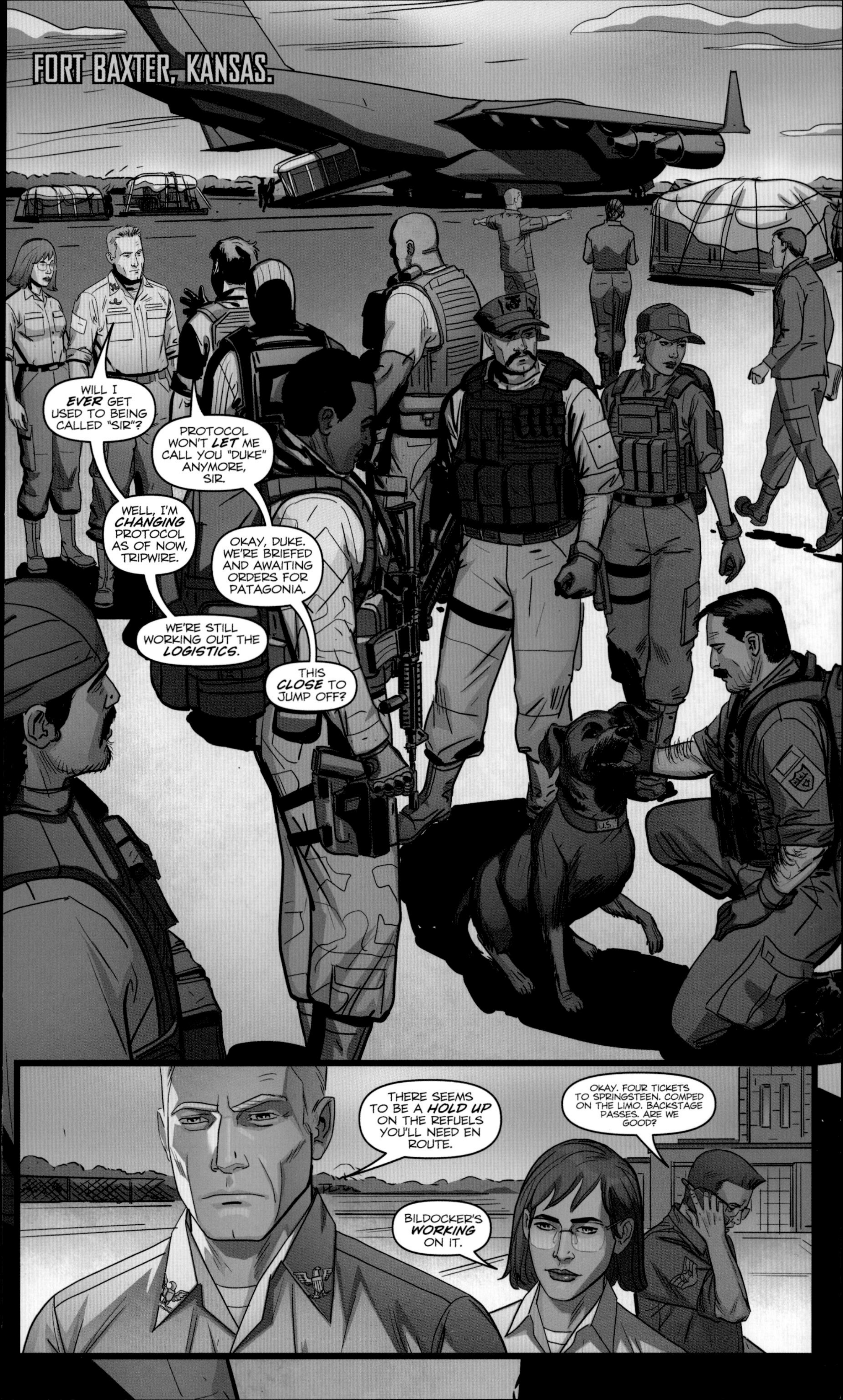
FORT BAXTER, KANSAS.
WILL I EVER GET USED TO BEING CALLED "SIR"?
PROTOCOL WON'T LET ME CALL YOU "DUKE" ANYMORE, SIR.
WELL, I'M CHANGING PROTOCOL AS OF NOW, TRIPWIRE.
OKAY, DUKE. WE'RE BRIEFED AND AWAITING ORDERS FOR PATAGONIA.
WE'RE STILL WORKING OUT THE LOGISTICS.
THIS CLOSE TO JUMP OFF?
THERE SEEMS TO BE A HOLD UP ON THE REFUELS YOU'LL NEED EN ROUTE.
OKAY. FOUR TICKETS TO SPRINGSTEEN. COMPED ON THE LIMO. BACKSTAGE PASSES. ARE WE GOOD?
BILDOCKER'S WORKING ON IT.

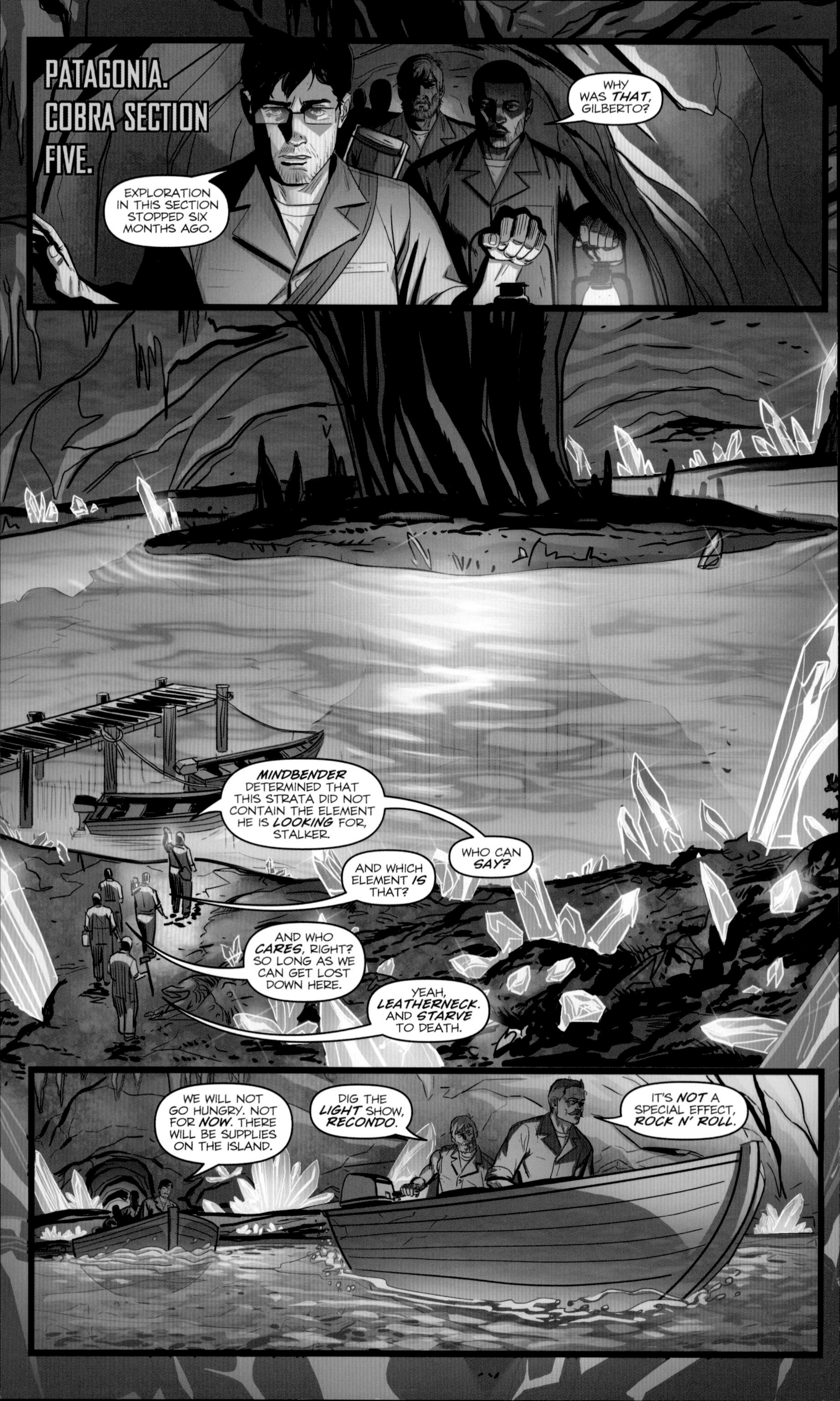
PATAGONIA. COBRA SECTION FIVE.
EXPLORATION IN THIS SECTION STOPPED SIX MONTHS AGO.
WHY WAS THAT, GILBERTO?
MINDBENDER DETERMINED THAT THIS STRATA DID NOT CONTAIN THE ELEMENT HE IS LOOKING FOR, STALKER.
AND WHICH ELEMENT IS THAT?
WHO CAN SAY?
AND WHO CARES, RIGHT? SO LONG AS WE CAN GET LOST DOWN HERE.
YEAH, LEATHERNECK. AND STARVE TO DEATH.
WE WILL NOT GO HUNGRY. NOT FOR NOW. THERE WILL BE SUPPLIES ON THE ISLAND.
DIG THE LIGHT SHOW, RECONDO.
IT'S NOT A SPECIAL EFFECT, ROCK N' ROLL.

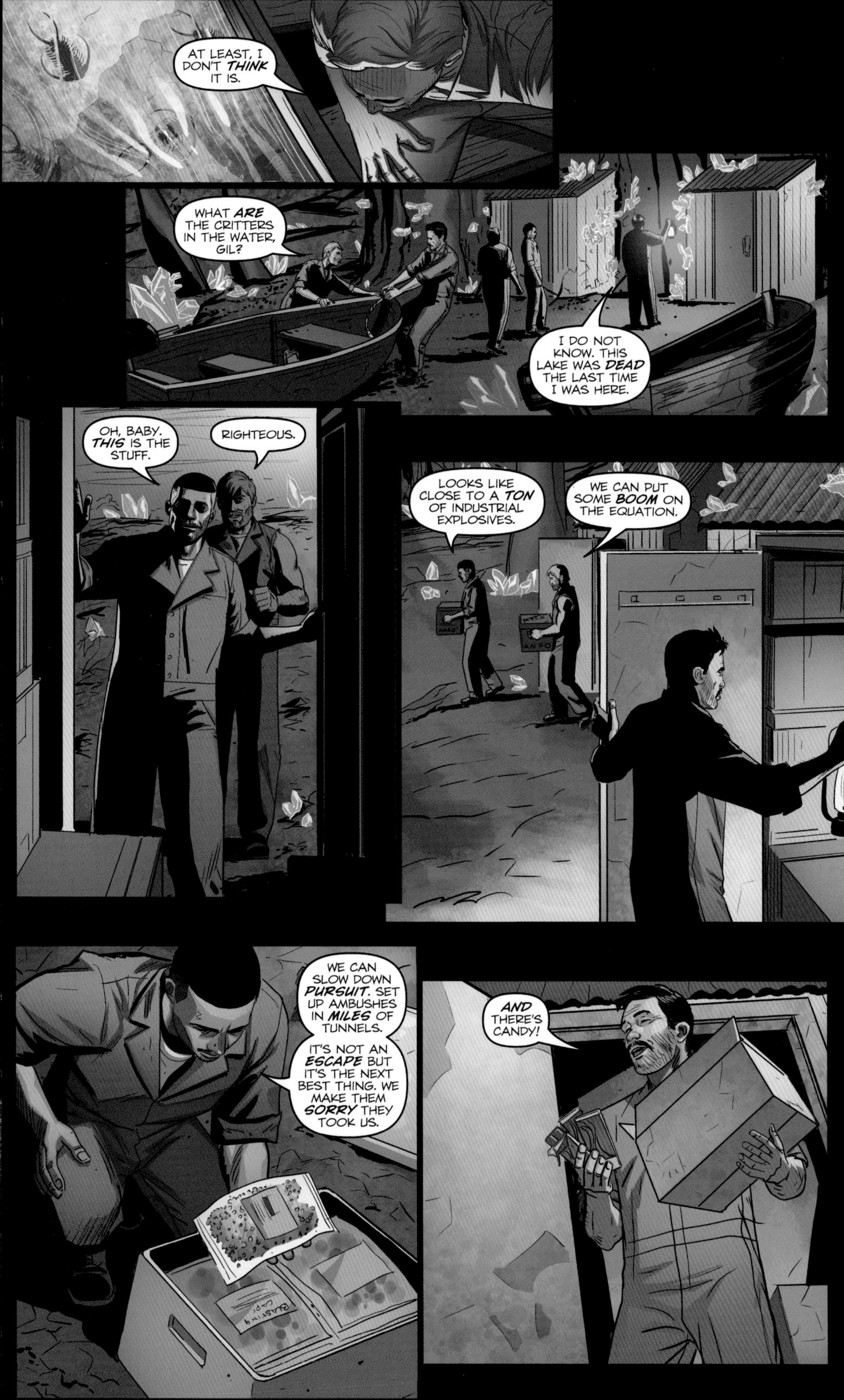
AT LEAST, I DON'T *THINK* IT IS.
WHAT *ARE* THE CRITTERS IN THE WATER, GIL?
I DO NOT KNOW. THIS LAKE WAS *DEAD* THE LAST TIME I WAS HERE.
OH, BABY. *THIS* IS THE STUFF.
RIGHTEOUS.
LOOKS LIKE CLOSE TO A *TON* OF INDUSTRIAL EXPLOSIVES.
WE CAN PUT SOME *BOOM* ON THE EQUATION.
WE CAN SLOW DOWN *PURSUIT*. SET UP AMBUSHES IN *MILES* OF TUNNELS.
IT'S NOT AN *ESCAPE* BUT IT'S THE NEXT BEST THING. WE MAKE THEM *SORRY* THEY TOOK US.
AND THERE'S CANDY!

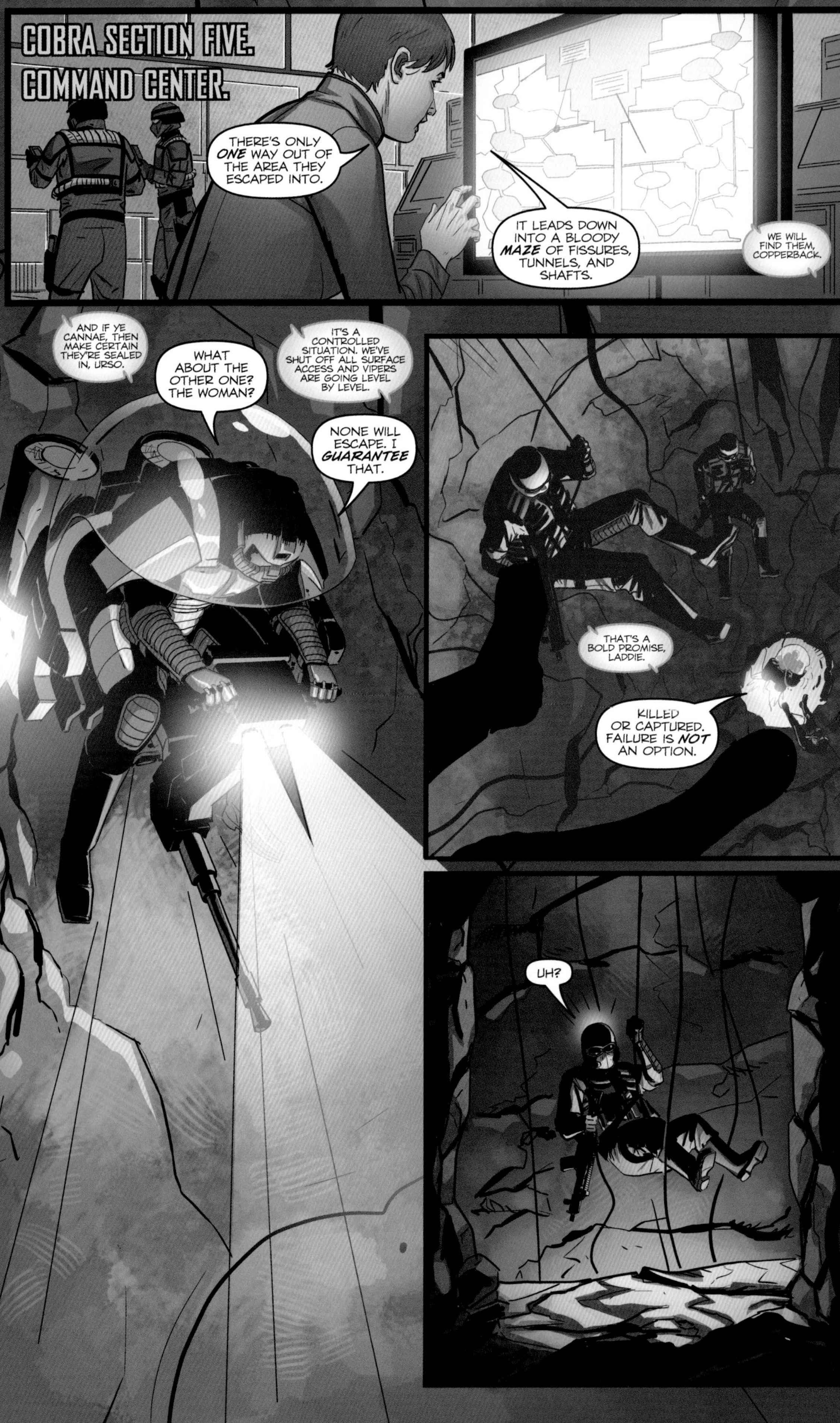
COBRA SECTION FIVE. COMMAND CENTER.
THERE'S ONLY ONE WAY OUT OF THE AREA THEY ESCAPED INTO.
IT LEADS DOWN INTO A BLOODY MAZE OF FISSURES, TUNNELS, AND SHAFTS.
WE WILL FIND THEM, COPPERBACK.
AND IF YE CANNAE, THEN MAKE CERTAIN THEY'RE SEALED IN, URSO.
WHAT ABOUT THE OTHER ONE? THE WOMAN?
IT'S A CONTROLLED SITUATION. WE'VE SHUT OFF ALL SURFACE ACCESS AND VIPERS ARE GOING LEVEL BY LEVEL.
NONE WILL ESCAPE. I GUARANTEE THAT.
THAT'S A BOLD PROMISE, LADDIE.
KILLED OR CAPTURED. FAILURE IS NOT AN OPTION.
UH?

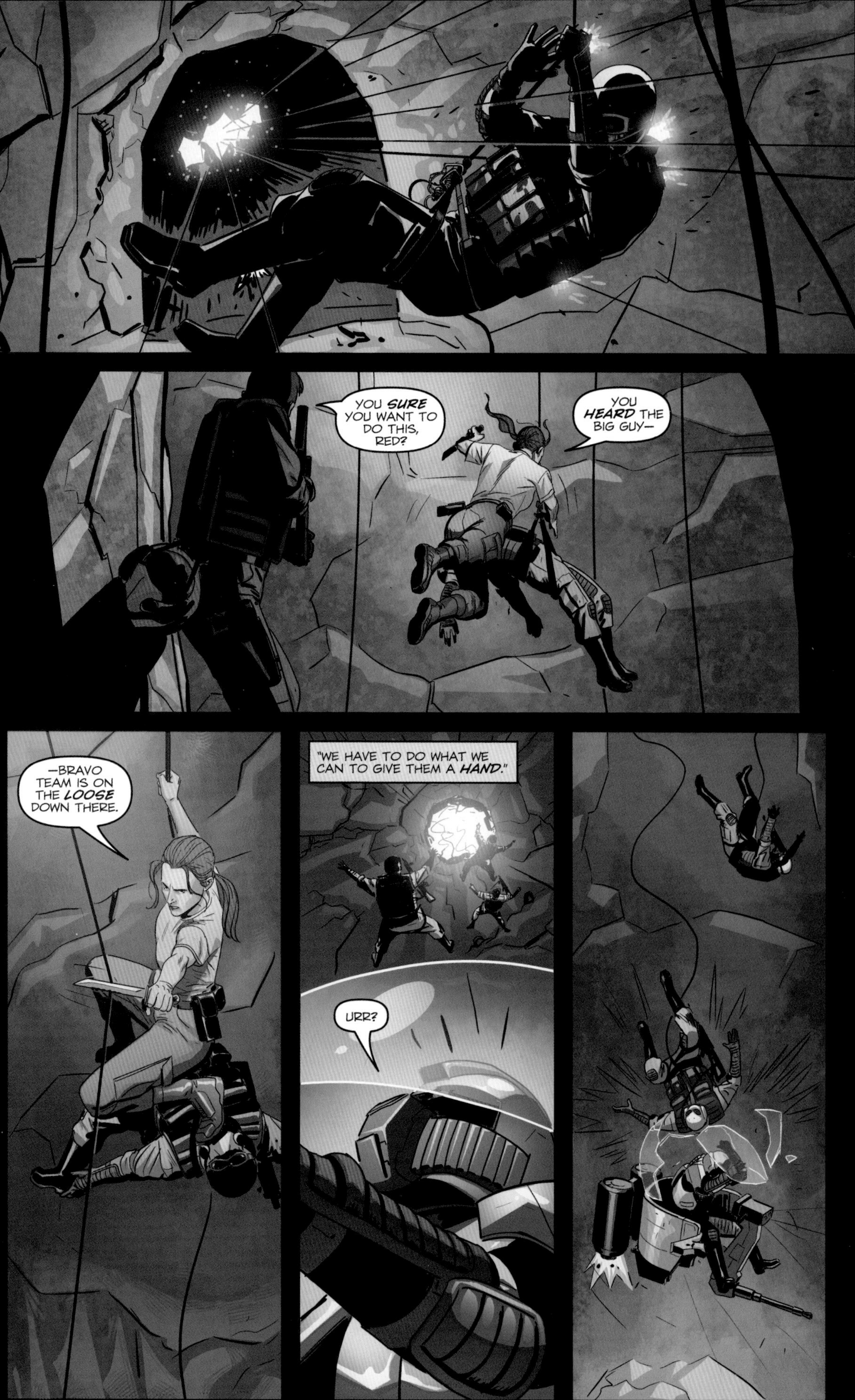
YOU SURE YOU WANT TO DO THIS, RED?
YOU HEARD THE BIG GUY—
—BRAVO TEAM IS ON THE LOOSE DOWN THERE.
"WE HAVE TO DO WHAT WE CAN TO GIVE THEM A HAND."
URR?

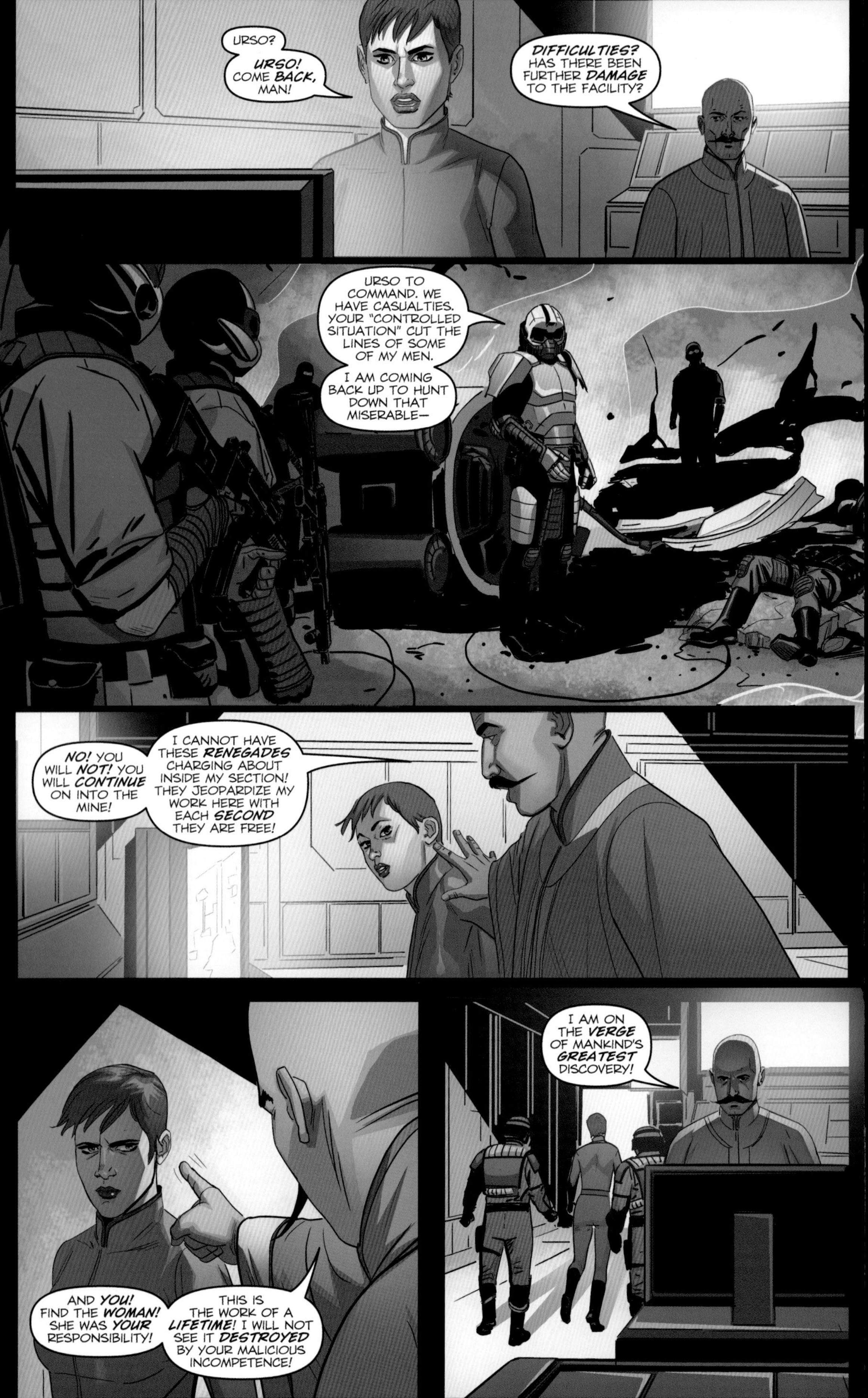
URSO? URSO! COME BACK, MAN!
DIFFICULTIES? HAS THERE BEEN FURTHER DAMAGE TO THE FACILITY?
URSO TO COMMAND. WE HAVE CASUALTIES. YOUR "CONTROLLED SITUATION" CUT THE LINES OF SOME OF MY MEN.
I AM COMING BACK UP TO HUNT DOWN THAT MISERABLE—
NO! YOU WILL NOT! YOU WILL CONTINUE ON INTO THE MINE!
I CANNOT HAVE THESE RENEGADES CHARGING ABOUT INSIDE MY SECTION! THEY JEOPARDIZE MY WORK HERE WITH EACH SECOND THEY ARE FREE!
AND YOU! FIND THE WOMAN! SHE WAS YOUR RESPONSIBILITY!
THIS IS THE WORK OF A LIFETIME! I WILL NOT SEE IT DESTROYED BY YOUR MALICIOUS INCOMPETENCE!
I AM ON THE VERGE OF MANKIND'S GREATEST DISCOVERY!

THEY CAME THIS WAY. IT IS THE ONLY POSSIBLE PATH FROM THE TUNNEL ABOVE.
THE PERFECT PLACE FOR AN AMBUSH, URSO.
THAT'S WHY WE HAVE A BLOODHOUND.
SOMETHING ABOUT ONE HUNDRED METERS AHEAD. WHAT DOES THAT LOOK LIKE TO YOU?
BACK! EVERYONE BACK!
OH.
00:00:05
RUN!
OUT OF MY WAY!

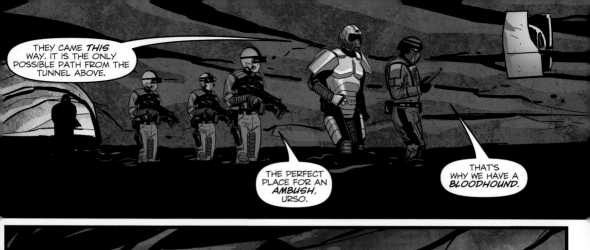

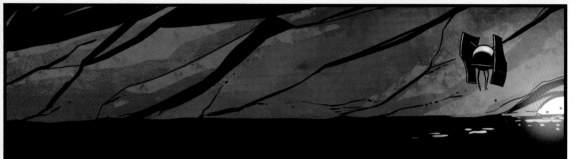

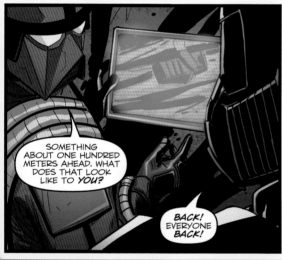

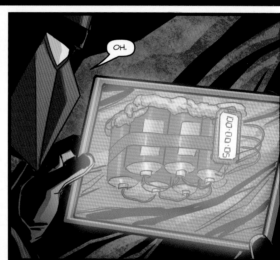

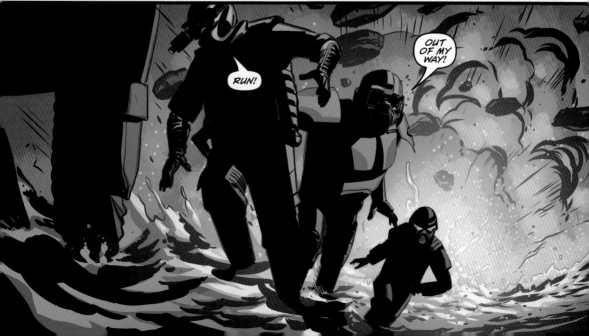

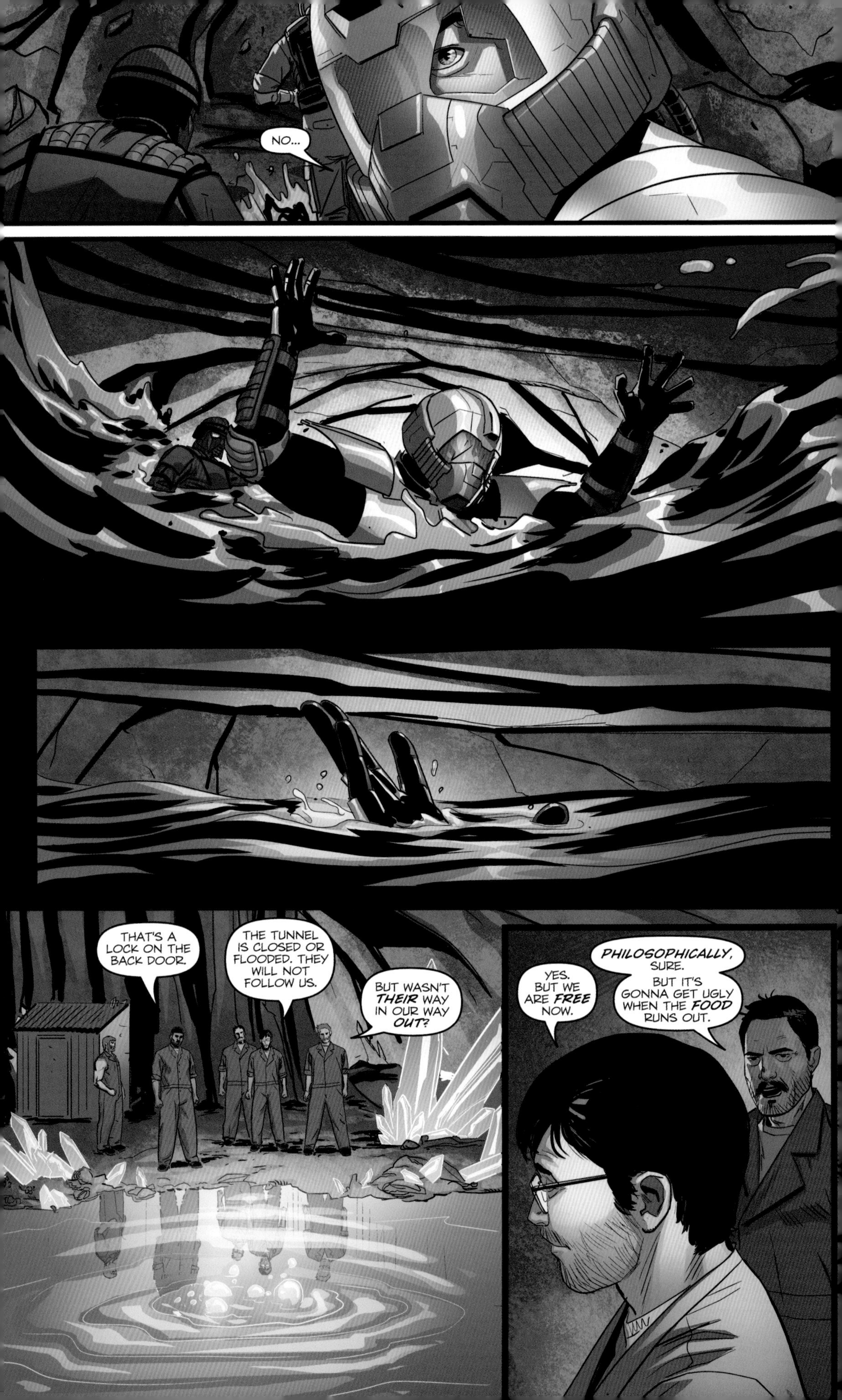
NO...
THAT'S A LOCK ON THE BACK DOOR.
THE TUNNEL IS CLOSED OR FLOODED. THEY WILL NOT FOLLOW US.
BUT WASN'T *THEIR* WAY IN OUR WAY *OUT*?
YES. BUT WE ARE *FREE* NOW.
PHILOSOPHICALLY, SURE. BUT IT'S GONNA GET UGLY WHEN THE *FOOD* RUNS OUT.

THEY'RE FINALLY OFF.

AND THEY'RE SET UP FOR IN-FLIGHT REFUELS. *RIGHT*, BILDOCKER?

MOSTLY.

MOSTLY?

LITTLE HANG-UP ON THE FINAL *LEG*. I'LL HAVE IT SQUARED AWAY BEFORE THEY *GET* THERE, SIR.

NORTH GATE TO JOE CENTRAL.

SO I HAVE A HEAVY DUE TO RUN OUT OF *GAS* OVER BOLIVIA?

NEVER GONNA *HAPPEN*. IT'S JUST A MATTER OF LEVERAGE.

IF YOU CAN'T DO IT, I'LL HAVE YOUR *HEAD*. IF YOU *CAN* DO IT, I DON'T WANT TO KNOW HOW.

ROGER THAT!

SIR?

GO FOR DUKE.

UM... WE HAVE A... SITUATION HERE AT THE NORTH GATE, SIR.

SITUATION?

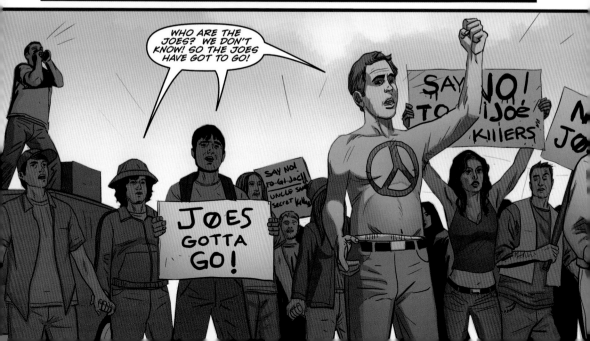

WHO ARE THE JOES? WE DON'T KNOW! SO THE JOES HAVE GOT TO GO!

SAY NO! TO iJOé KiIIerS

JOES GOTTA GO!

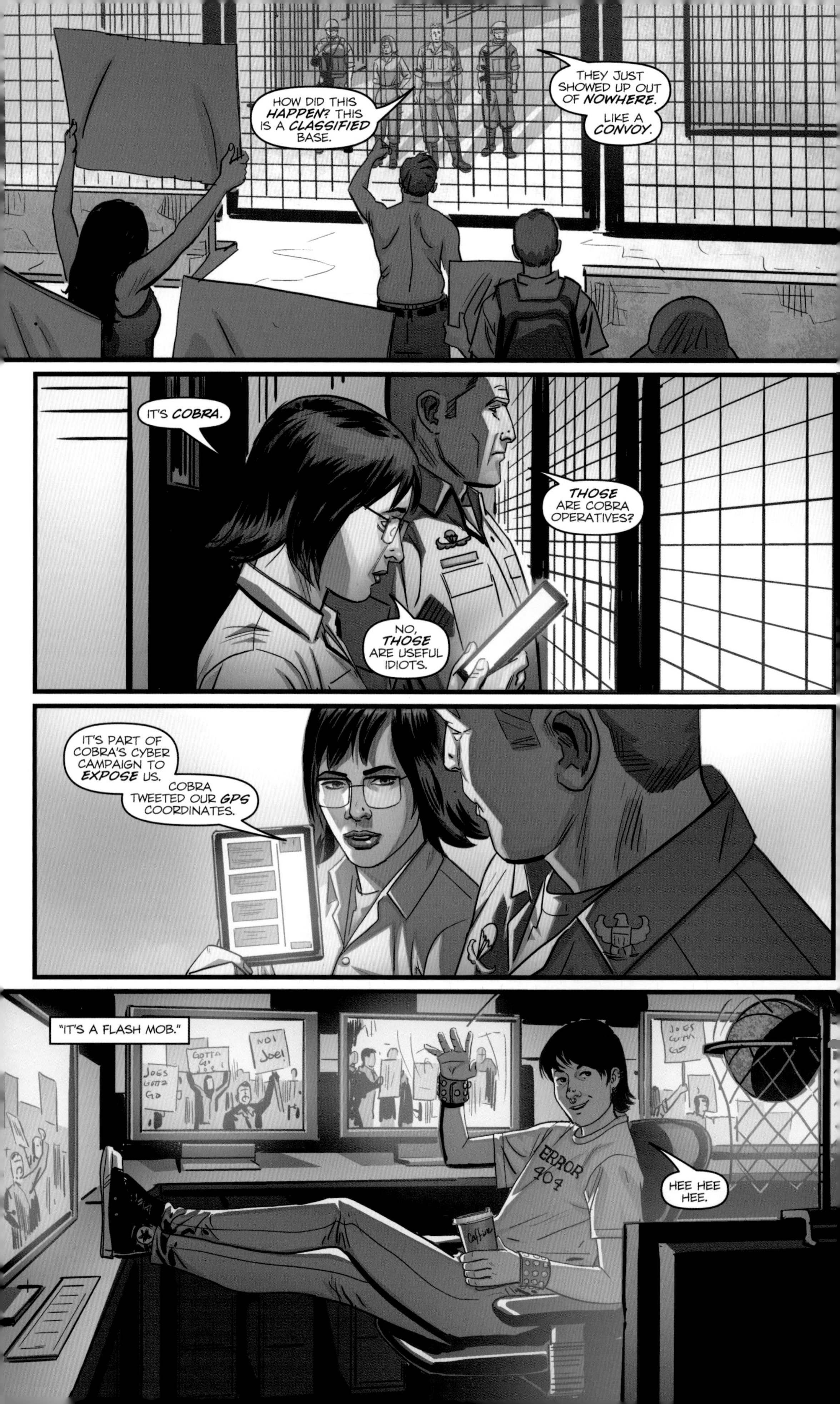
HOW DID THIS *HAPPEN?* THIS IS A *CLASSIFIED* BASE.
THEY JUST SHOWED UP OUT OF *NOWHERE*.
LIKE A *CONVOY*.
IT'S *COBRA*.
THOSE ARE COBRA OPERATIVES?
NO, *THOSE* ARE USEFUL IDIOTS.
IT'S PART OF COBRA'S CYBER CAMPAIGN TO *EXPOSE* US.
COBRA TWEETED OUR *GPS* COORDINATES.
"IT'S A FLASH MOB."
ERROR 404
HEE HEE HEE.

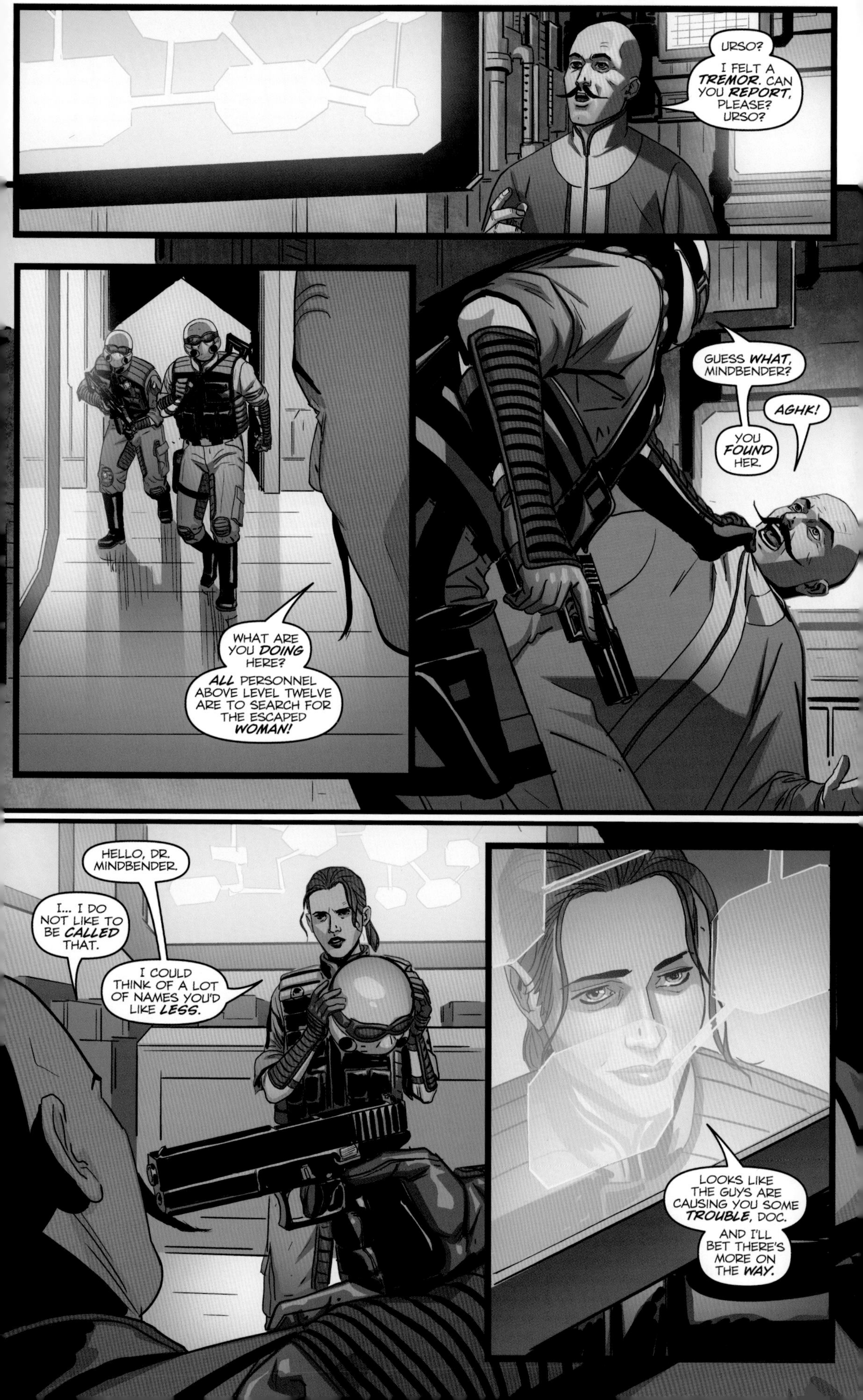
URSO?
I FELT A TREMOR. CAN YOU REPORT, PLEASE? URSO?
WHAT ARE YOU DOING HERE?
ALL PERSONNEL ABOVE LEVEL TWELVE ARE TO SEARCH FOR THE ESCAPED WOMAN!
GUESS WHAT, MINDBENDER?
YOU FOUND HER.
AGHK!
HELLO, DR. MINDBENDER.
I... I DO NOT LIKE TO BE CALLED THAT.
I COULD THINK OF A LOT OF NAMES YOU'D LIKE LESS.
LOOKS LIKE THE GUYS ARE CAUSING YOU SOME TROUBLE, DOC.
AND I'LL BET THERE'S MORE ON THE WAY.

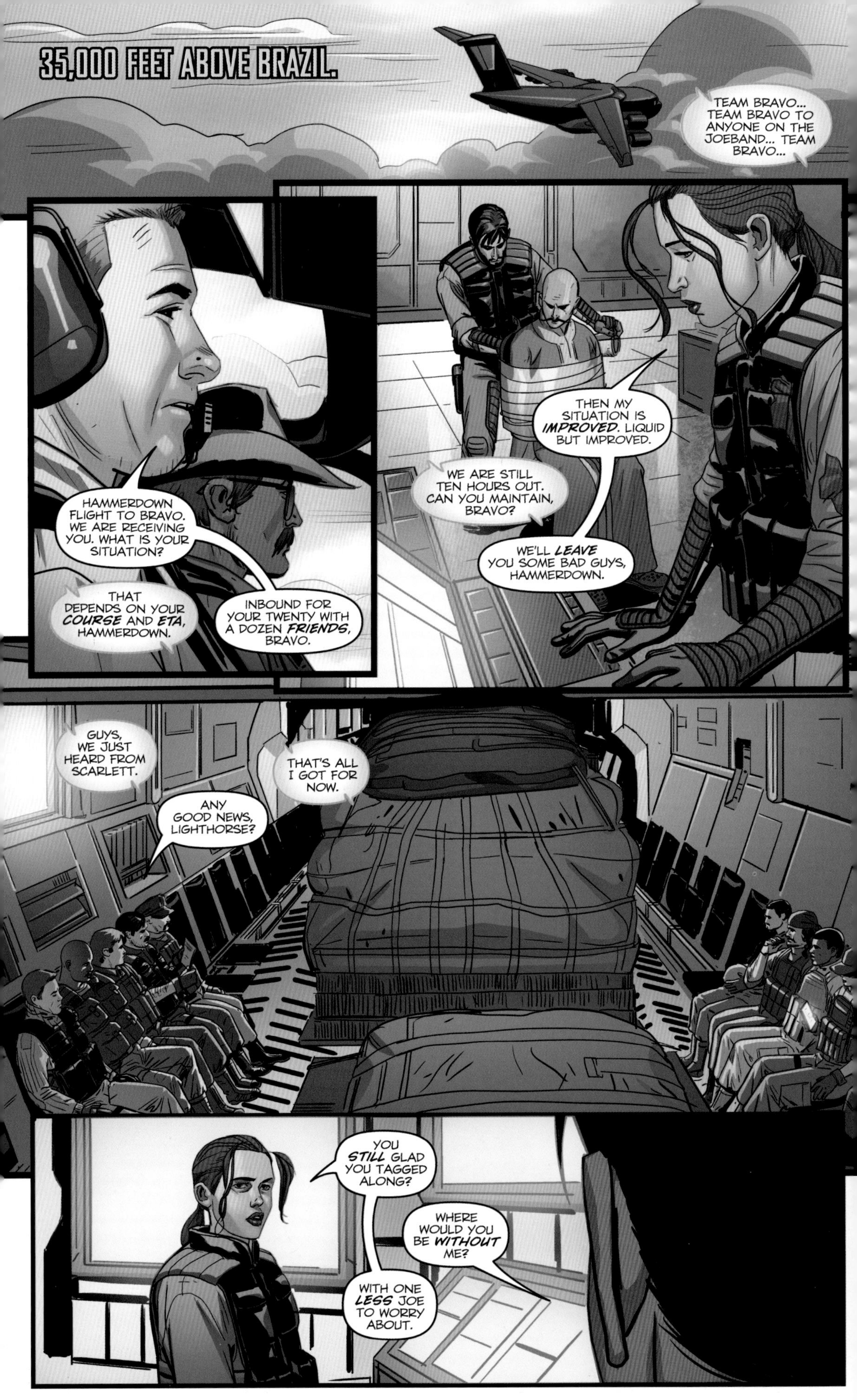
35,000 FEET ABOVE BRAZIL.
TEAM BRAVO... TEAM BRAVO TO ANYONE ON THE JOEBAND... TEAM BRAVO...
HAMMERDOWN FLIGHT TO BRAVO. WE ARE RECEIVING YOU. WHAT IS YOUR SITUATION?
THAT DEPENDS ON YOUR COURSE AND ETA, HAMMERDOWN.
INBOUND FOR YOUR TWENTY WITH A DOZEN FRIENDS, BRAVO.
THEN MY SITUATION IS IMPROVED. LIQUID BUT IMPROVED.
WE ARE STILL TEN HOURS OUT. CAN YOU MAINTAIN, BRAVO?
WE'LL LEAVE YOU SOME BAD GUYS, HAMMERDOWN.
GUYS, WE JUST HEARD FROM SCARLETT.
ANY GOOD NEWS, LIGHTHORSE?
THAT'S ALL I GOT FOR NOW.
YOU STILL GLAD YOU TAGGED ALONG?
WHERE WOULD YOU BE WITHOUT ME?
WITH ONE LESS JOE TO WORRY ABOUT.

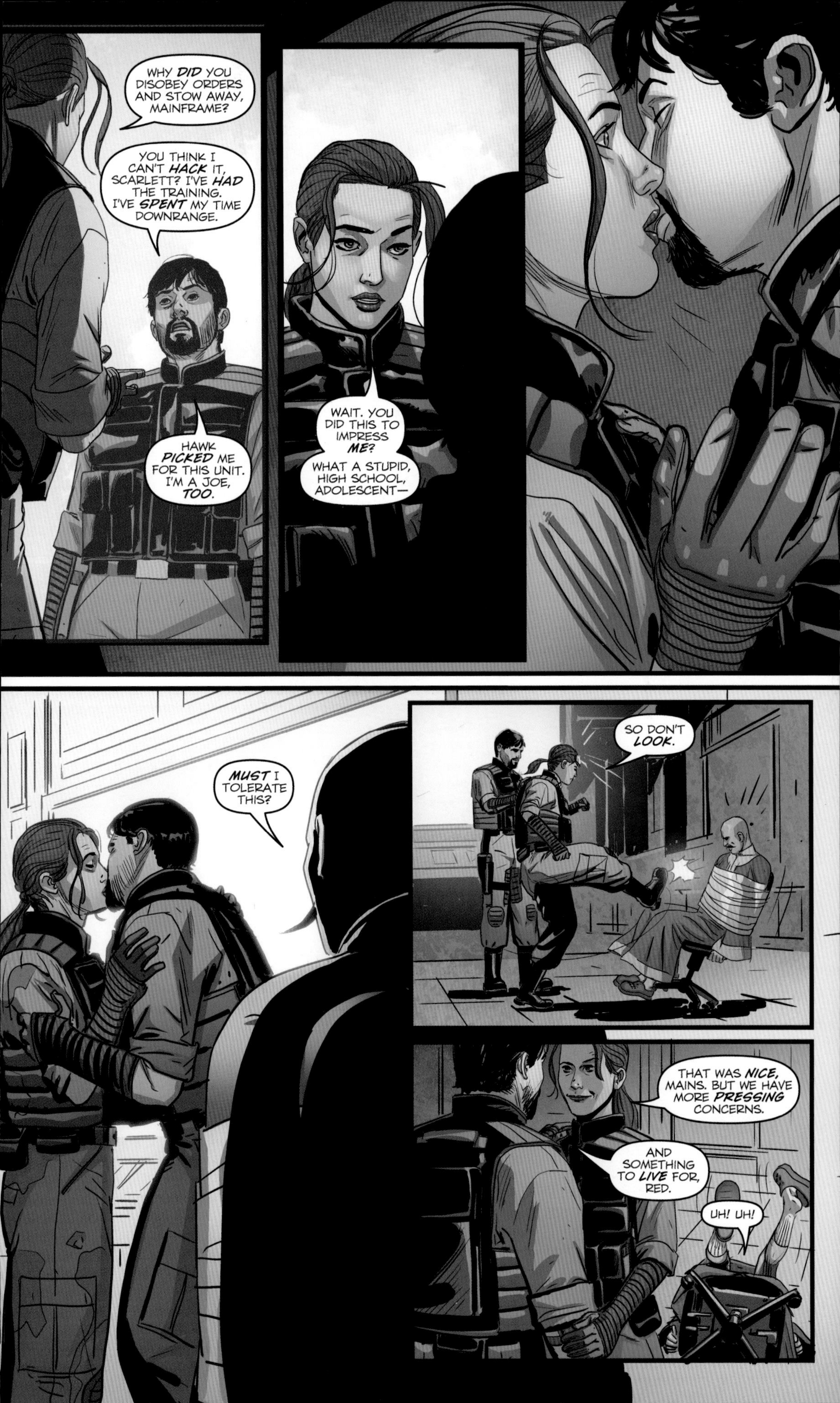
WHY DID YOU DISOBEY ORDERS AND STOW AWAY, MAINFRAME?
YOU THINK I CAN'T HACK IT, SCARLETT? I'VE HAD THE TRAINING. I'VE SPENT MY TIME DOWNRANGE.
HAWK PICKED ME FOR THIS UNIT. I'M A JOE, TOO.
WAIT. YOU DID THIS TO IMPRESS ME?
WHAT A STUPID, HIGH SCHOOL, ADOLESCENT—
MUST I TOLERATE THIS?
SO DON'T LOOK.
THAT WAS NICE, MAINS. BUT WE HAVE MORE PRESSING CONCERNS.
AND SOMETHING TO LIVE FOR, RED.
UH! UH!

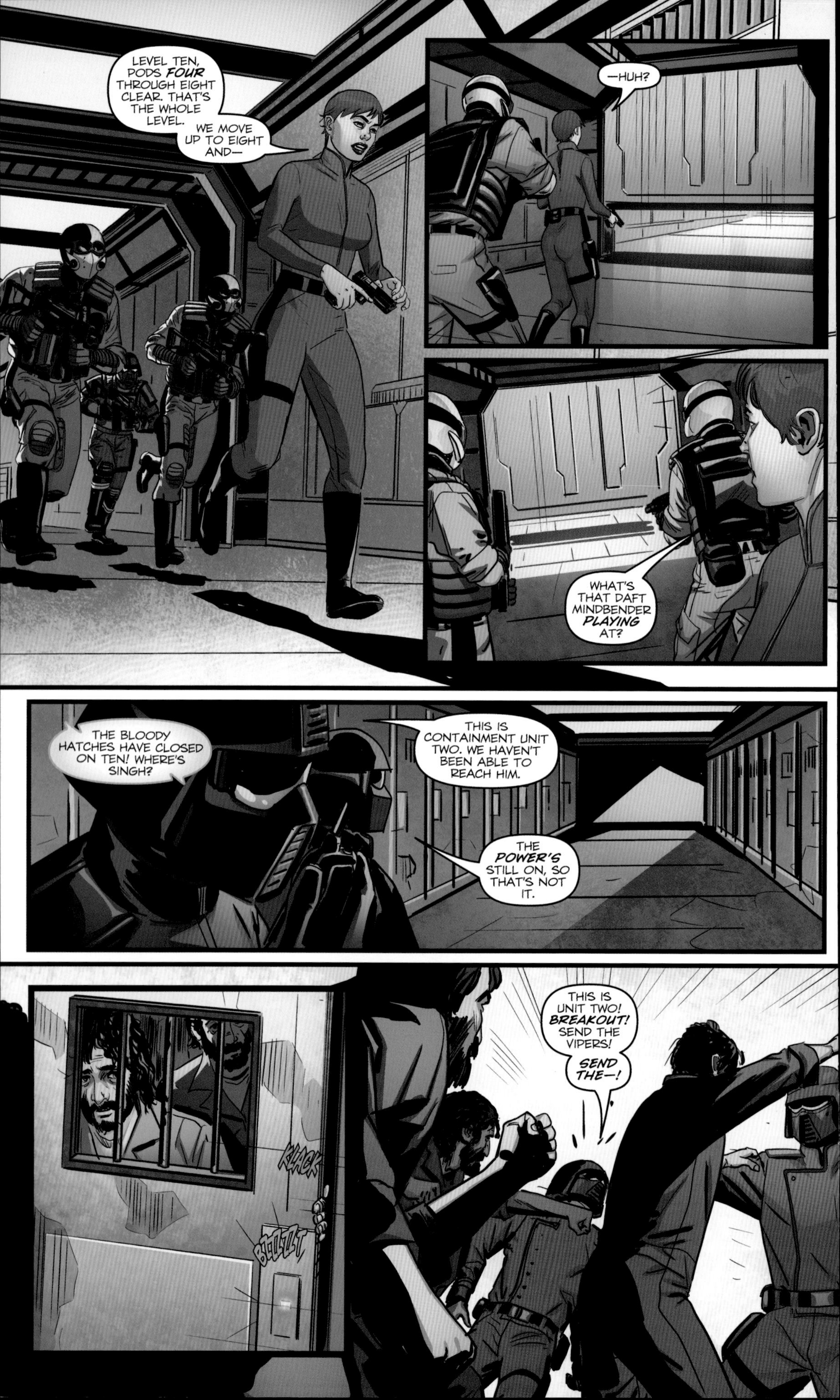
LEVEL TEN, PODS FOUR THROUGH EIGHT CLEAR. THAT'S THE WHOLE LEVEL.
WE MOVE UP TO EIGHT AND—
—HUH?
WHAT'S THAT DAFT MINDBENDER PLAYING AT?
THE BLOODY HATCHES HAVE CLOSED ON TEN! WHERE'S SINGH?
THIS IS CONTAINMENT UNIT TWO. WE HAVEN'T BEEN ABLE TO REACH HIM.
THE POWER'S STILL ON, SO THAT'S NOT IT.
KLACK
BZZZT
THIS IS UNIT TWO! BREAKOUT! SEND THE VIPERS!
SEND THE—!

I HAVE MOST OF THEIR SEARCH UNITS LOCKED *DOWN* AND *ISOLATED.*

AND THE CELL BLOCKS ARE *WIDE* OPEN.

GOOD WORK, MAINS.

THIS IS SCARLETT TO ANY JOES. BRAVO, YOU COPY?

STALKER HERE, RED. HOW AM I *HEARING* YOU?

COBRA WIRED THE WHOLE MINE WITH A WI-FI RELAY. SO, YOU BOYS ARE ON THE RUN.

ROGER THAT. WE'RE GOING *DEEP* HERE.

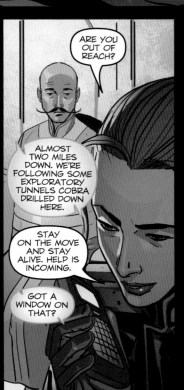

ARE YOU OUT OF REACH?

ALMOST TWO MILES DOWN. WE'RE FOLLOWING SOME EXPLORATORY TUNNELS COBRA DRILLED DOWN HERE.

STAY ON THE MOVE AND STAY ALIVE. HELP IS INCOMING.

GOT A WINDOW ON THAT?

CANNOT CONFIRM. CAN YOU GIVE ME YOUR TWENTY?

THERE'S MARKINGS ON THE WALL EVERY HUNDRED FEET OR SO. A LOCATION CODE?

FIVE-X-X-FIVE.

NO...

HAS TO BE SIGNIFICANT. WE'LL LOOK FOR IT ON THE CHARTS HERE.

WE?

MAINFRAME IS HERE.

JUST MAINFRAME? HOLD ON, RED...

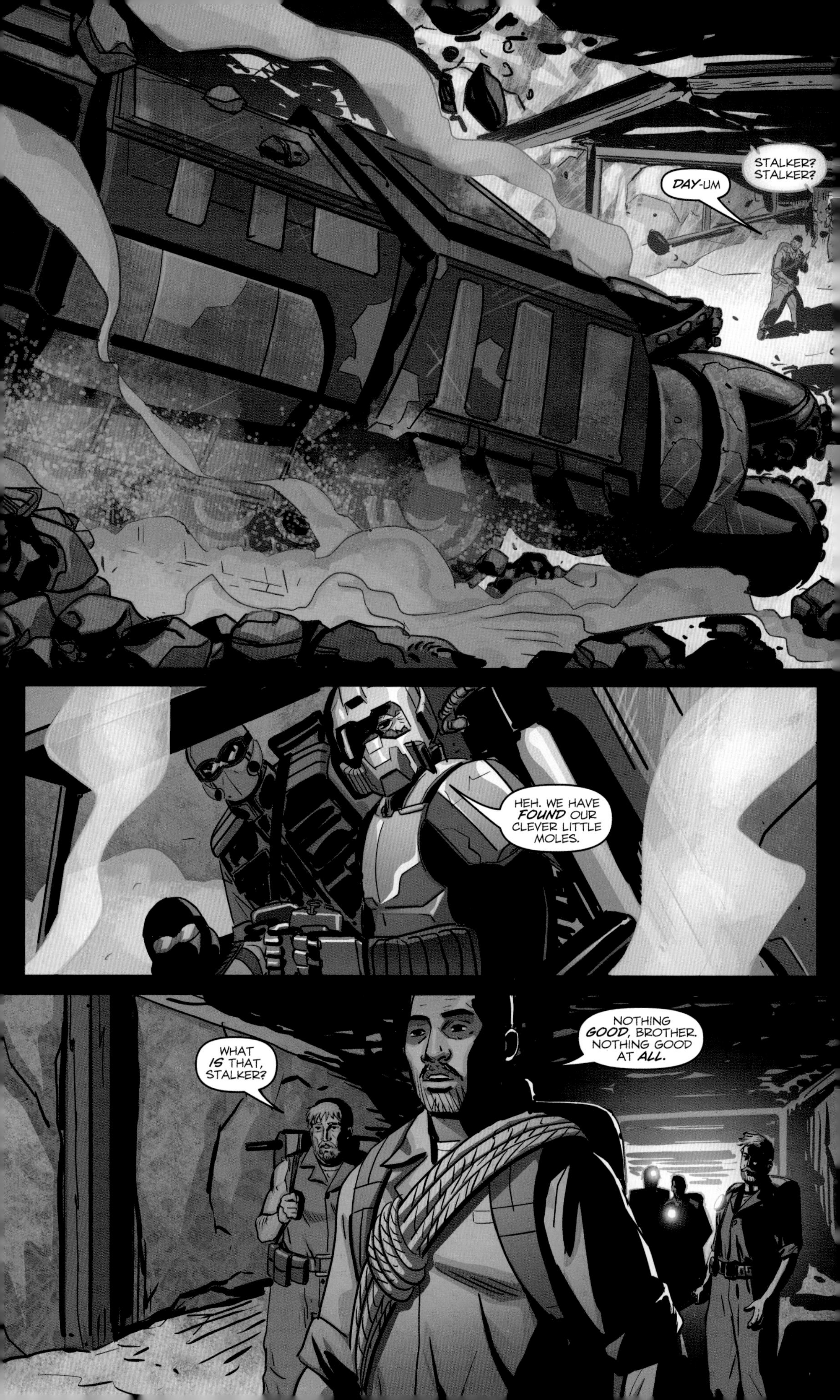
STALKER? STALKER?
DAY-UM
HEH. WE HAVE FOUND OUR CLEVER LITTLE MOLES.
WHAT IS THAT, STALKER?
NOTHING GOOD, BROTHER. NOTHING GOOD AT ALL.

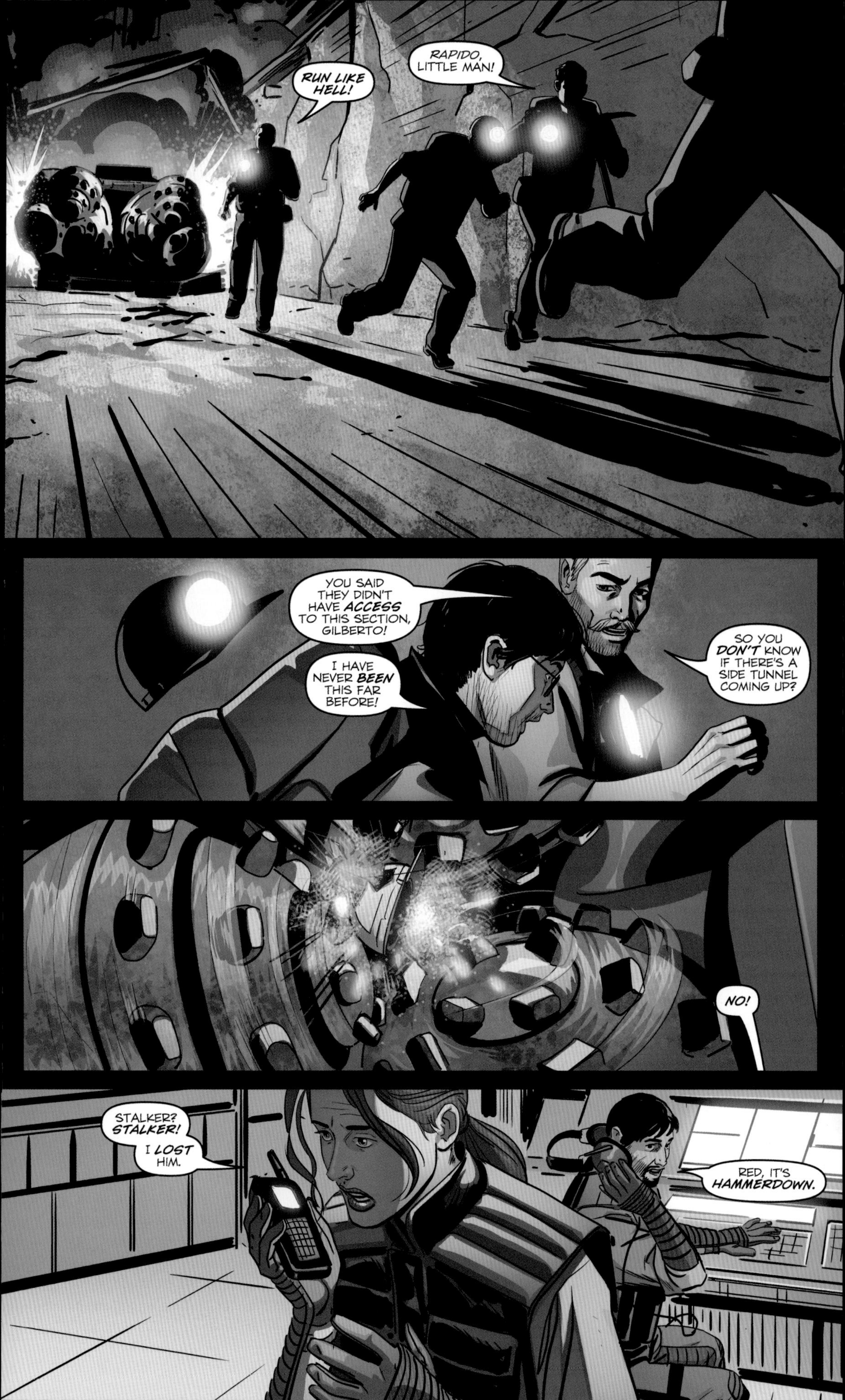
RUN LIKE HELL!
RAPIDO, LITTLE MAN!
YOU SAID THEY DIDN'T HAVE ACCESS TO THIS SECTION, GILBERTO!
I HAVE NEVER BEEN THIS FAR BEFORE!
SO YOU DON'T KNOW IF THERE'S A SIDE TUNNEL COMING UP?
NO!
STALKER? STALKER!
I LOST HIM.
RED, IT'S HAMMERDOWN.

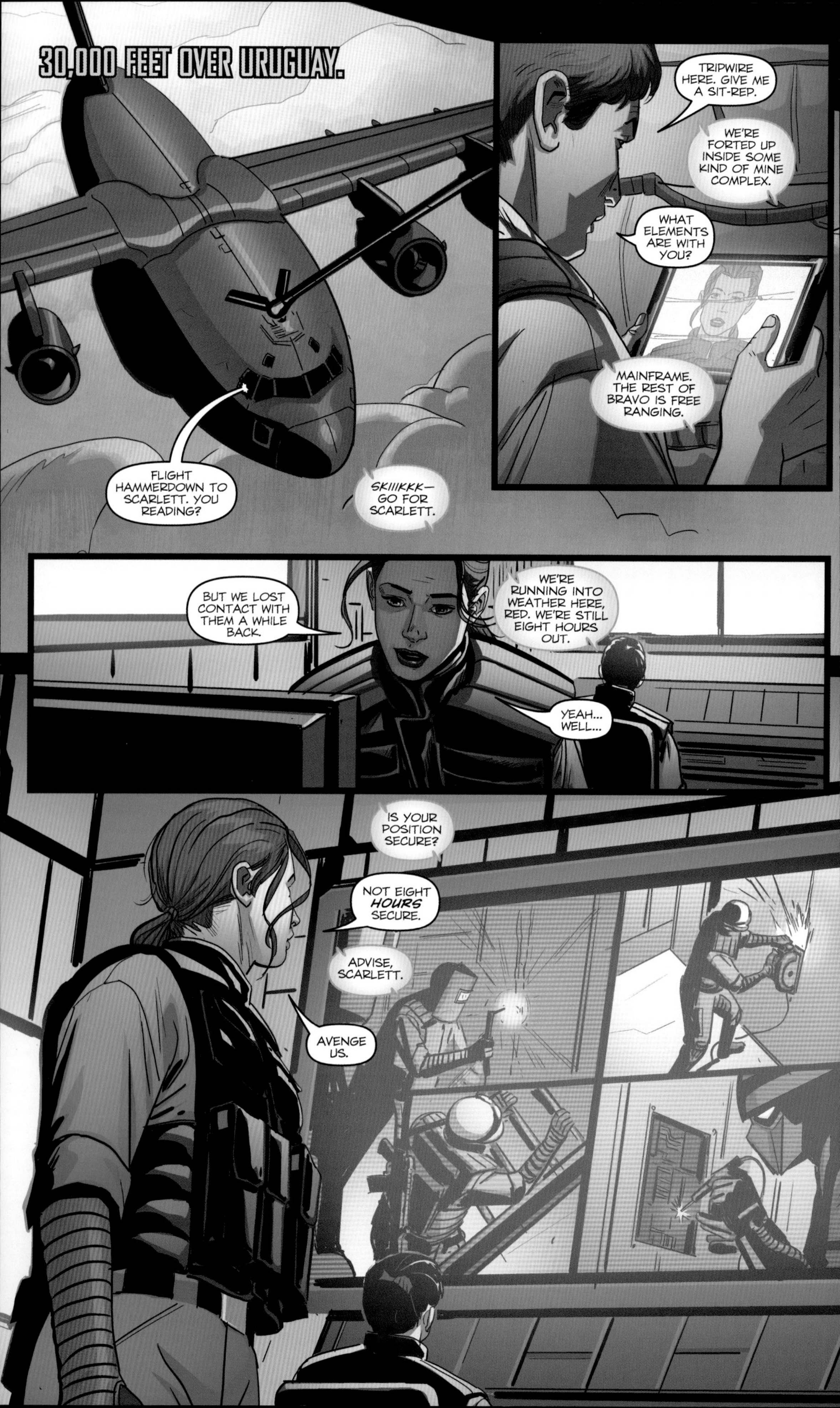
30,000 FEET OVER URUGUAY.
FLIGHT HAMMERDOWN TO SCARLETT. YOU READING?
SKIIIKKK— GO FOR SCARLETT.
TRIPWIRE HERE. GIVE ME A SIT-REP.
WE'RE FORTED UP INSIDE SOME KIND OF MINE COMPLEX.
WHAT ELEMENTS ARE WITH YOU?
MAINFRAME. THE REST OF BRAVO IS FREE RANGING.
BUT WE LOST CONTACT WITH THEM A WHILE BACK.
WE'RE RUNNING INTO WEATHER HERE, RED. WE'RE STILL EIGHT HOURS OUT.
YEAH... WELL...
IS YOUR POSITION SECURE?
NOT EIGHT HOURS SECURE.
ADVISE, SCARLETT.
AVENGE US.

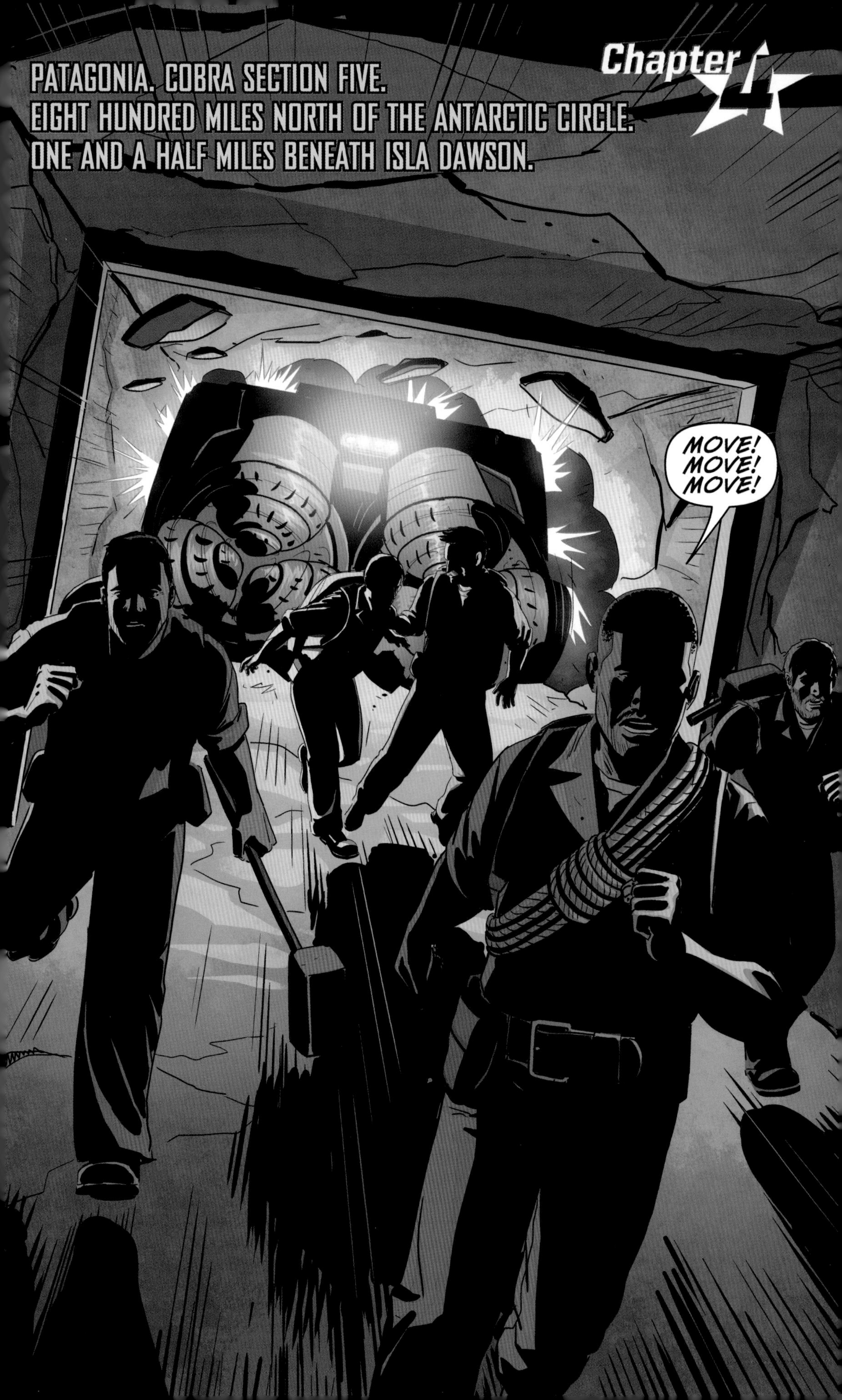
Chapter 4
PATAGONIA. COBRA SECTION FIVE.
EIGHT HUNDRED MILES NORTH OF THE ANTARCTIC CIRCLE.
ONE AND A HALF MILES BENEATH ISLA DAWSON.
MOVE! MOVE! MOVE!

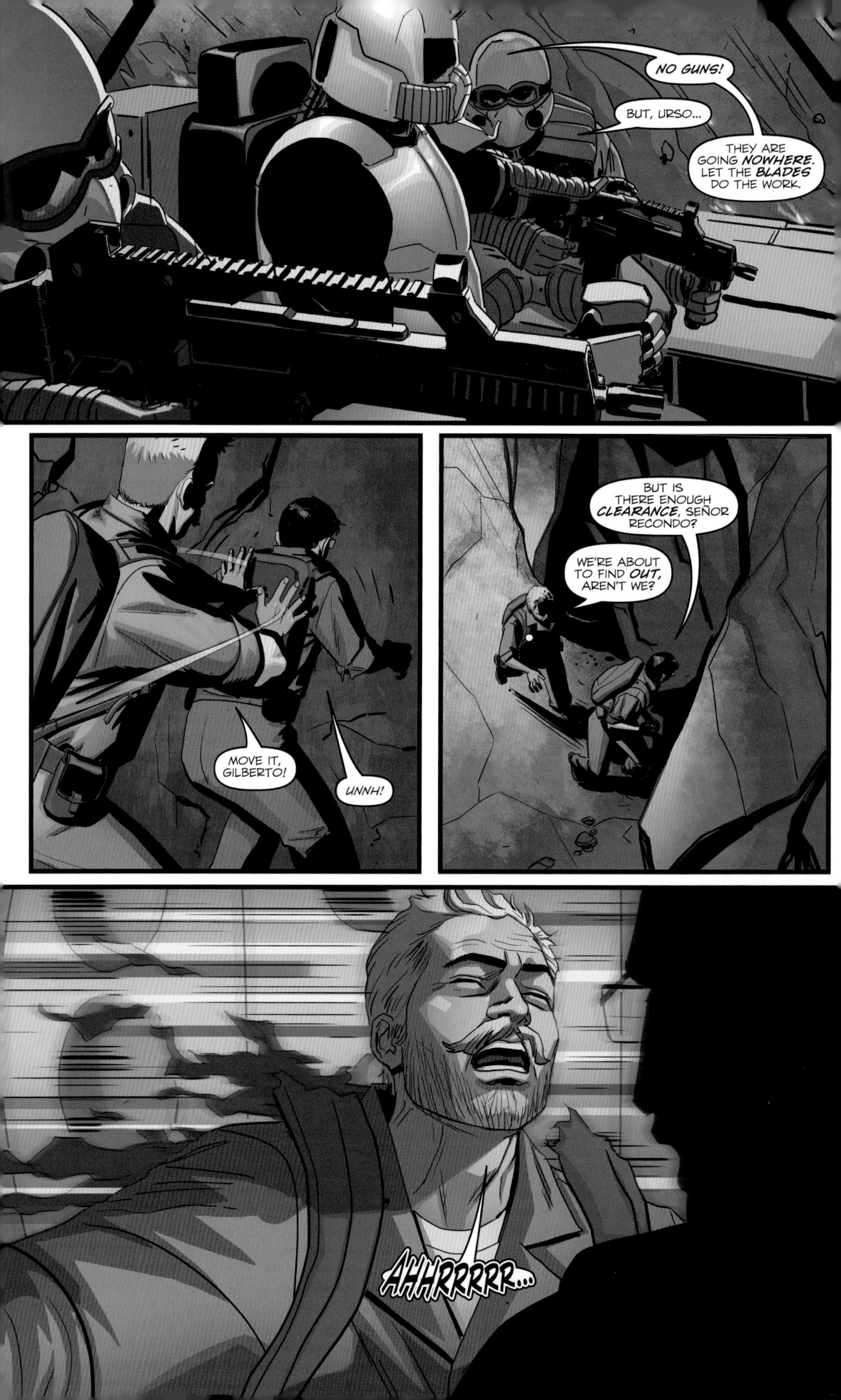
NO GUNS!
BUT, URSO...
THEY ARE GOING NOWHERE. LET THE BLADES DO THE WORK.
MOVE IT, GILBERTO!
UNNH!
BUT IS THERE ENOUGH CLEARANCE, SEÑOR RECONDO?
WE'RE ABOUT TO FIND OUT, AREN'T WE?
AHHRRRRR...

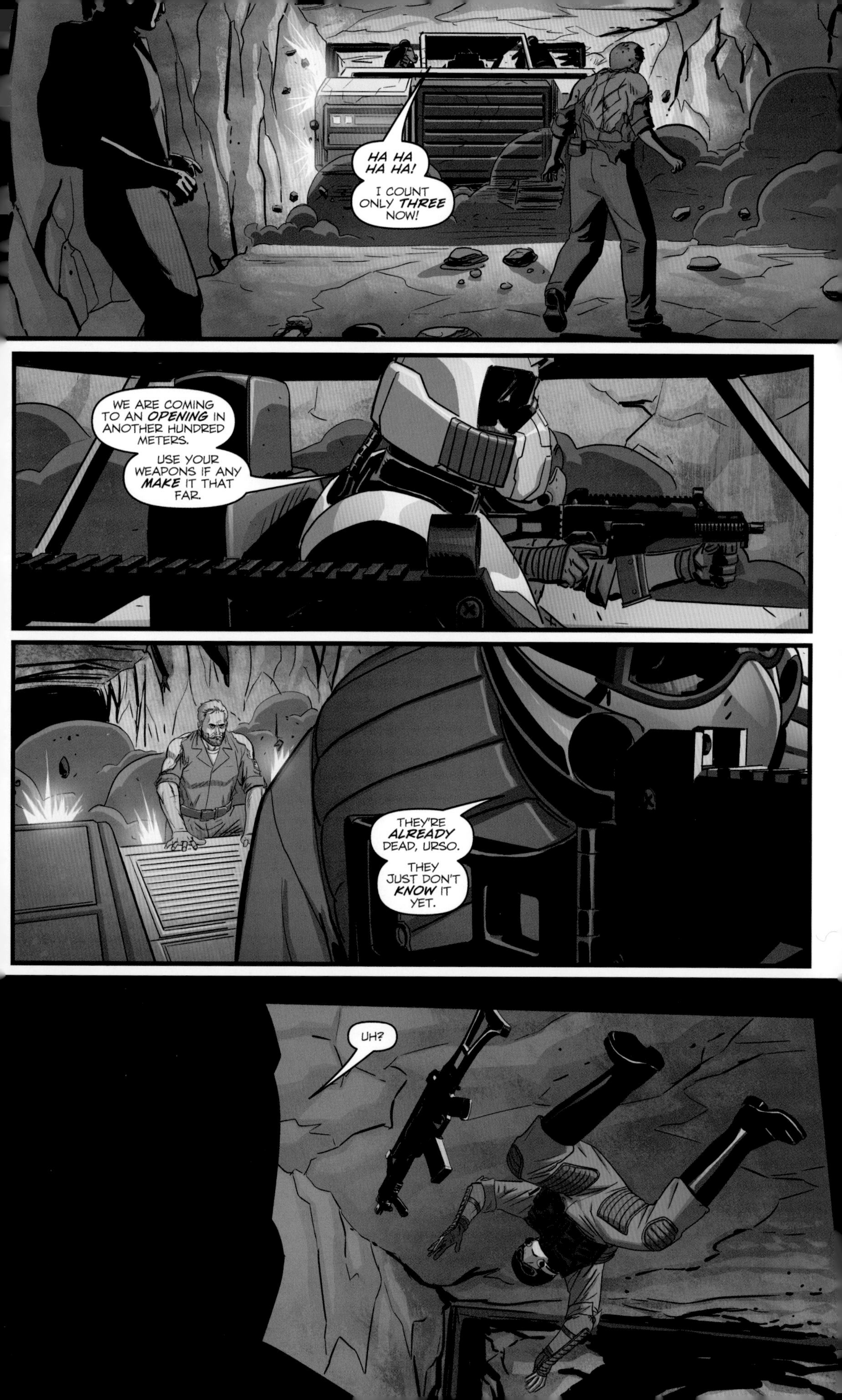
HA HA HA HA! I COUNT ONLY THREE NOW!
WE ARE COMING TO AN OPENING IN ANOTHER HUNDRED METERS.
USE YOUR WEAPONS IF ANY MAKE IT THAT FAR.
THEY'RE ALREADY DEAD, URSO.
THEY JUST DON'T KNOW IT YET.
UH?

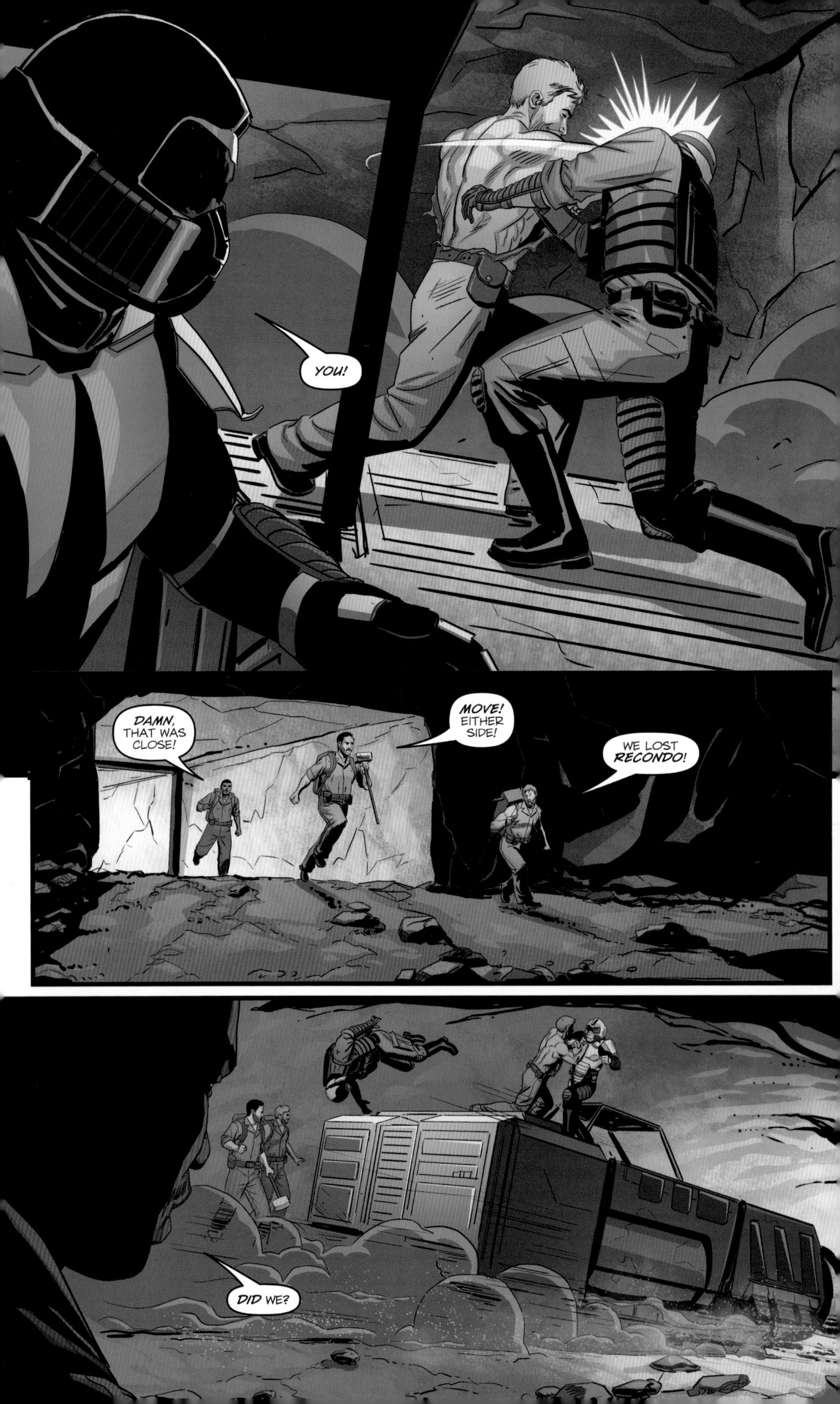
YOU!
DAMN, THAT WAS CLOSE!
MOVE! EITHER SIDE!
WE LOST RECONDO!
DID WE?

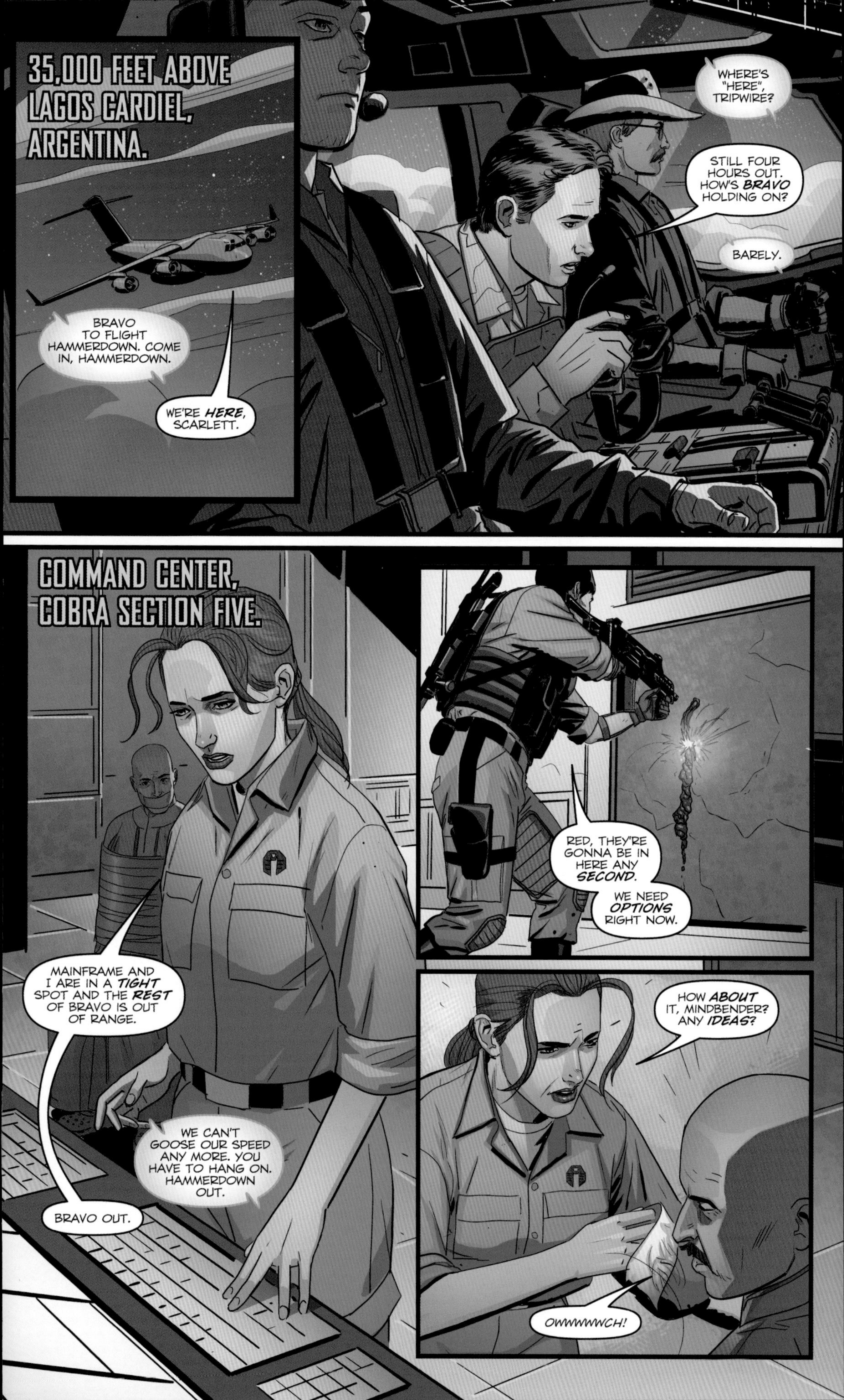
35,000 FEET ABOVE LAGOS CARDIEL, ARGENTINA.
BRAVO TO FLIGHT HAMMERDOWN. COME IN, HAMMERDOWN.
WE'RE HERE, SCARLETT.
WHERE'S "HERE", TRIPWIRE?
STILL FOUR HOURS OUT. HOW'S BRAVO HOLDING ON?
BARELY.
COMMAND CENTER, COBRA SECTION FIVE.
MAINFRAME AND I ARE IN A TIGHT SPOT AND THE REST OF BRAVO IS OUT OF RANGE.
WE CAN'T GOOSE OUR SPEED ANY MORE. YOU HAVE TO HANG ON. HAMMERDOWN OUT.
BRAVO OUT.
RED, THEY'RE GONNA BE IN HERE ANY SECOND.
WE NEED OPTIONS RIGHT NOW.
HOW ABOUT IT, MINDBENDER? ANY IDEAS?
OWWWWWCH!

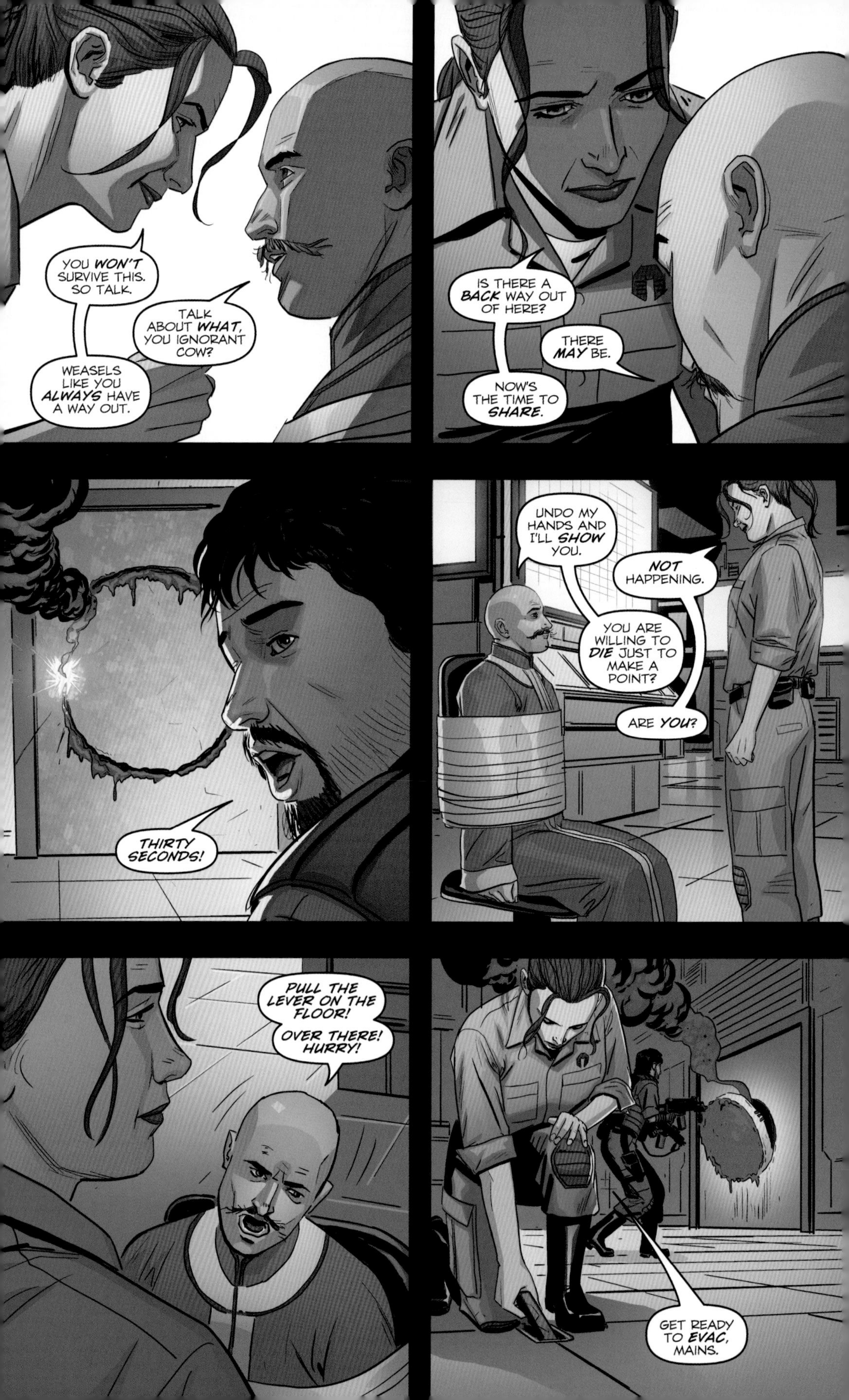
YOU WON'T SURVIVE THIS. SO TALK.
TALK ABOUT WHAT, YOU IGNORANT COW?
WEASELS LIKE YOU ALWAYS HAVE A WAY OUT.
IS THERE A BACK WAY OUT OF HERE?
THERE MAY BE.
NOW'S THE TIME TO SHARE.
THIRTY SECONDS!
UNDO MY HANDS AND I'LL SHOW YOU.
NOT HAPPENING.
YOU ARE WILLING TO DIE JUST TO MAKE A POINT?
ARE YOU?
PULL THE LEVER ON THE FLOOR!
OVER THERE! HURRY!
GET READY TO EVAC, MAINS.

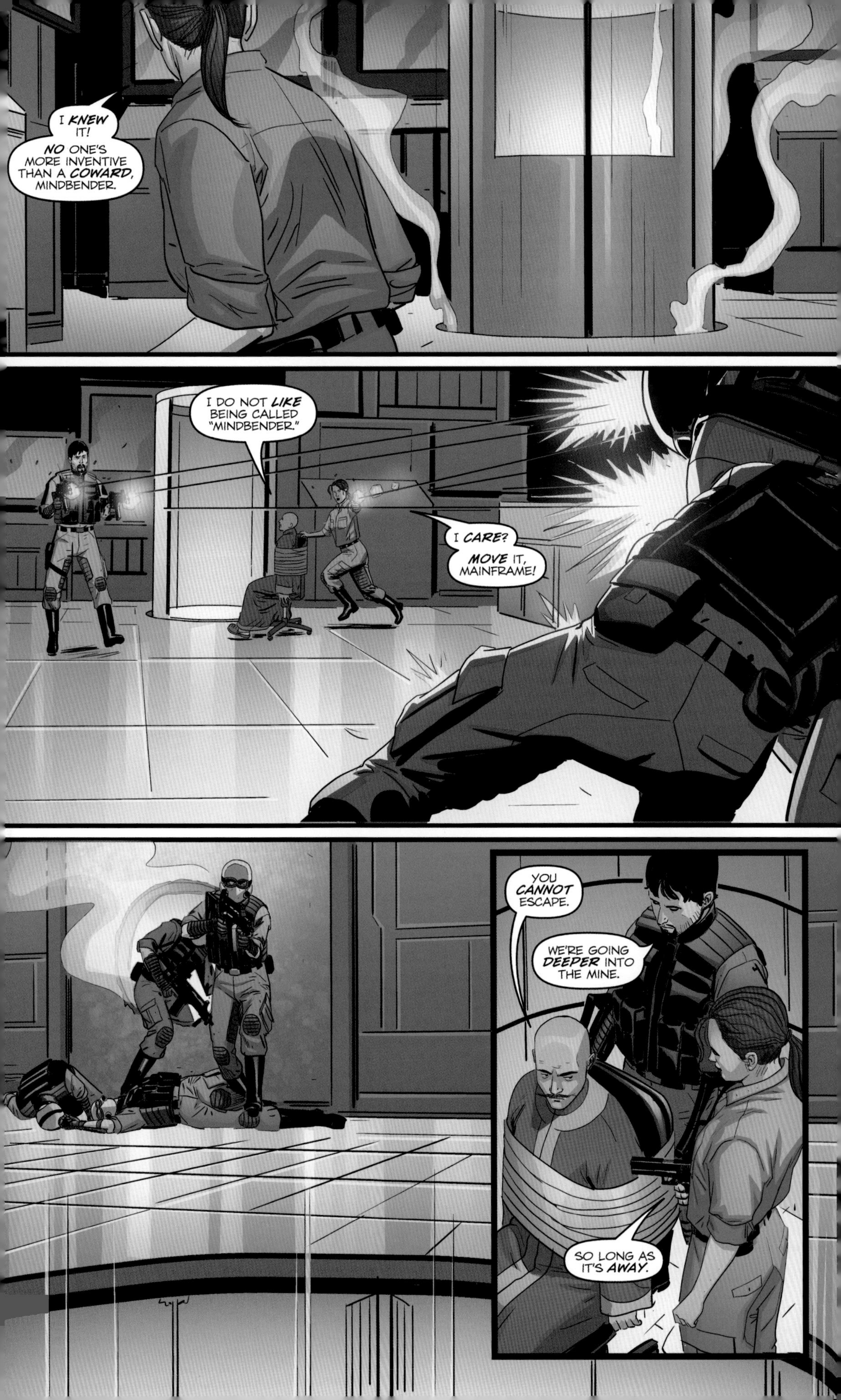
I KNEW IT!
NO ONE'S MORE INVENTIVE THAN A COWARD, MINDBENDER.
I DO NOT LIKE BEING CALLED "MINDBENDER."
I CARE?
MOVE IT, MAINFRAME!
YOU CANNOT ESCAPE.
WE'RE GOING DEEPER INTO THE MINE.
SO LONG AS IT'S AWAY.

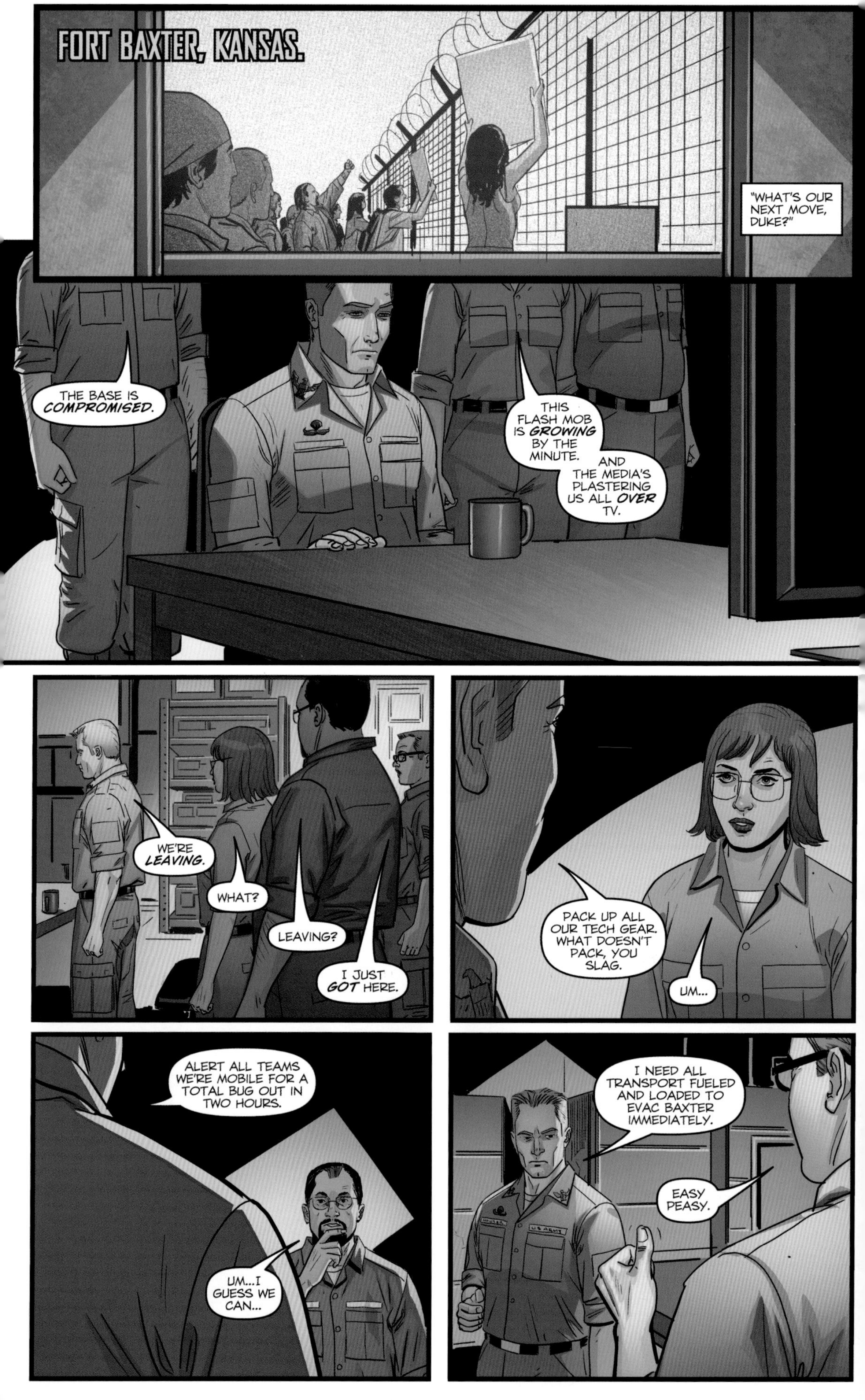
FORT BAXTER, KANSAS.
"WHAT'S OUR NEXT MOVE, DUKE?"
THE BASE IS COMPROMISED.
THIS FLASH MOB IS GROWING BY THE MINUTE.
AND THE MEDIA'S PLASTERING US ALL OVER TV.
WE'RE LEAVING.
WHAT?
LEAVING?
I JUST GOT HERE.
PACK UP ALL OUR TECH GEAR. WHAT DOESN'T PACK, YOU SLAG.
UM...
ALERT ALL TEAMS WE'RE MOBILE FOR A TOTAL BUG OUT IN TWO HOURS.
UM...I GUESS WE CAN...
I NEED ALL TRANSPORT FUELED AND LOADED TO EVAC BAXTER IMMEDIATELY.
EASY PEASY.

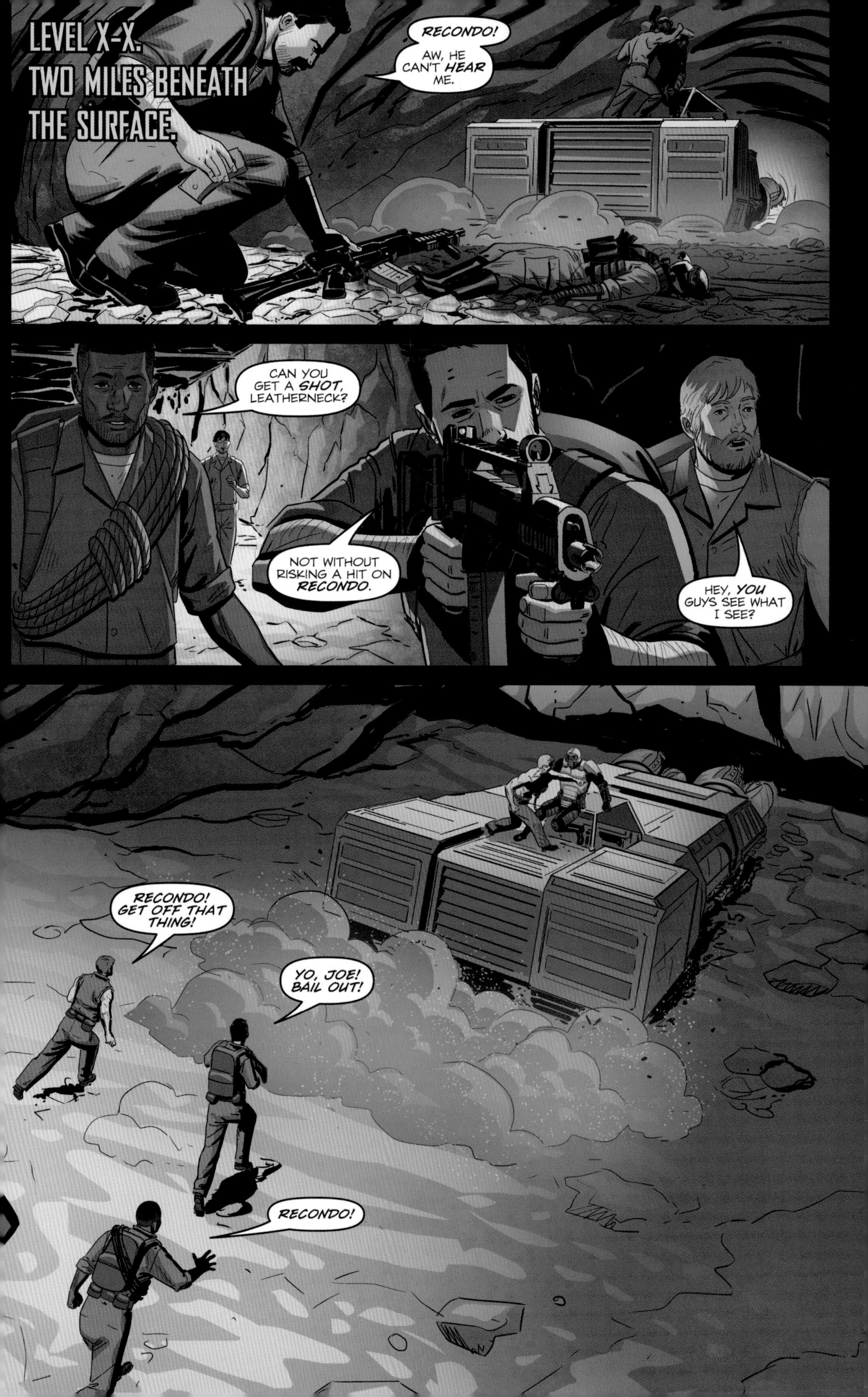
LEVEL X-X.
TWO MILES BENEATH THE SURFACE.
RECONDO!
AW, HE CAN'T HEAR ME.
CAN YOU GET A SHOT, LEATHERNECK?
NOT WITHOUT RISKING A HIT ON RECONDO.
HEY, YOU GUYS SEE WHAT I SEE?
RECONDO! GET OFF THAT THING!
YO, JOE! BAIL OUT!
RECONDO!

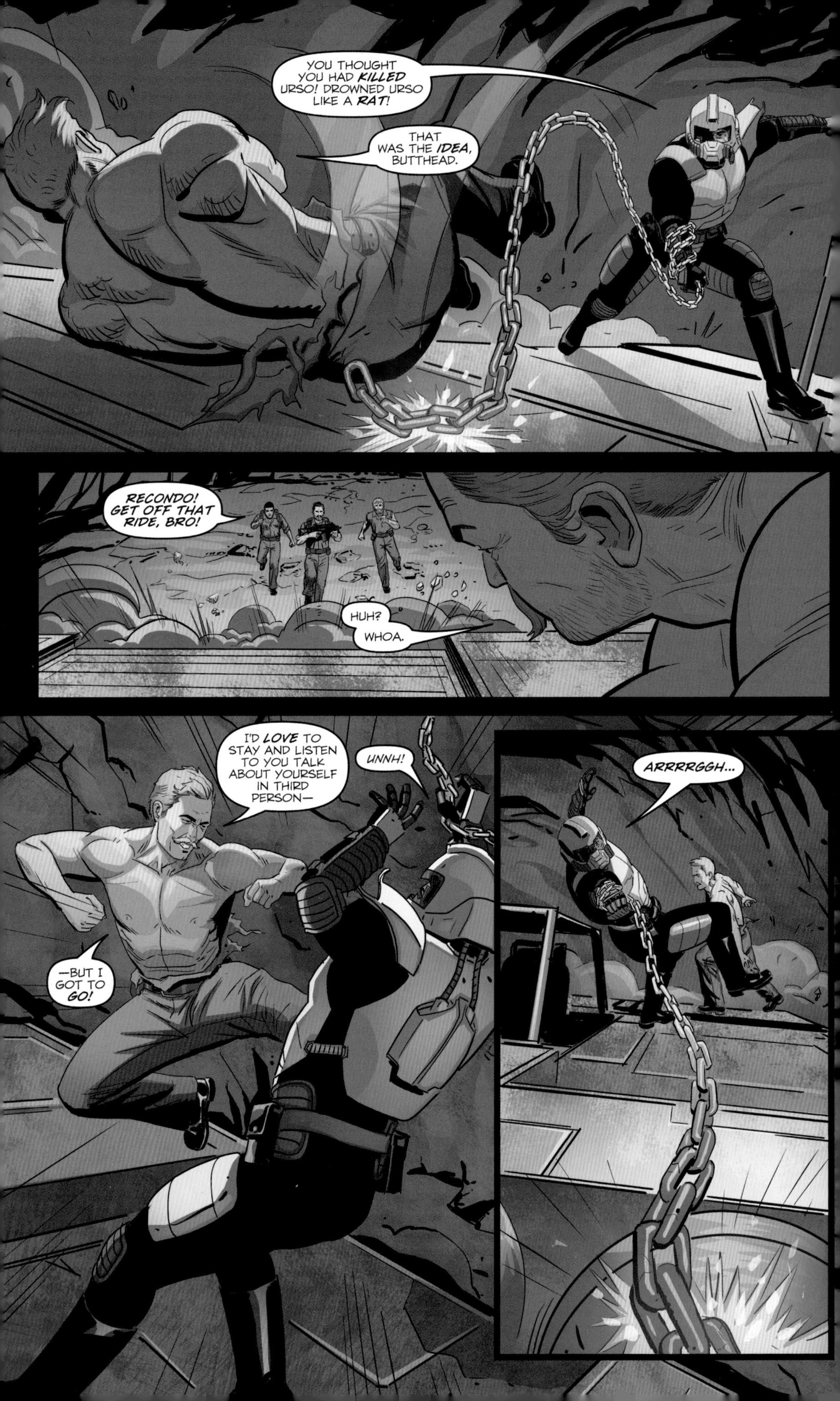
YOU THOUGHT YOU HAD KILLED URSO! DROWNED URSO LIKE A RAT!
THAT WAS THE IDEA, BUTTHEAD.
RECONDO! GET OFF THAT RIDE, BRO!
HUH?
WHOA.
I'D LOVE TO STAY AND LISTEN TO YOU TALK ABOUT YOURSELF IN THIRD PERSON—
UNNH!
—BUT I GOT TO GO!
ARRRRGGH...

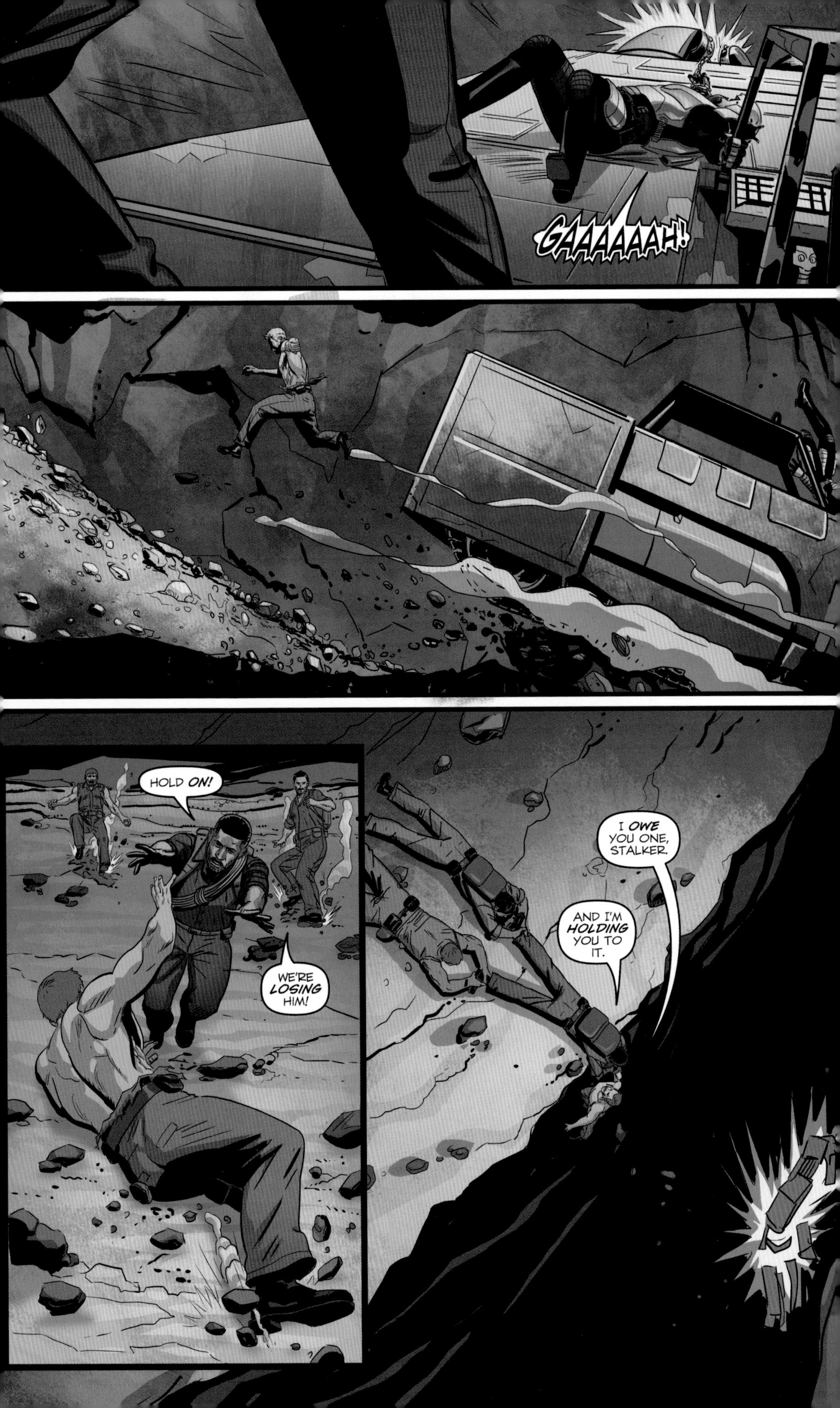
GAAAAAAH!
HOLD ON!
WE'RE LOSING HIM!
I OWE YOU ONE, STALKER.
AND I'M HOLDING YOU TO IT.

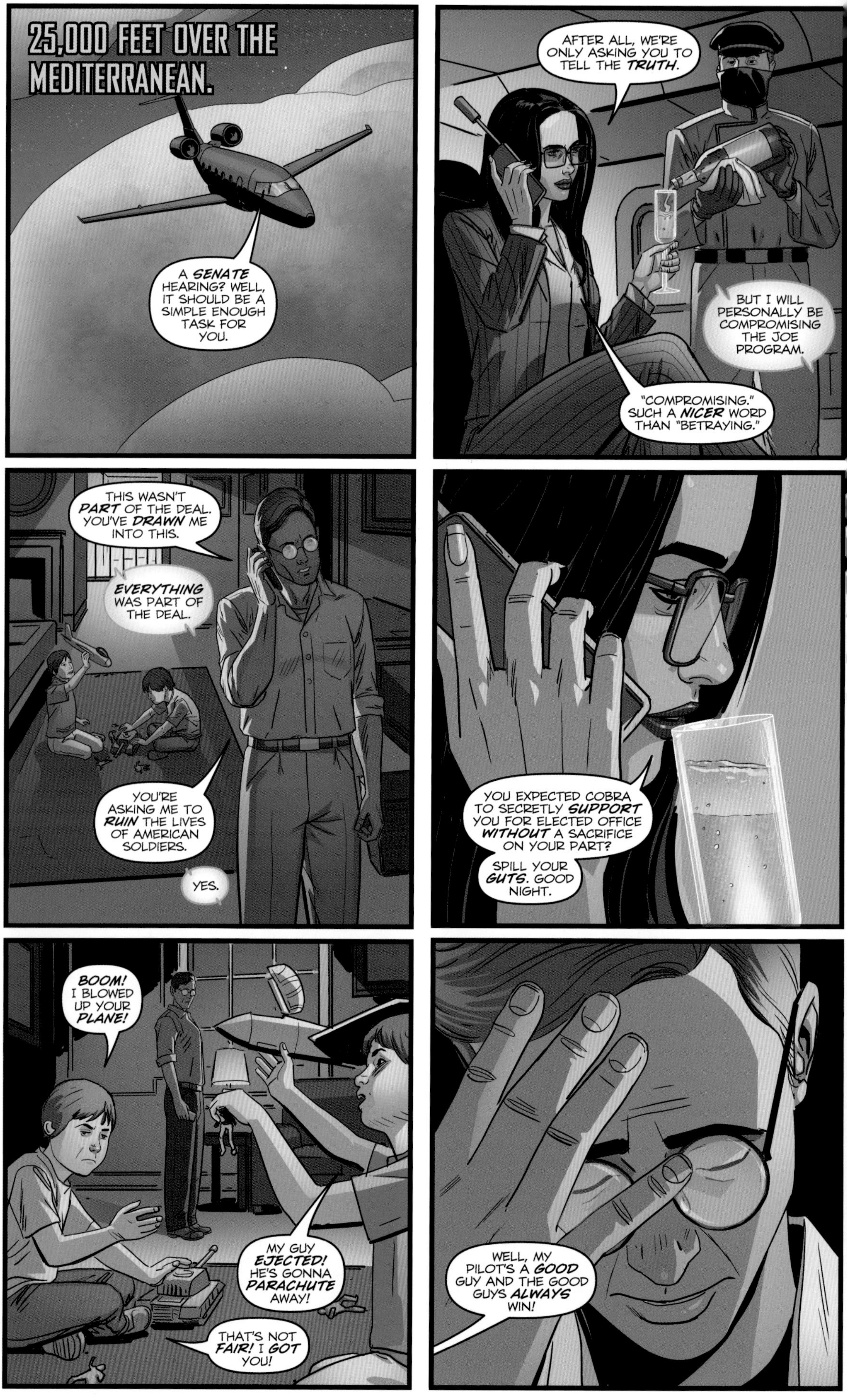
25,000 FEET OVER THE MEDITERRANEAN.
A SENATE HEARING? WELL, IT SHOULD BE A SIMPLE ENOUGH TASK FOR YOU.
AFTER ALL, WE'RE ONLY ASKING YOU TO TELL THE TRUTH.
BUT I WILL PERSONALLY BE COMPROMISING THE JOE PROGRAM.
"COMPROMISING." SUCH A NICER WORD THAN "BETRAYING."
THIS WASN'T PART OF THE DEAL. YOU'VE DRAWN ME INTO THIS.
EVERYTHING WAS PART OF THE DEAL.
YOU'RE ASKING ME TO RUIN THE LIVES OF AMERICAN SOLDIERS.
YES.
YOU EXPECTED COBRA TO SECRETLY SUPPORT YOU FOR ELECTED OFFICE WITHOUT A SACRIFICE ON YOUR PART?
SPILL YOUR GUTS. GOOD NIGHT.
BOOM! I BLOWED UP YOUR PLANE!
MY GUY EJECTED! HE'S GONNA PARACHUTE AWAY!
THAT'S NOT FAIR! I GOT YOU!
WELL, MY PILOT'S A GOOD GUY AND THE GOOD GUYS ALWAYS WIN!

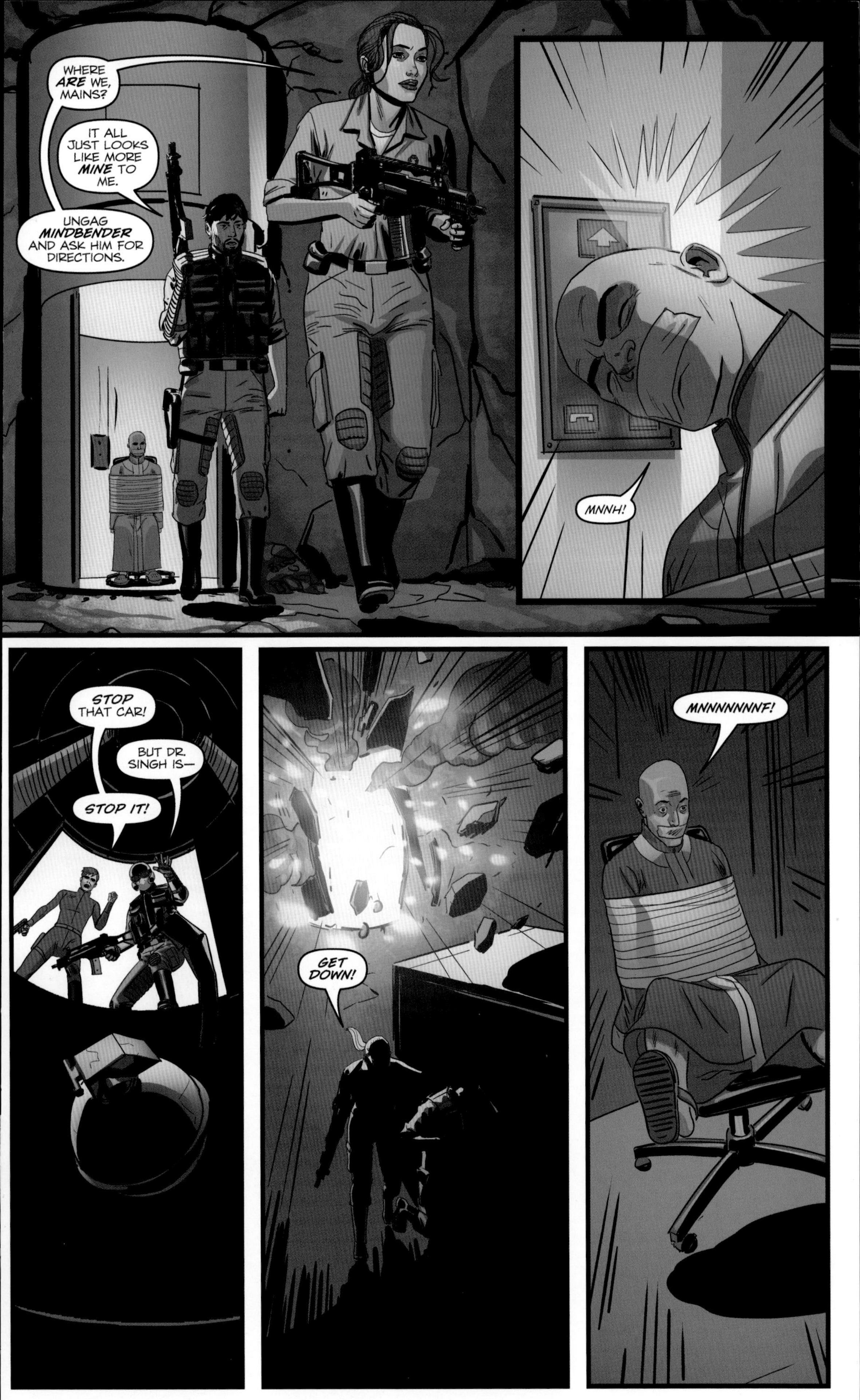
WHERE ARE WE, MAINS?
IT ALL JUST LOOKS LIKE MORE MINE TO ME.
UNGAG MINDBENDER AND ASK HIM FOR DIRECTIONS.
MNNH!
STOP THAT CAR!
BUT DR. SINGH IS—
STOP IT!
GET DOWN!
MNNNNNNNF!

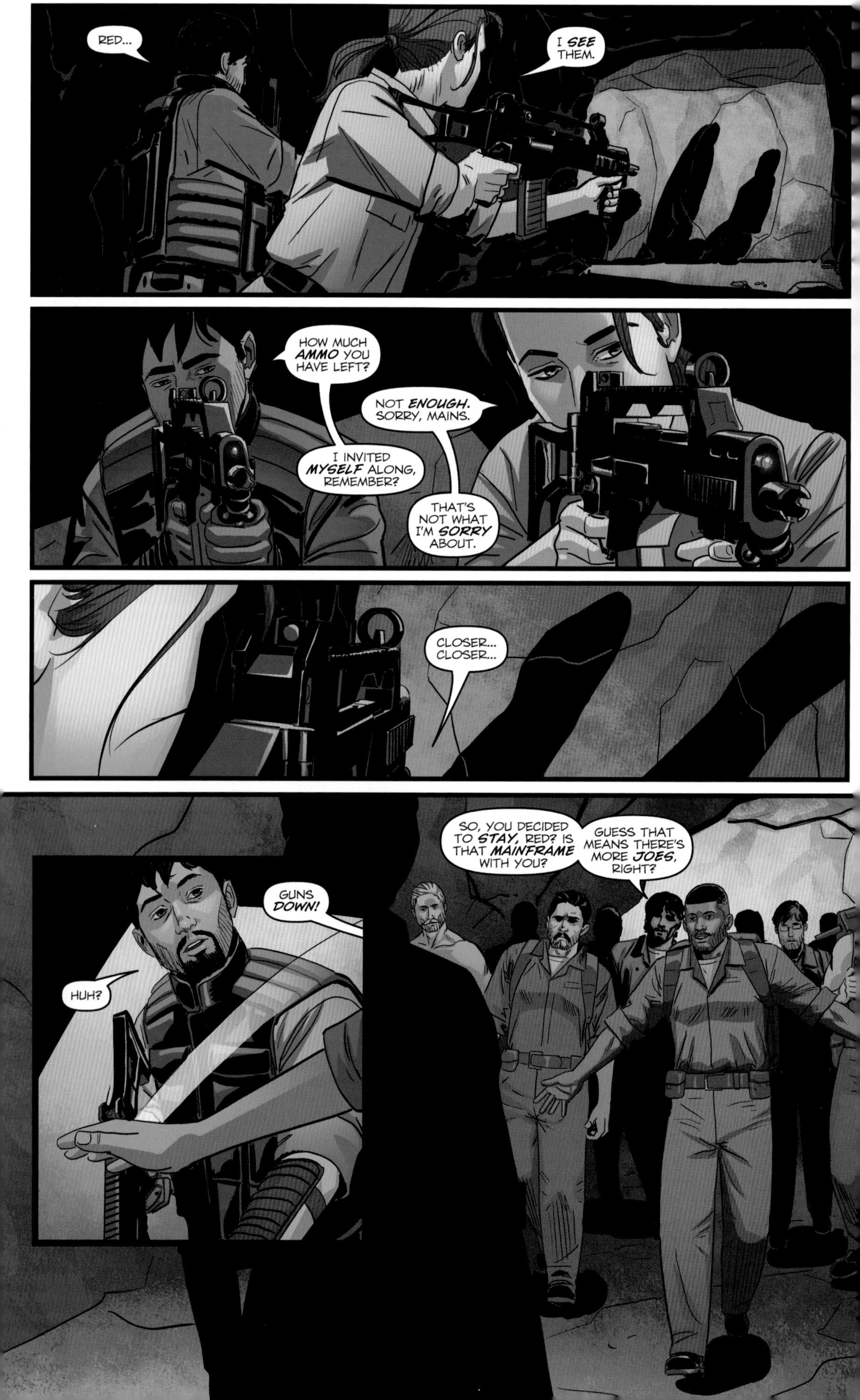
RED...
I SEE THEM.
HOW MUCH AMMO YOU HAVE LEFT?
NOT ENOUGH. SORRY, MAINS.
I INVITED MYSELF ALONG, REMEMBER?
THAT'S NOT WHAT I'M SORRY ABOUT.
CLOSER... CLOSER...
GUNS DOWN!
HUH?
SO, YOU DECIDED TO STAY, RED? IS THAT MAINFRAME WITH YOU?
GUESS THAT MEANS THERE'S MORE JOES, RIGHT?

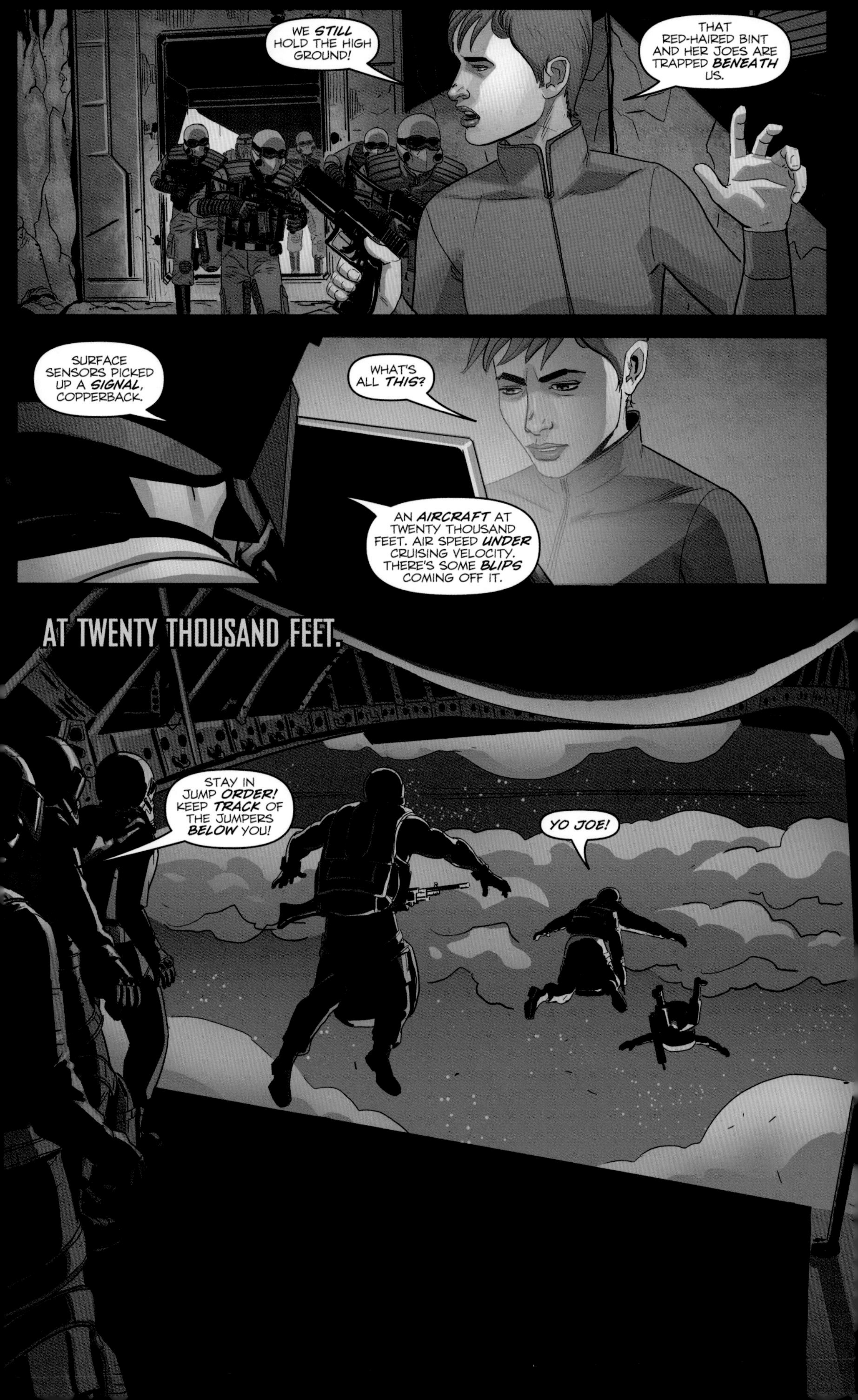
WE STILL HOLD THE HIGH GROUND!
THAT RED-HAIRED BINT AND HER JOES ARE TRAPPED BENEATH US.
SURFACE SENSORS PICKED UP A SIGNAL, COPPERBACK.
WHAT'S ALL THIS?
AN AIRCRAFT AT TWENTY THOUSAND FEET. AIR SPEED UNDER CRUISING VELOCITY. THERE'S SOME BLIPS COMING OFF IT.
AT TWENTY THOUSAND FEET.
STAY IN JUMP ORDER! KEEP TRACK OF THE JUMPERS BELOW YOU!
YO JOE!

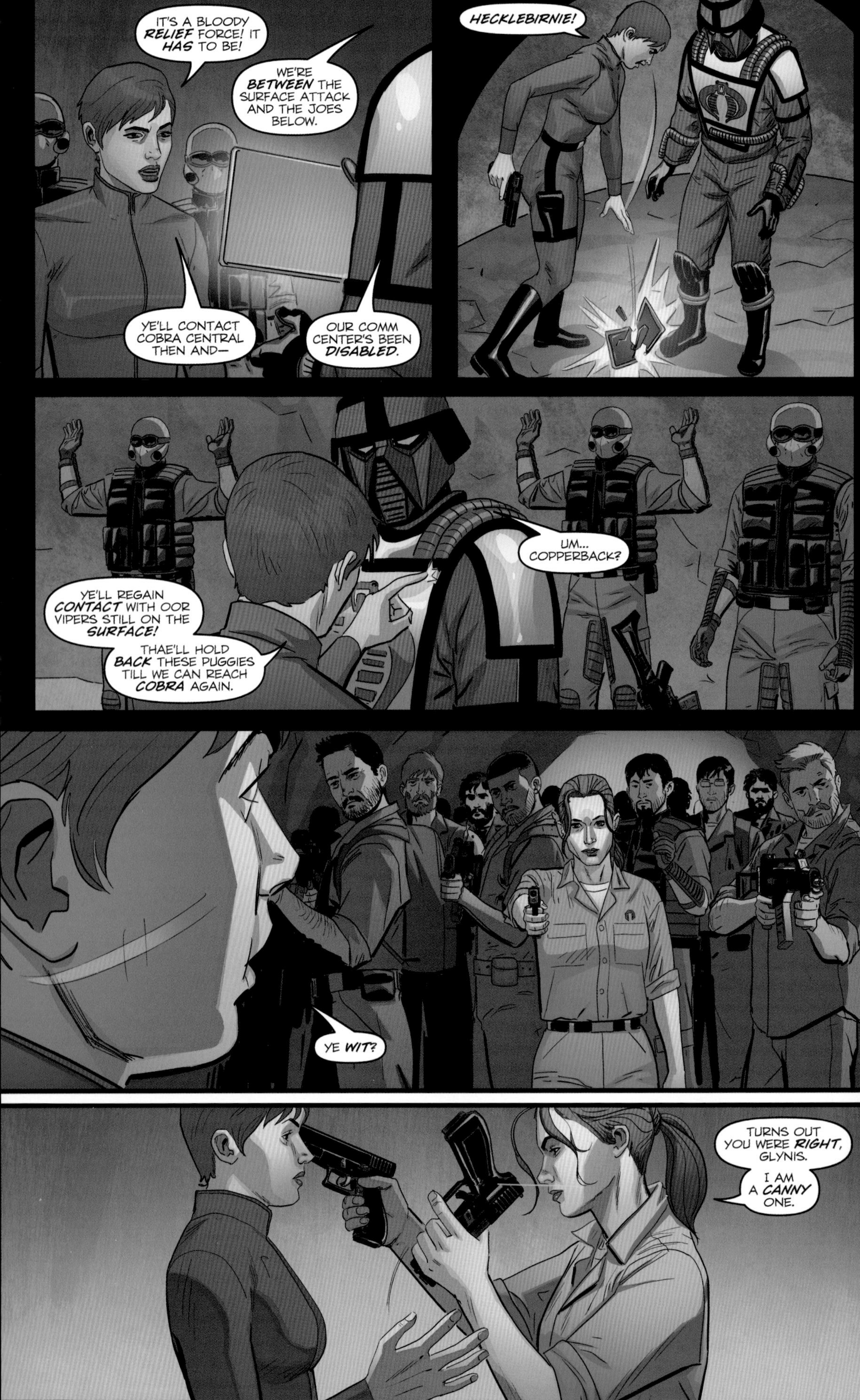
IT'S A BLOODY RELIEF FORCE! IT HAS TO BE!
WE'RE BETWEEN THE SURFACE ATTACK AND THE JOES BELOW.
YE'LL CONTACT COBRA CENTRAL THEN AND—
OUR COMM CENTER'S BEEN DISABLED.
HECKLEBIRNIE!
YE'LL REGAIN CONTACT WITH OOR VIPERS STILL ON THE SURFACE!
THAE'LL HOLD BACK THESE PUGGIES TILL WE CAN REACH COBRA AGAIN.
UM... COPPERBACK?
YE WIT?
TURNS OUT YOU WERE RIGHT, GLYNIS.
I AM A CANNY ONE.

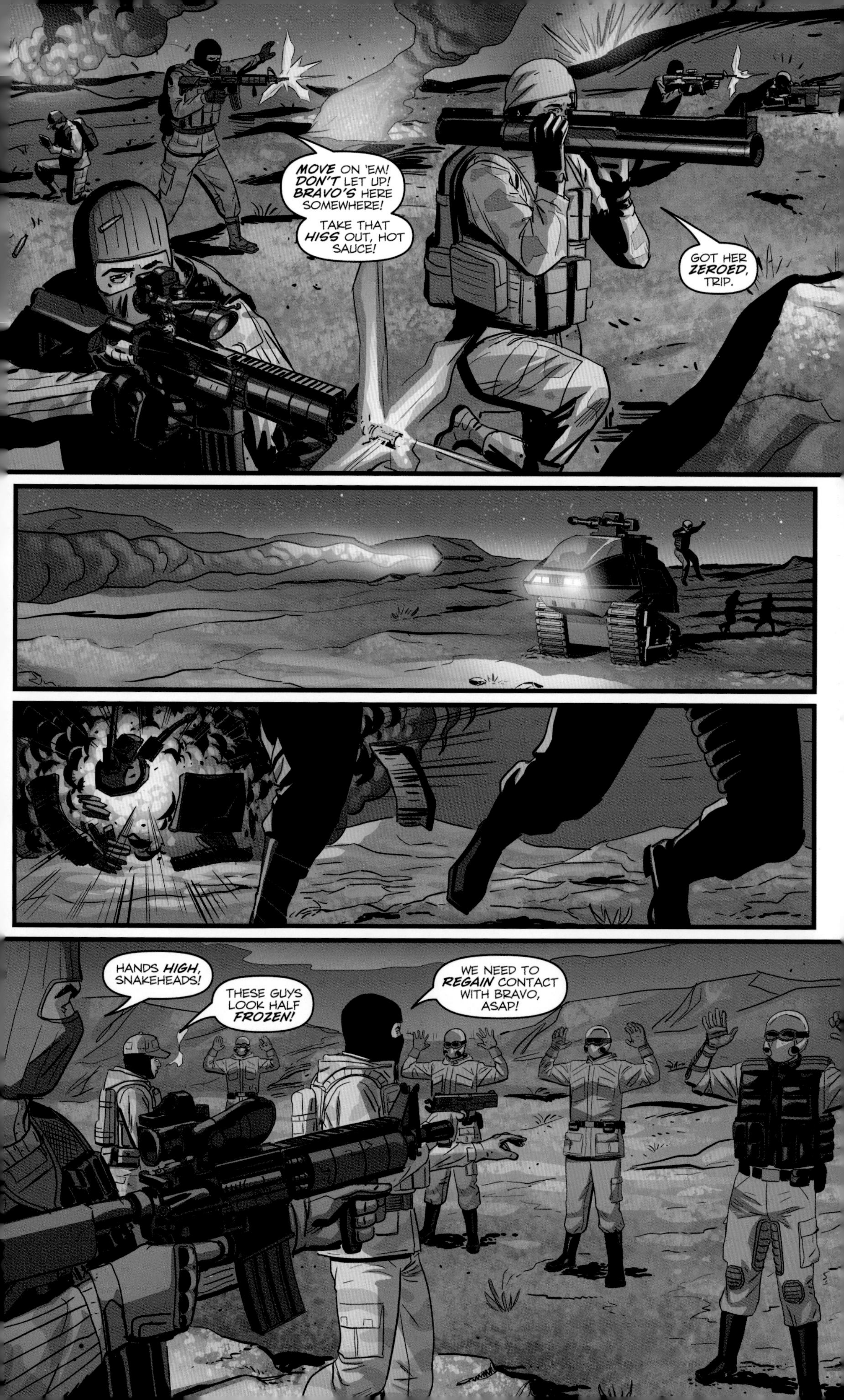
MOVE ON 'EM! DON'T LET UP! BRAVO'S HERE SOMEWHERE!
TAKE THAT HISS OUT, HOT SAUCE!
GOT HER ZEROED, TRIP.
HANDS HIGH, SNAKEHEADS!
THESE GUYS LOOK HALF FROZEN!
WE NEED TO REGAIN CONTACT WITH BRAVO, ASAP!

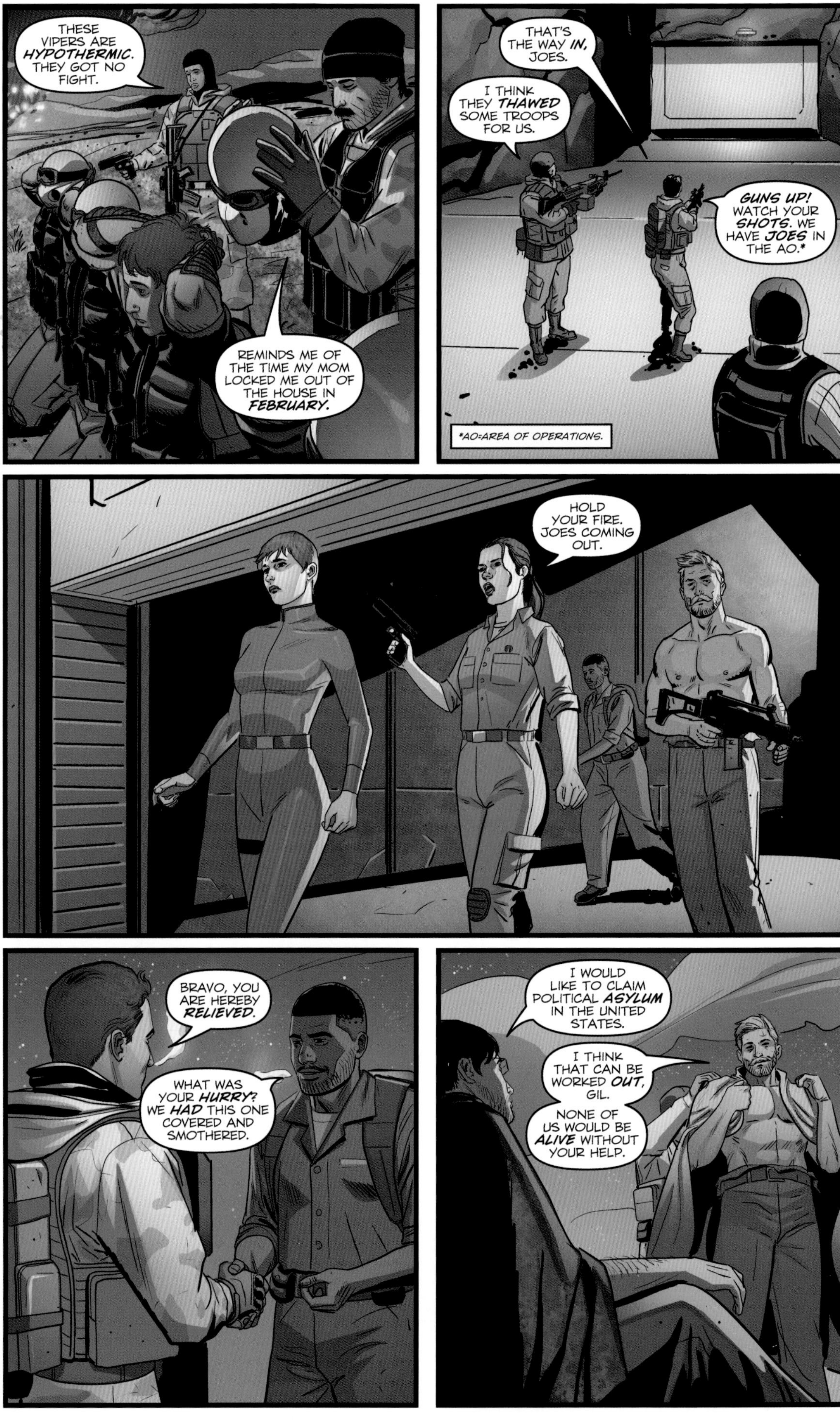

THESE VIPERS ARE HYPOTHERMIC. THEY GOT NO FIGHT.
REMINDS ME OF THE TIME MY MOM LOCKED ME OUT OF THE HOUSE IN FEBRUARY.
THAT'S THE WAY IN, JOES.
I THINK THEY THAWED SOME TROOPS FOR US.
GUNS UP! WATCH YOUR SHOTS. WE HAVE JOES IN THE AO.*
*AO=AREA OF OPERATIONS.
HOLD YOUR FIRE. JOES COMING OUT.
BRAVO, YOU ARE HEREBY RELIEVED.
WHAT WAS YOUR HURRY? WE HAD THIS ONE COVERED AND SMOTHERED.
I WOULD LIKE TO CLAIM POLITICAL ASYLUM IN THE UNITED STATES.
I THINK THAT CAN BE WORKED OUT, GIL.
NONE OF US WOULD BE ALIVE WITHOUT YOUR HELP.

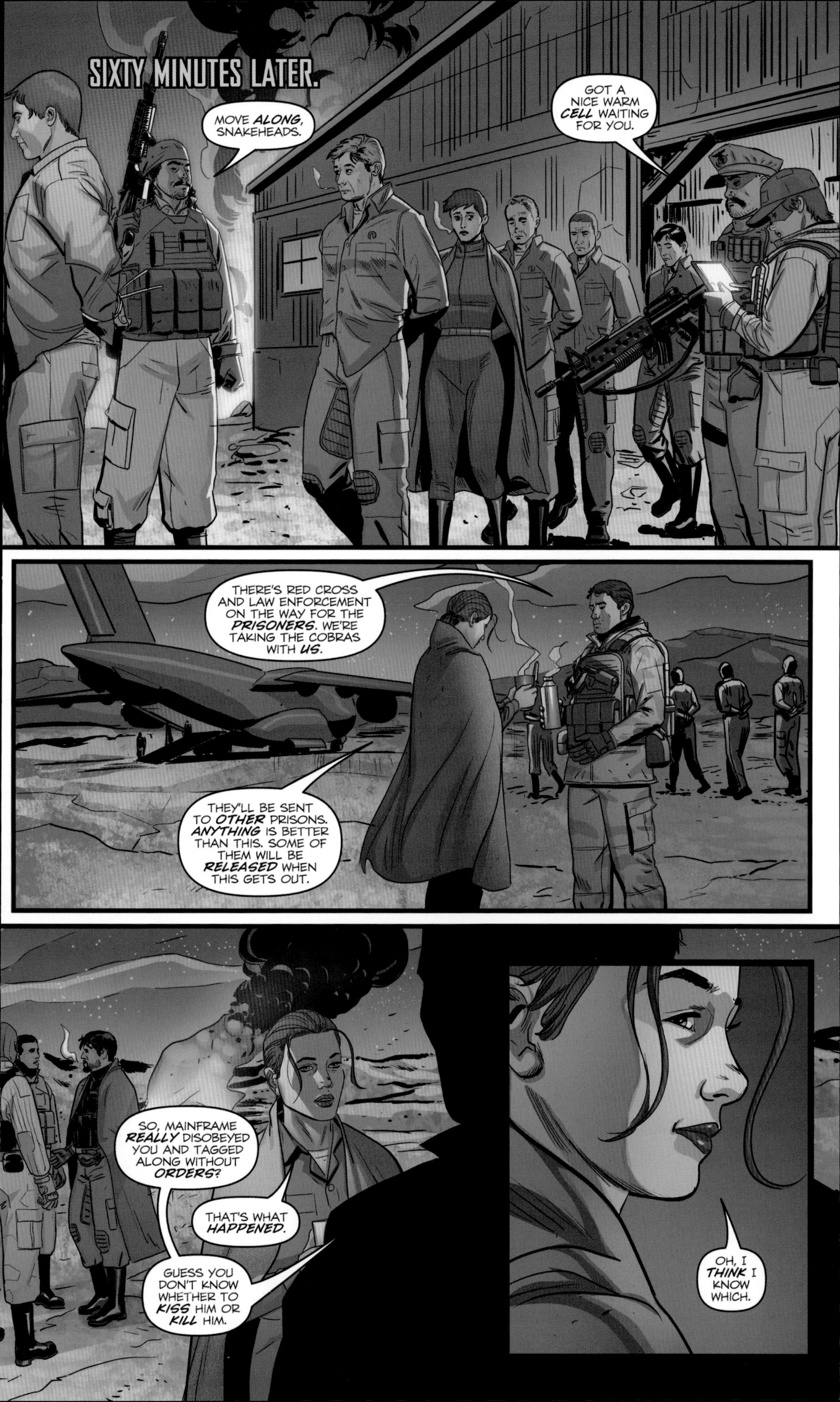
SIXTY MINUTES LATER.
MOVE ALONG, SNAKEHEADS.
GOT A NICE WARM CELL WAITING FOR YOU.
THERE'S RED CROSS AND LAW ENFORCEMENT ON THE WAY FOR THE PRISONERS. WE'RE TAKING THE COBRAS WITH US.
THEY'LL BE SENT TO OTHER PRISONS. ANYTHING IS BETTER THAN THIS. SOME OF THEM WILL BE RELEASED WHEN THIS GETS OUT.
SO, MAINFRAME REALLY DISOBEYED YOU AND TAGGED ALONG WITHOUT ORDERS?
THAT'S WHAT HAPPENED.
GUESS YOU DON'T KNOW WHETHER TO KISS HIM OR KILL HIM.
OH, I THINK I KNOW WHICH.

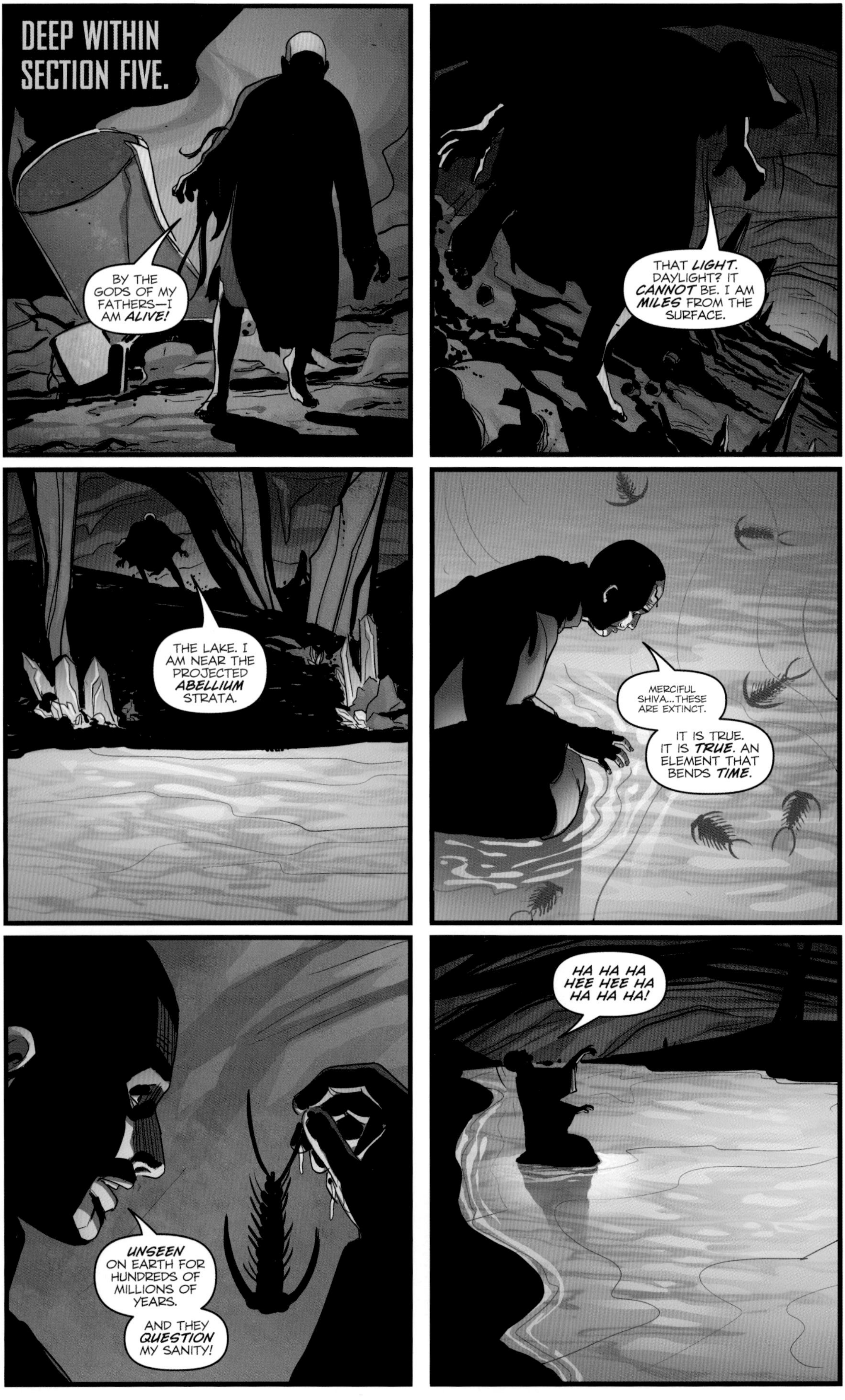
DEEP WITHIN SECTION FIVE.
BY THE GODS OF MY FATHERS—I AM ALIVE!
THAT LIGHT. DAYLIGHT? IT CANNOT BE. I AM MILES FROM THE SURFACE.
THE LAKE. I AM NEAR THE PROJECTED ABELLIUM STRATA.
MERCIFUL SHIVA...THESE ARE EXTINCT.
IT IS TRUE. IT IS TRUE. AN ELEMENT THAT BENDS TIME.
UNSEEN ON EARTH FOR HUNDREDS OF MILLIONS OF YEARS.
AND THEY QUESTION MY SANITY!
HA HA HA HEE HEE HA HA HA HA!

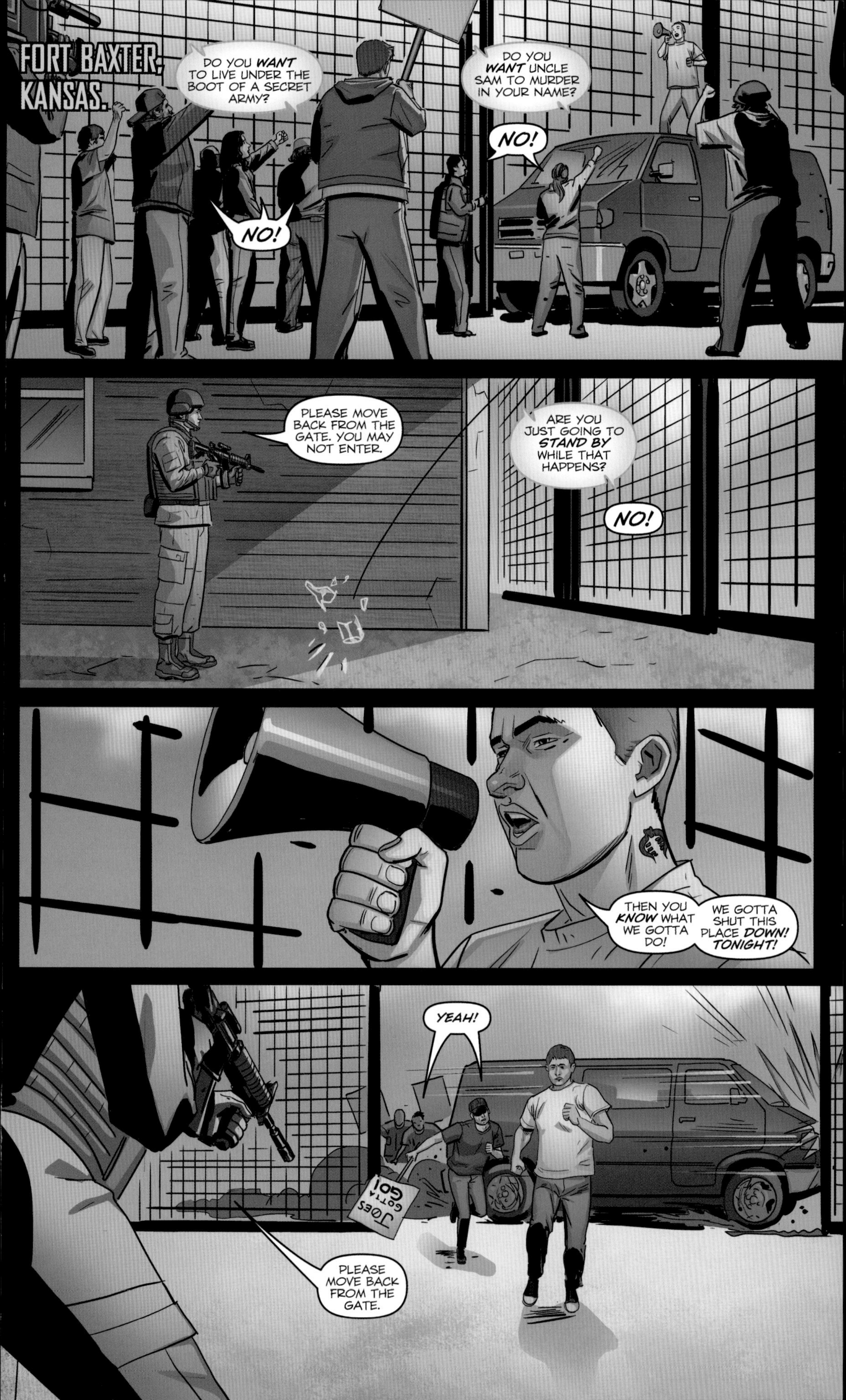
FORT BAXTER, KANSAS.
DO YOU WANT TO LIVE UNDER THE BOOT OF A SECRET ARMY?
NO!
DO YOU WANT UNCLE SAM TO MURDER IN YOUR NAME?
NO!
PLEASE MOVE BACK FROM THE GATE. YOU MAY NOT ENTER.
ARE YOU JUST GOING TO STAND BY WHILE THAT HAPPENS?
NO!
THEN YOU KNOW WHAT WE GOTTA DO!
WE GOTTA SHUT THIS PLACE DOWN! TONIGHT!
YEAH!
JOES GOTTA GO!
PLEASE MOVE BACK FROM THE GATE.

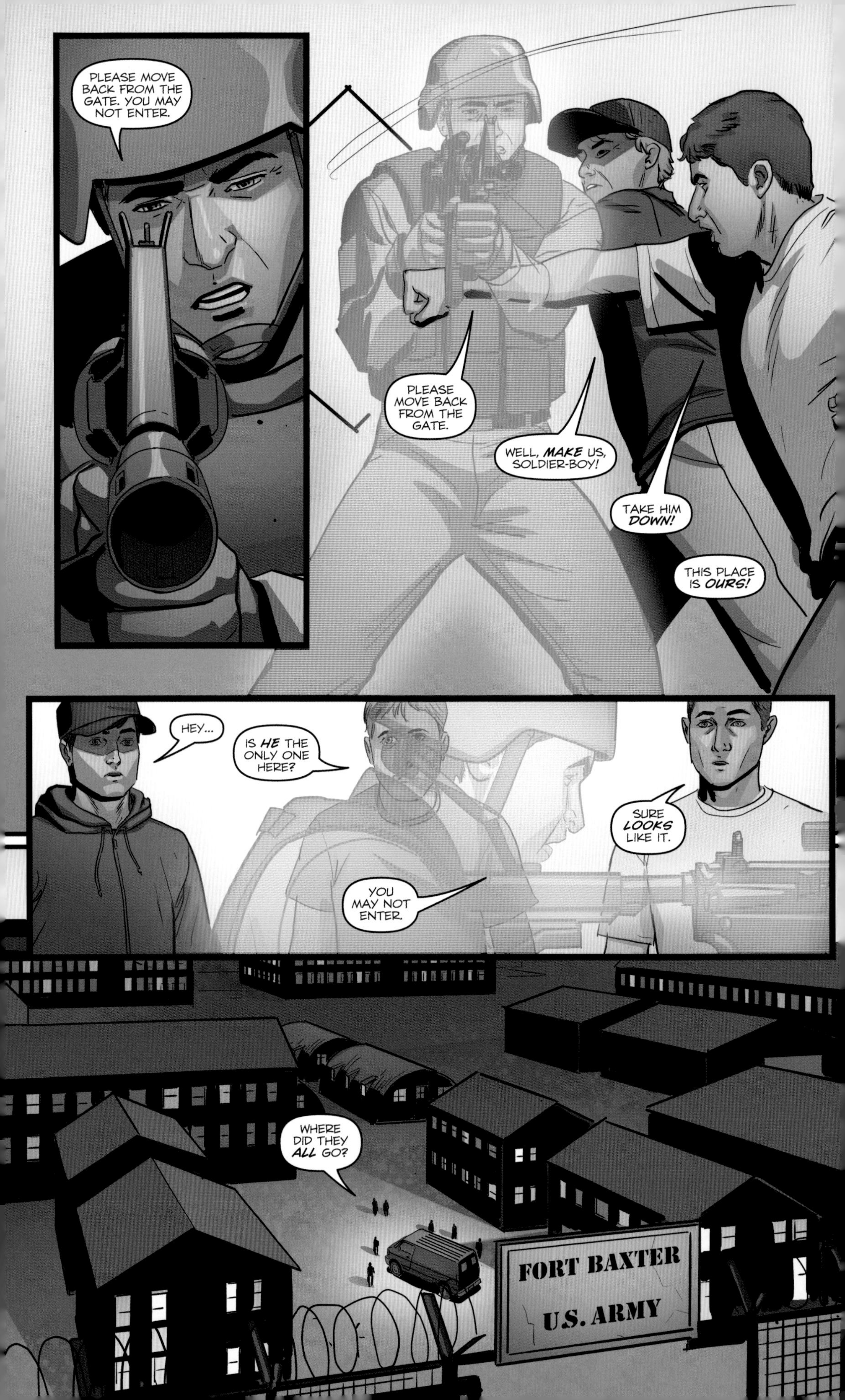
PLEASE MOVE BACK FROM THE GATE. YOU MAY NOT ENTER.
PLEASE MOVE BACK FROM THE GATE.
WELL, MAKE US, SOLDIER-BOY!
TAKE HIM DOWN!
THIS PLACE IS OURS!
HEY...
IS HE THE ONLY ONE HERE?
SURE LOOKS LIKE IT.
YOU MAY NOT ENTER.
WHERE DID THEY ALL GO?
FORT BAXTER
U.S. ARMY

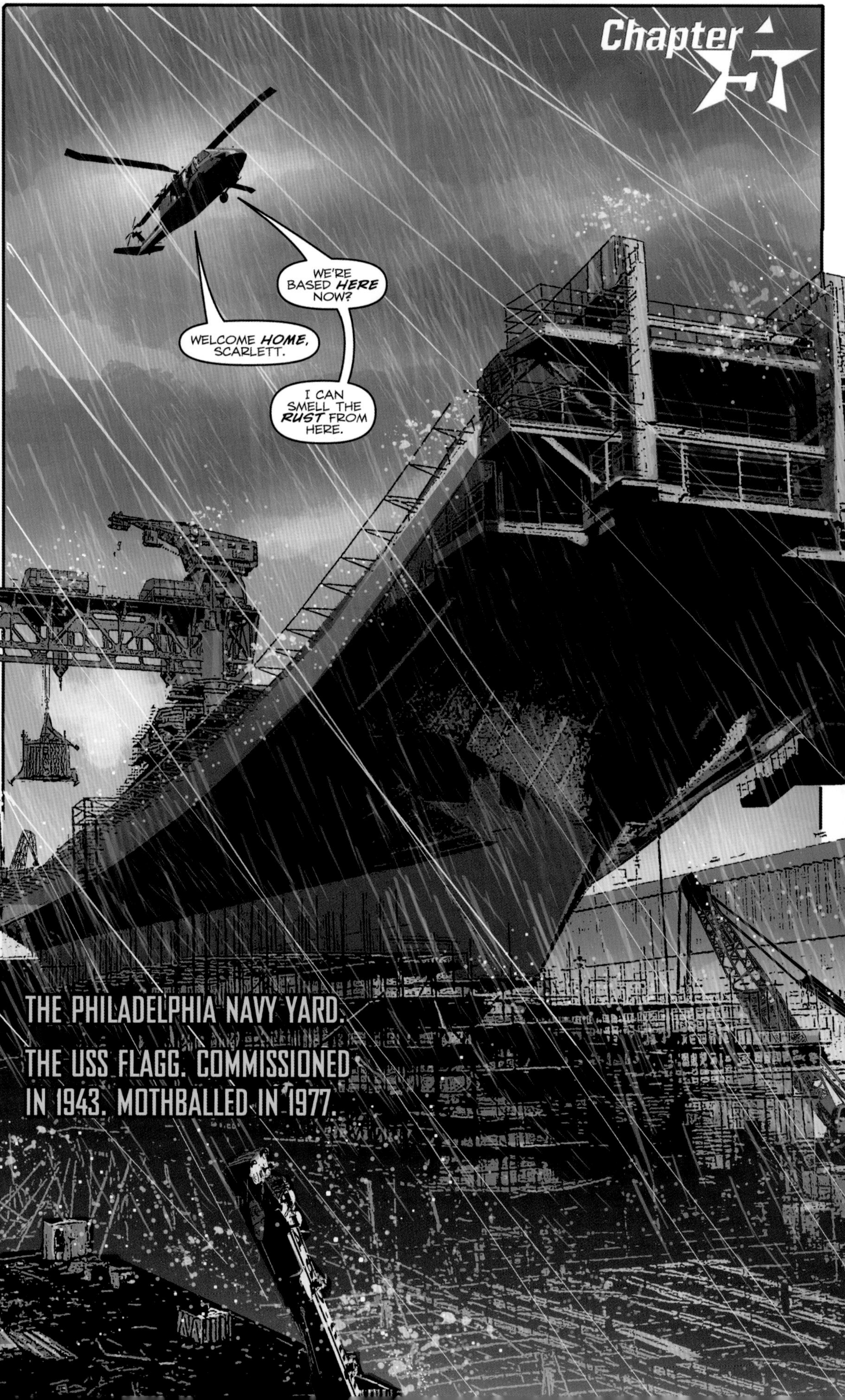

Chapter 5
WE'RE BASED HERE NOW?
WELCOME HOME, SCARLETT.
I CAN SMELL THE RUST FROM HERE.
THE PHILADELPHIA NAVY YARD.
THE USS FLAGG. COMMISSIONED IN 1943. MOTHBALLED IN 1977.

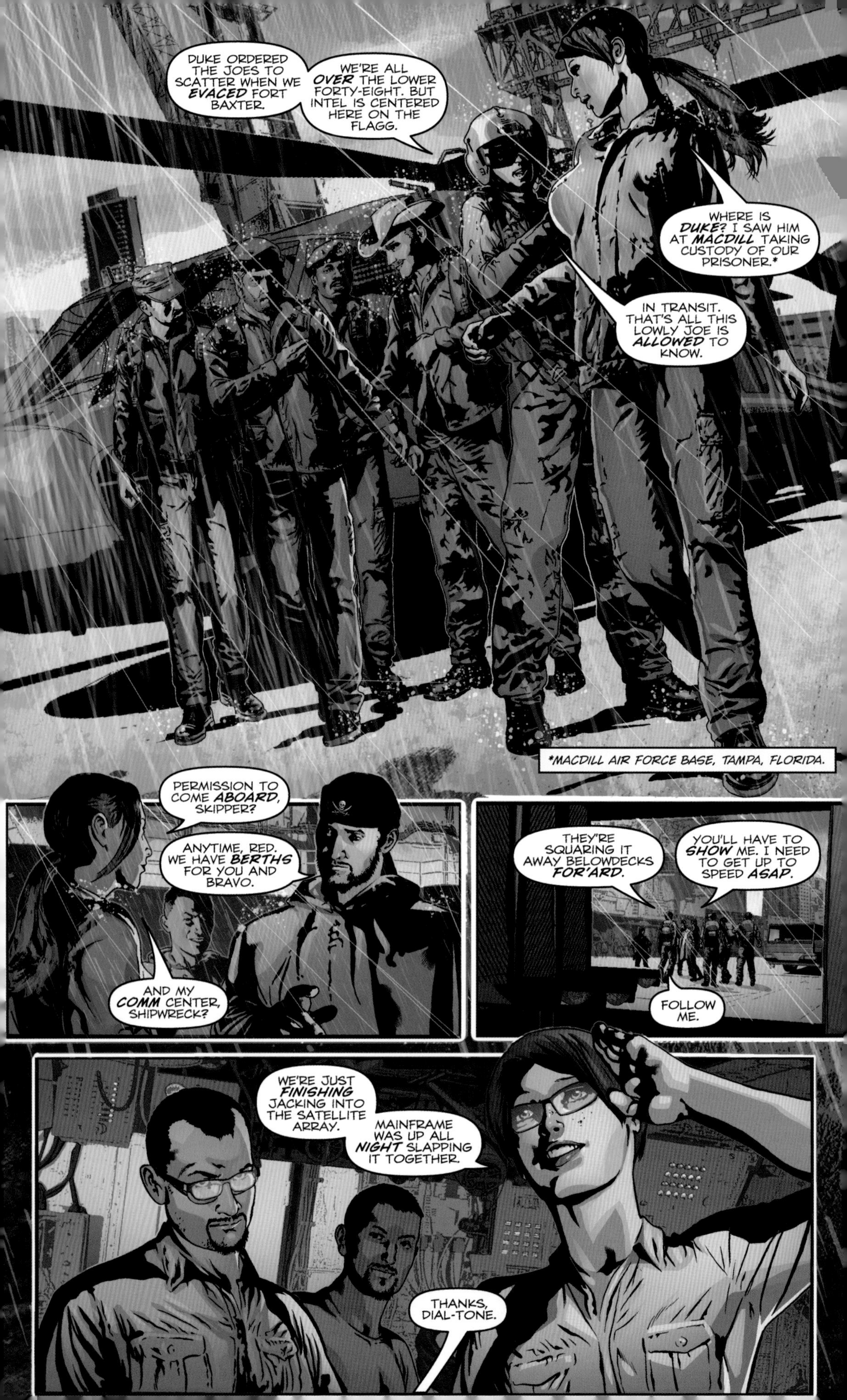

DUKE ORDERED THE JOES TO SCATTER WHEN WE *EVACED* FORT BAXTER.
WE'RE ALL *OVER* THE LOWER FORTY-EIGHT. BUT INTEL IS CENTERED HERE ON THE FLAGG.
WHERE IS *DUKE*? I SAW HIM AT *MACDILL* TAKING CUSTODY OF OUR PRISONER.*
IN TRANSIT. THAT'S ALL THIS LOWLY JOE IS *ALLOWED* TO KNOW.
*MACDILL AIR FORCE BASE, TAMPA, FLORIDA.
PERMISSION TO COME *ABOARD*, SKIPPER?
ANYTIME, RED. WE HAVE *BERTHS* FOR YOU AND BRAVO.
AND MY *COMM* CENTER, SHIPWRECK?
THEY'RE SQUARING IT AWAY BELOWDECKS *FOR'ARD*.
YOU'LL HAVE TO *SHOW* ME. I NEED TO GET UP TO SPEED *ASAP*.
FOLLOW ME.
WE'RE JUST *FINISHING* JACKING INTO THE SATELLITE ARRAY.
MAINFRAME WAS UP ALL *NIGHT* SLAPPING IT TOGETHER.
THANKS, DIAL-TONE.

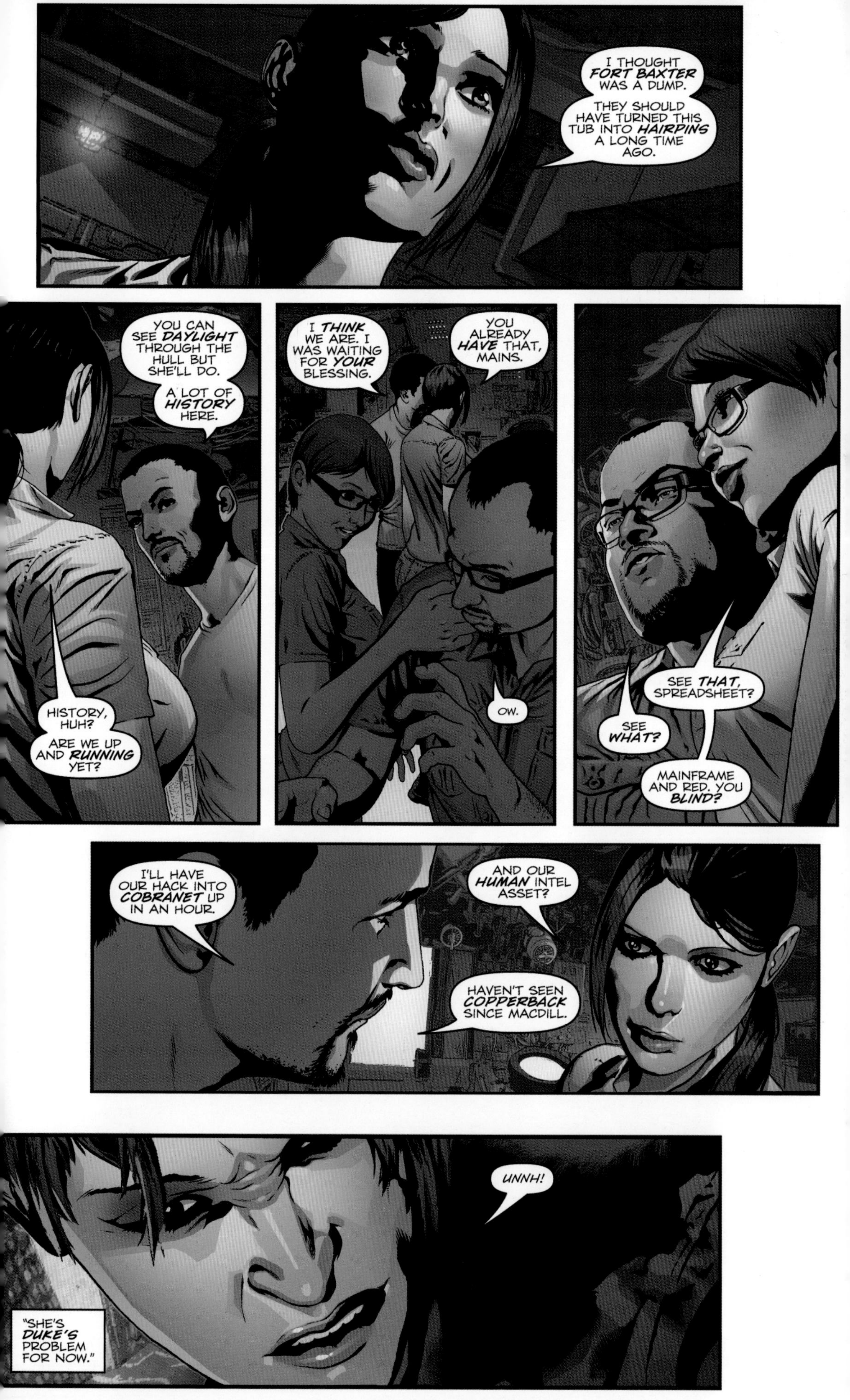
I THOUGHT FORT BAXTER WAS A DUMP.
THEY SHOULD HAVE TURNED THIS TUB INTO HAIRPINS A LONG TIME AGO.
YOU CAN SEE DAYLIGHT THROUGH THE HULL BUT SHE'LL DO.
A LOT OF HISTORY HERE.
HISTORY, HUH?
ARE WE UP AND RUNNING YET?
I THINK WE ARE. I WAS WAITING FOR YOUR BLESSING.
YOU ALREADY HAVE THAT, MAINS.
OW.
SEE THAT, SPREADSHEET?
SEE WHAT?
MAINFRAME AND RED. YOU BLIND?
I'LL HAVE OUR HACK INTO COBRANET UP IN AN HOUR.
AND OUR HUMAN INTEL ASSET?
HAVEN'T SEEN COPPERBACK SINCE MACDILL.
UNNH!
"SHE'S DUKE'S PROBLEM FOR NOW."

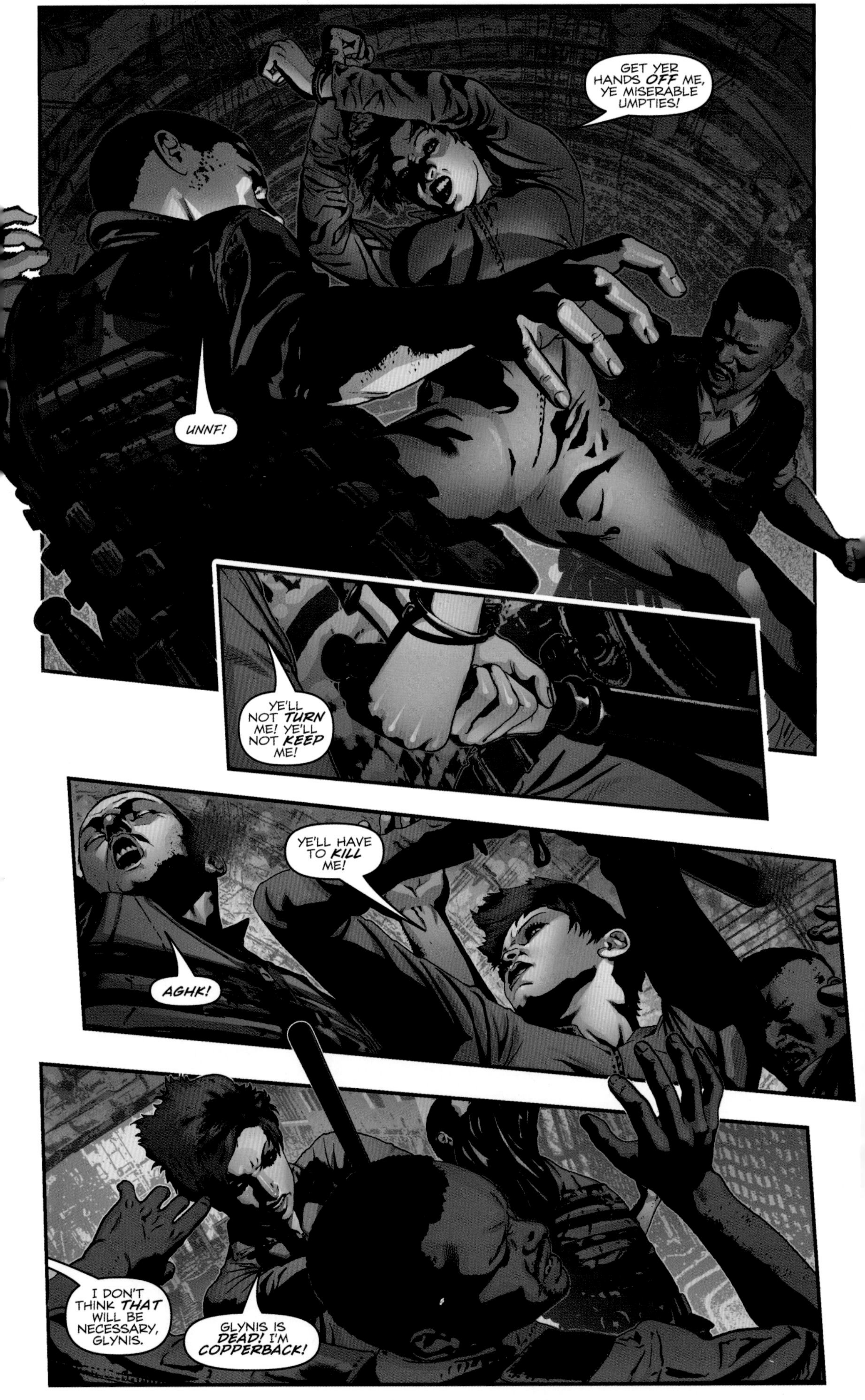
GET YER HANDS OFF ME, YE MISERABLE UMPTIES!
UNNF!
YE'LL NOT TURN ME! YE'LL NOT KEEP ME!
YE'LL HAVE TO KILL ME!
AGHK!
I DON'T THINK THAT WILL BE NECESSARY, GLYNIS.
GLYNIS IS DEAD! I'M COPPERBACK!

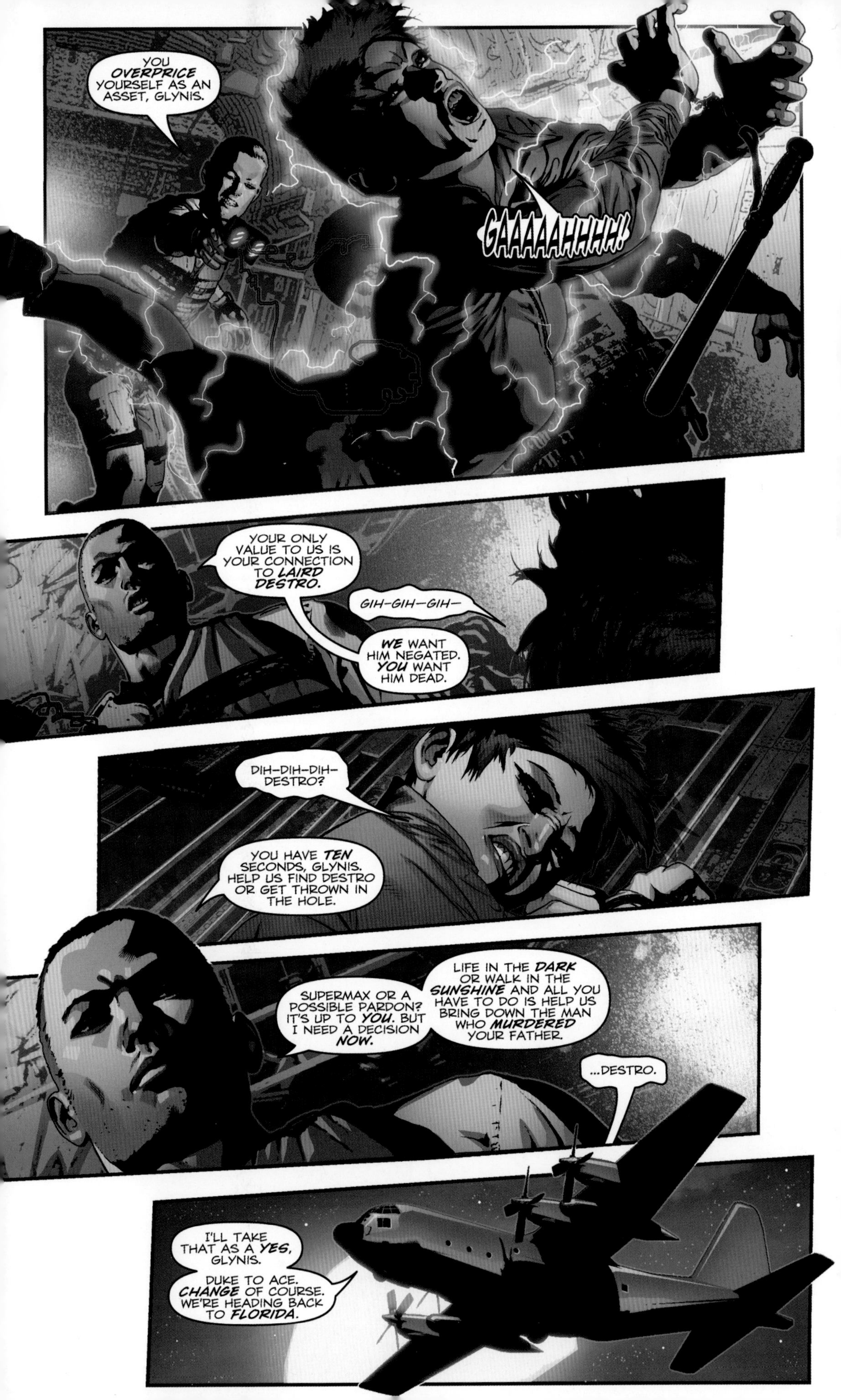
YOU OVERPRICE YOURSELF AS AN ASSET, GLYNIS.
GAAAAAHHHH!
YOUR ONLY VALUE TO US IS YOUR CONNECTION TO LAIRD DESTRO.
GIH-GIH-GIH-
WE WANT HIM NEGATED. YOU WANT HIM DEAD.
DIH-DIH-DIH-DESTRO?
YOU HAVE TEN SECONDS, GLYNIS. HELP US FIND DESTRO OR GET THROWN IN THE HOLE.
SUPERMAX OR A POSSIBLE PARDON? IT'S UP TO YOU. BUT I NEED A DECISION NOW.
LIFE IN THE DARK OR WALK IN THE SUNSHINE AND ALL YOU HAVE TO DO IS HELP US BRING DOWN THE MAN WHO MURDERED YOUR FATHER.
...DESTRO.
I'LL TAKE THAT AS A YES, GLYNIS.
DUKE TO ACE. CHANGE OF COURSE. WE'RE HEADING BACK TO FLORIDA.

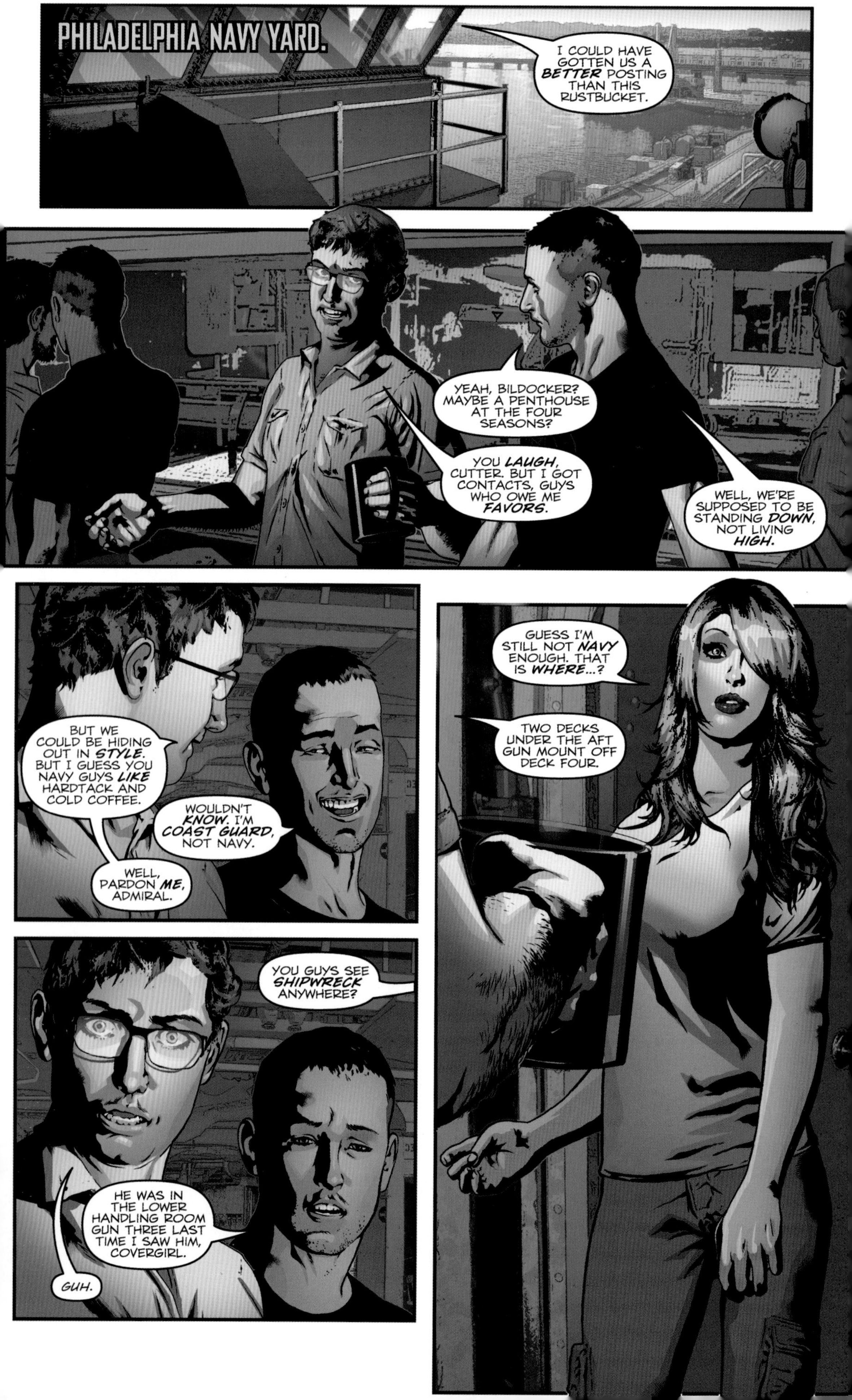
PHILADELPHIA NAVY YARD.
I COULD HAVE GOTTEN US A BETTER POSTING THAN THIS RUSTBUCKET.
YEAH, BILDOCKER? MAYBE A PENTHOUSE AT THE FOUR SEASONS?
YOU LAUGH, CUTTER. BUT I GOT CONTACTS, GUYS WHO OWE ME FAVORS.
WELL, WE'RE SUPPOSED TO BE STANDING DOWN, NOT LIVING HIGH.
BUT WE COULD BE HIDING OUT IN STYLE. BUT I GUESS YOU NAVY GUYS LIKE HARDTACK AND COLD COFFEE.
WOULDN'T KNOW. I'M COAST GUARD, NOT NAVY.
WELL, PARDON ME, ADMIRAL.
YOU GUYS SEE SHIPWRECK ANYWHERE?
HE WAS IN THE LOWER HANDLING ROOM GUN THREE LAST TIME I SAW HIM, COVERGIRL.
GUH.
GUESS I'M STILL NOT NAVY ENOUGH. THAT IS WHERE...?
TWO DECKS UNDER THE AFT GUN MOUNT OFF DECK FOUR.

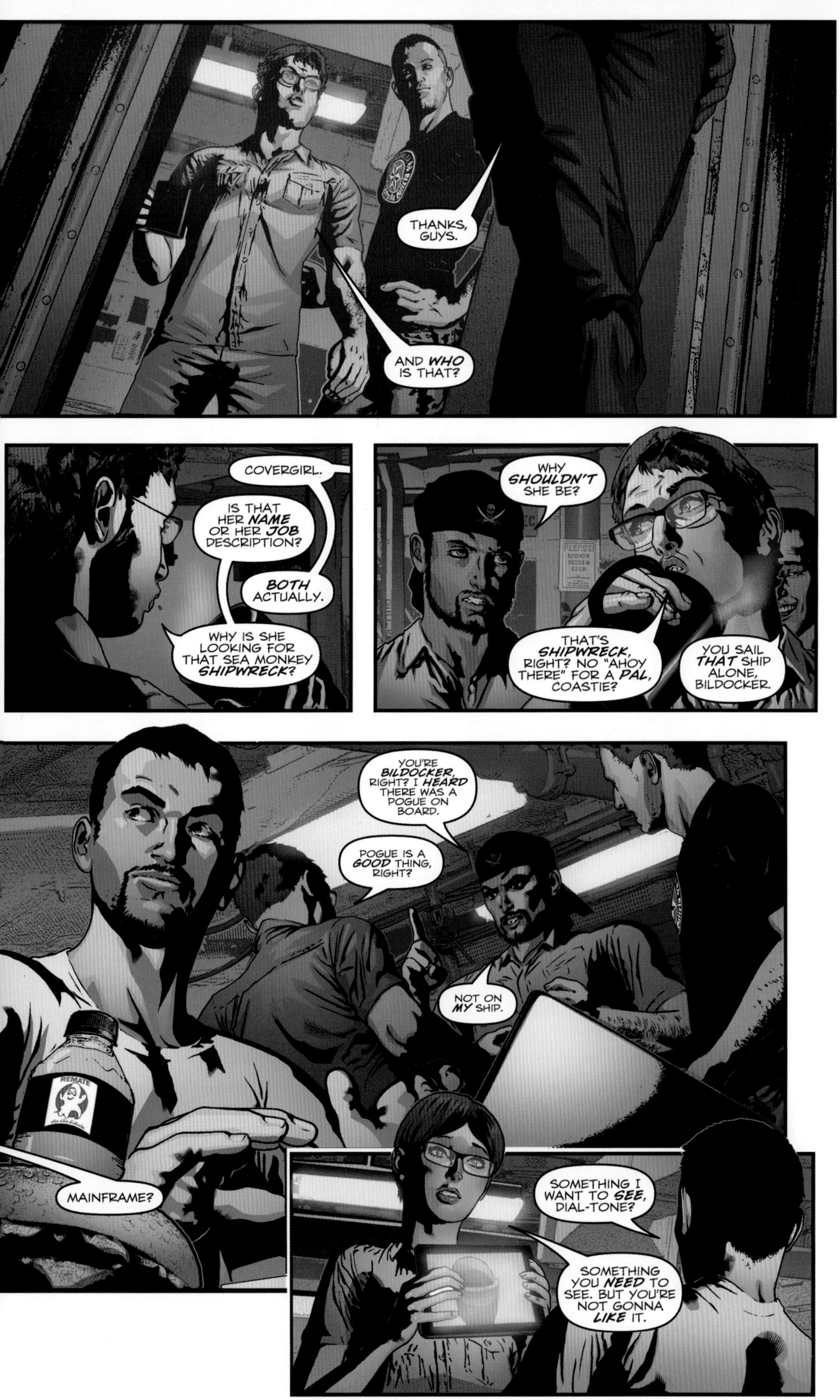
THANKS, GUYS.
AND WHO IS THAT?
COVERGIRL.
IS THAT HER NAME OR HER JOB DESCRIPTION?
BOTH ACTUALLY.
WHY IS SHE LOOKING FOR THAT SEA MONKEY SHIPWRECK?
WHY SHOULDN'T SHE BE?
THAT'S SHIPWRECK, RIGHT? NO "AHOY THERE" FOR A PAL, COASTIE?
YOU SAIL THAT SHIP ALONE, BILDOCKER.
YOU'RE BILDOCKER, RIGHT? I HEARD THERE WAS A POGUE ON BOARD.
POGUE IS A GOOD THING, RIGHT?
NOT ON MY SHIP.
REMATE
MAINFRAME?
SOMETHING I WANT TO SEE, DIAL-TONE?
SOMETHING YOU NEED TO SEE. BUT YOU'RE NOT GONNA LIKE IT.

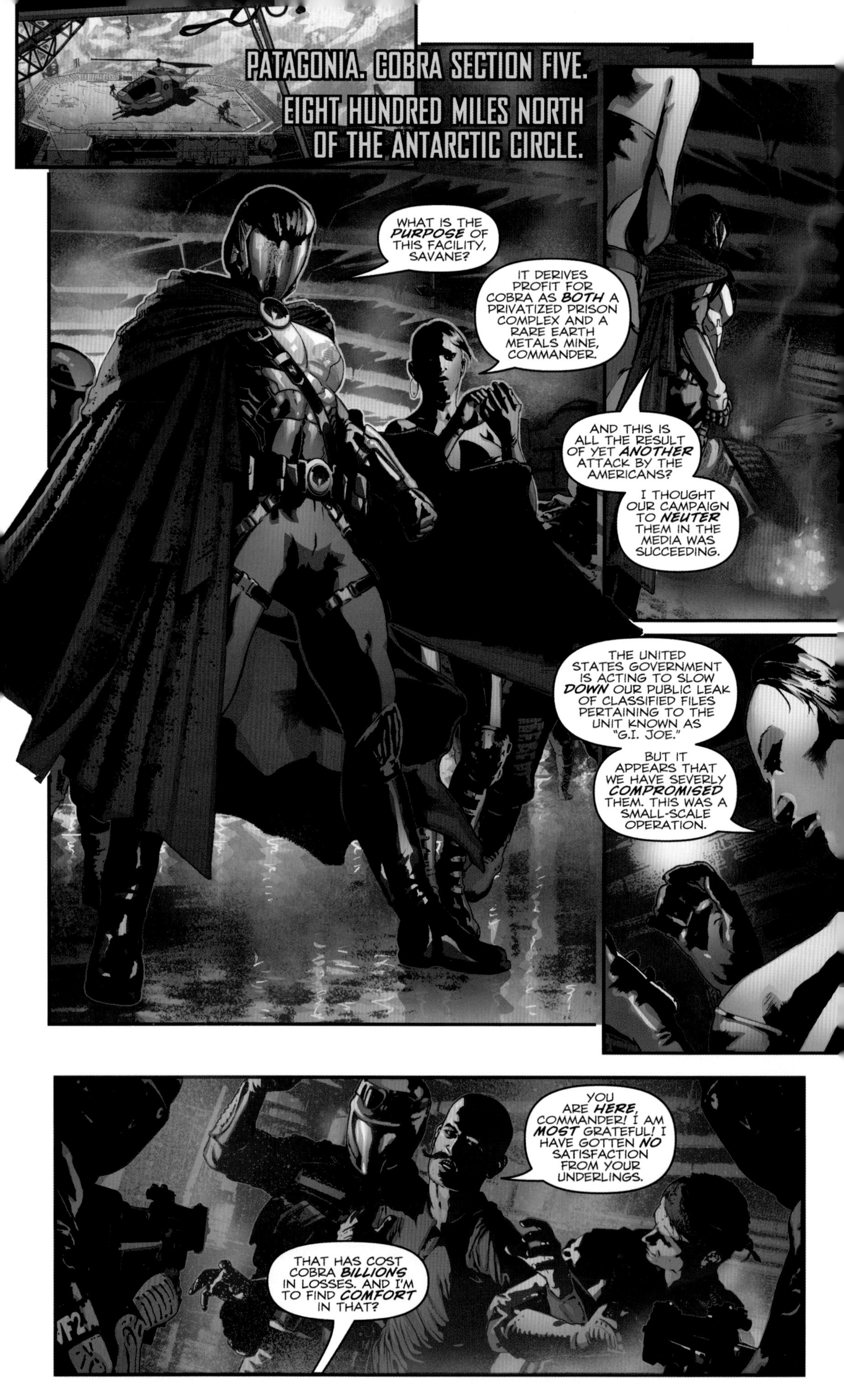
PATAGONIA. COBRA SECTION FIVE.
EIGHT HUNDRED MILES NORTH OF THE ANTARCTIC CIRCLE.
WHAT IS THE *PURPOSE* OF THIS FACILITY, SAVANE?
IT DERIVES PROFIT FOR COBRA AS *BOTH* A PRIVATIZED PRISON COMPLEX AND A RARE EARTH METALS MINE, COMMANDER.
AND THIS IS ALL THE RESULT OF YET *ANOTHER* ATTACK BY THE AMERICANS?
I THOUGHT OUR CAMPAIGN TO *NEUTER* THEM IN THE MEDIA WAS SUCCEEDING.
THE UNITED STATES GOVERNMENT IS ACTING TO SLOW *DOWN* OUR PUBLIC LEAK OF CLASSIFIED FILES PERTAINING TO THE UNIT KNOWN AS "G.I. JOE."
BUT IT APPEARS THAT WE HAVE SEVERLY *COMPROMISED* THEM. THIS WAS A SMALL-SCALE OPERATION.
YOU ARE *HERE*, COMMANDER! I AM *MOST* GRATEFUL! I HAVE GOTTEN *NO* SATISFACTION FROM YOUR UNDERLINGS.
THAT HAS COST COBRA *BILLIONS* IN LOSSES. AND I'M TO FIND *COMFORT* IN THAT?

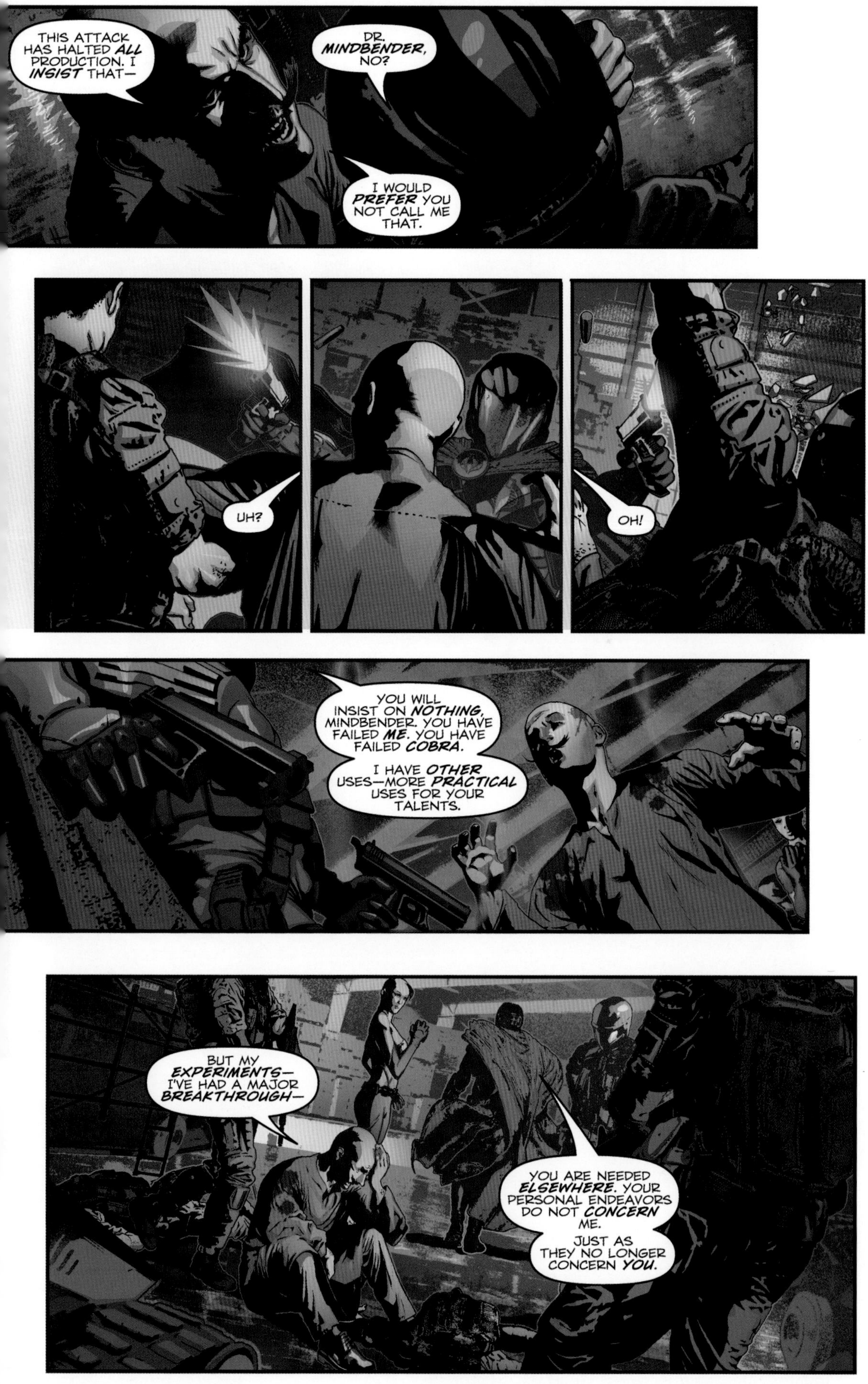

THIS ATTACK HAS HALTED ALL PRODUCTION. I INSIST THAT—
DR. MINDBENDER, NO?
I WOULD PREFER YOU NOT CALL ME THAT.
UH?
OH!
YOU WILL INSIST ON NOTHING, MINDBENDER. YOU HAVE FAILED ME. YOU HAVE FAILED COBRA.
I HAVE OTHER USES—MORE PRACTICAL USES FOR YOUR TALENTS.
BUT MY EXPERIMENTS— I'VE HAD A MAJOR BREAKTHROUGH—
YOU ARE NEEDED ELSEWHERE. YOUR PERSONAL ENDEAVORS DO NOT CONCERN ME.
JUST AS THEY NO LONGER CONCERN YOU.

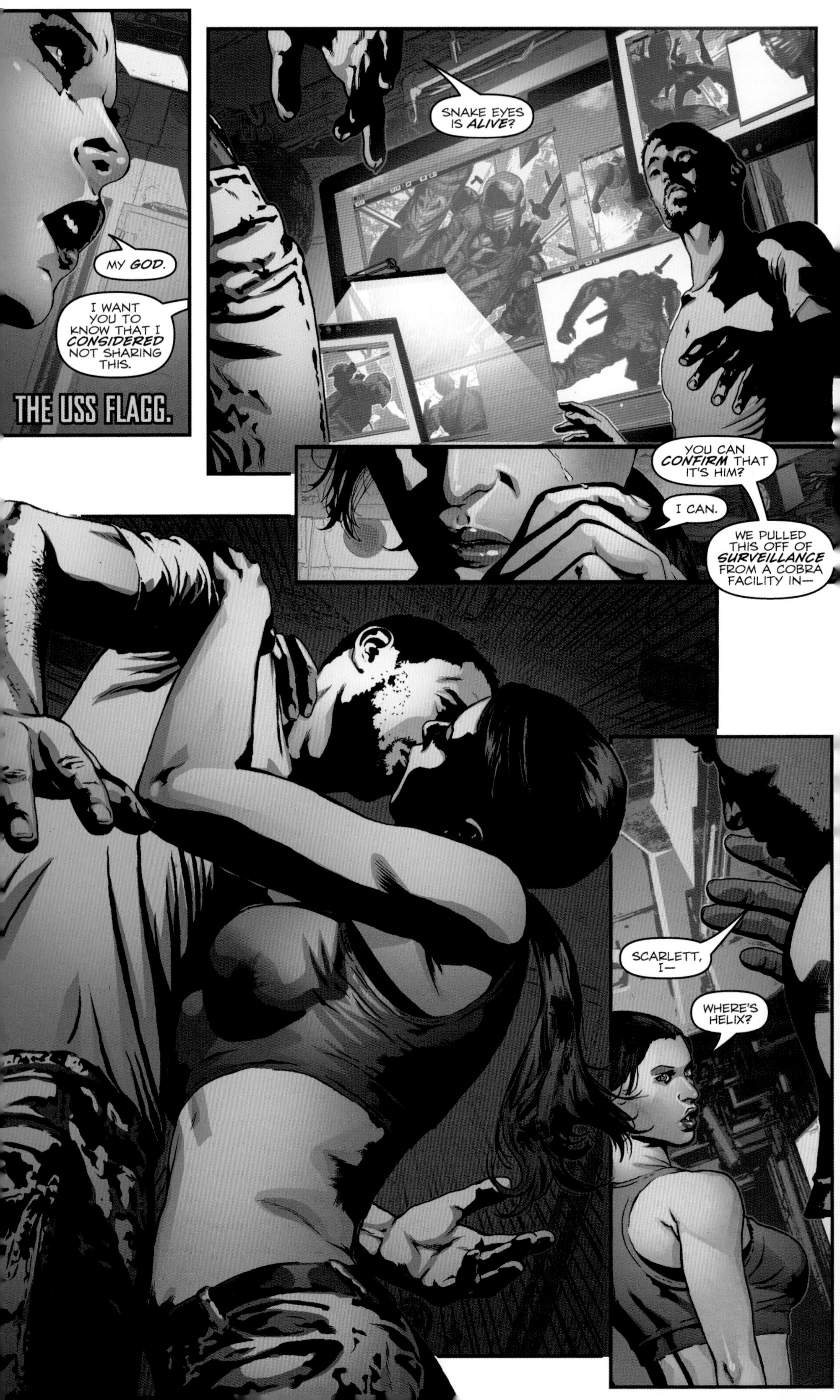
MY GOD.
I WANT YOU TO KNOW THAT I CONSIDERED NOT SHARING THIS.
THE USS FLAGG.
SNAKE EYES IS ALIVE?
YOU CAN CONFIRM THAT IT'S HIM?
I CAN.
WE PULLED THIS OFF OF SURVEILLANCE FROM A COBRA FACILITY IN—
SCARLETT, I—
WHERE'S HELIX?

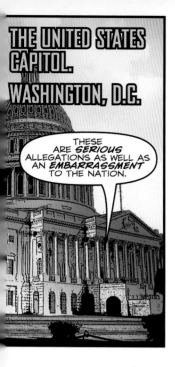

THE UNITED STATES CAPITOL. WASHINGTON, D.C.

THESE ARE *SERIOUS* ALLEGATIONS AS WELL AS AN *EMBARRASSMENT* TO THE NATION.

THE LEAKS OF PUBLIC INFORMATION CLAIM THERE IS A SECRET MILITARY UNIT MADE UP OF FORMER MEMBERS OF THE US MILITARY OFFICIALLY LISTED AS DECEASED.

DOCUMENTS SHOW THAT THIS UNIT WAS RUN FROM THE EXECUTIVE BRANCH WITHOUT THE DIRECT KNOWLEDGE OF THE PENTAGON OR JOINT CHIEFS.

HAVE YOU SEEN THESE DOCUMENTS?

I HAVE, SENATOR.

THESE FILES, WHICH ALL THE WORLD HAS BEEN EXPOSED TO, CLAIM THAT YOU ARE THE SPECIAL *LIAISON* BETWEEN THESE "G.I. JOES" AND THE WHITE HOUSE.

CAN YOU *CONFIRM* OR *DENY* THIS FOR THE PANEL?

I *AM* A SPECIAL ENVOY ASSIGNED TO THE WHITE HOUSE. BUT THAT IS THE *ONLY* TRUTH IN A MOUNTAIN OF LIES.

I WILL ATTEST AND CAN *PROVE* WITHOUT A SHADOW OF DOUBT THAT THE MILITARY ENTITY KNOWN AS G.I. JOE...

LIVE

...DOES *NOT* EXIST.

LIVE

HUH?

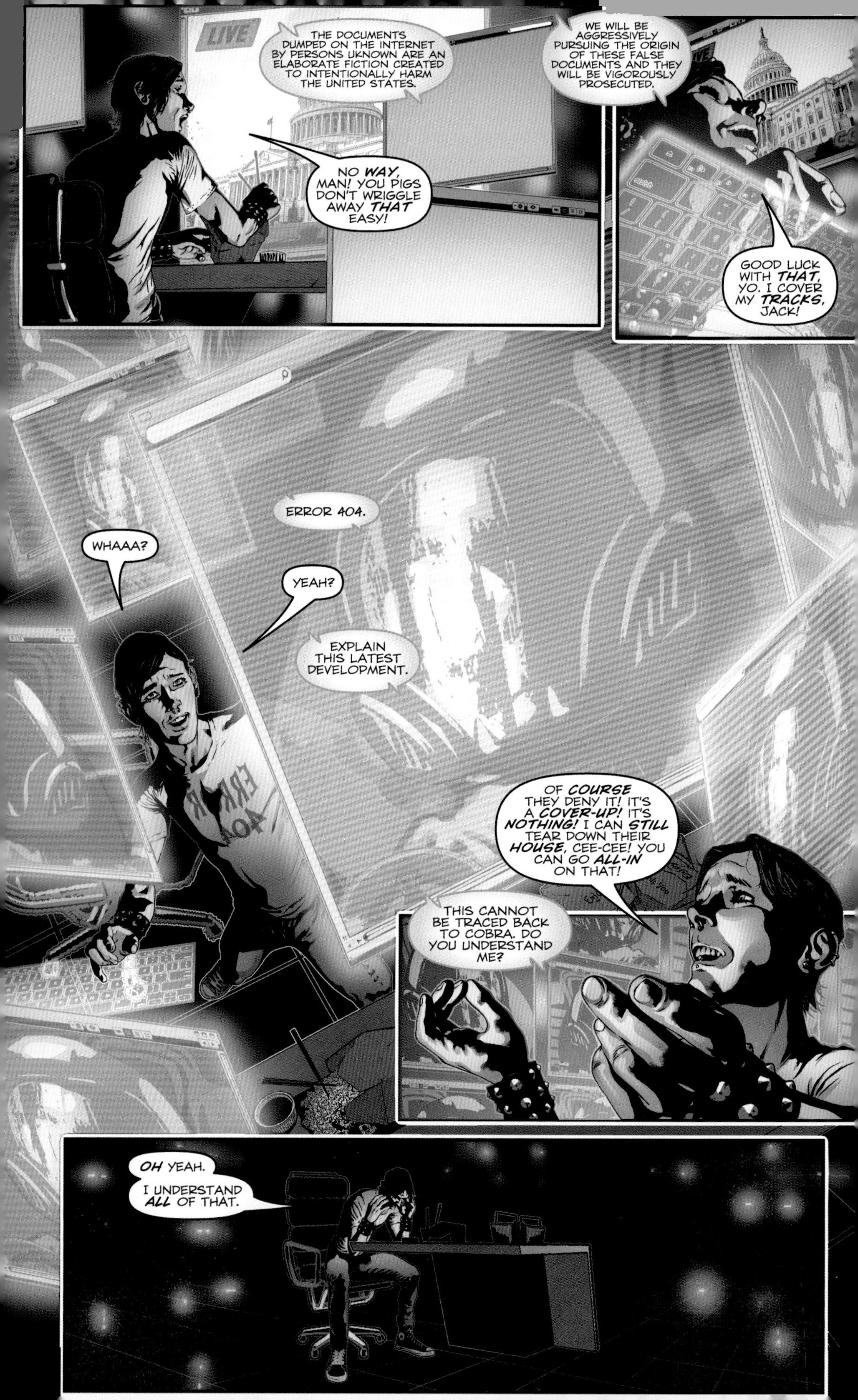
THE DOCUMENTS DUMPED ON THE INTERNET BY PERSONS UKNOWN ARE AN ELABORATE FICTION CREATED TO INTENTIONALLY HARM THE UNITED STATES.
NO WAY, MAN! YOU PIGS DON'T WRIGGLE AWAY THAT EASY!
WE WILL BE AGGRESSIVELY PURSUING THE ORIGIN OF THESE FALSE DOCUMENTS AND THEY WILL BE VIGOROUSLY PROSECUTED.
GOOD LUCK WITH THAT, YO. I COVER MY TRACKS, JACK!
ERROR 404.
WHAAA?
YEAH?
EXPLAIN THIS LATEST DEVELOPMENT.
OF COURSE THEY DENY IT! IT'S A COVER-UP! IT'S NOTHING! I CAN STILL TEAR DOWN THEIR HOUSE, CEE-CEE! YOU CAN GO ALL-IN ON THAT!
THIS CANNOT BE TRACED BACK TO COBRA. DO YOU UNDERSTAND ME?
OH YEAH.
I UNDERSTAND ALL OF THAT.

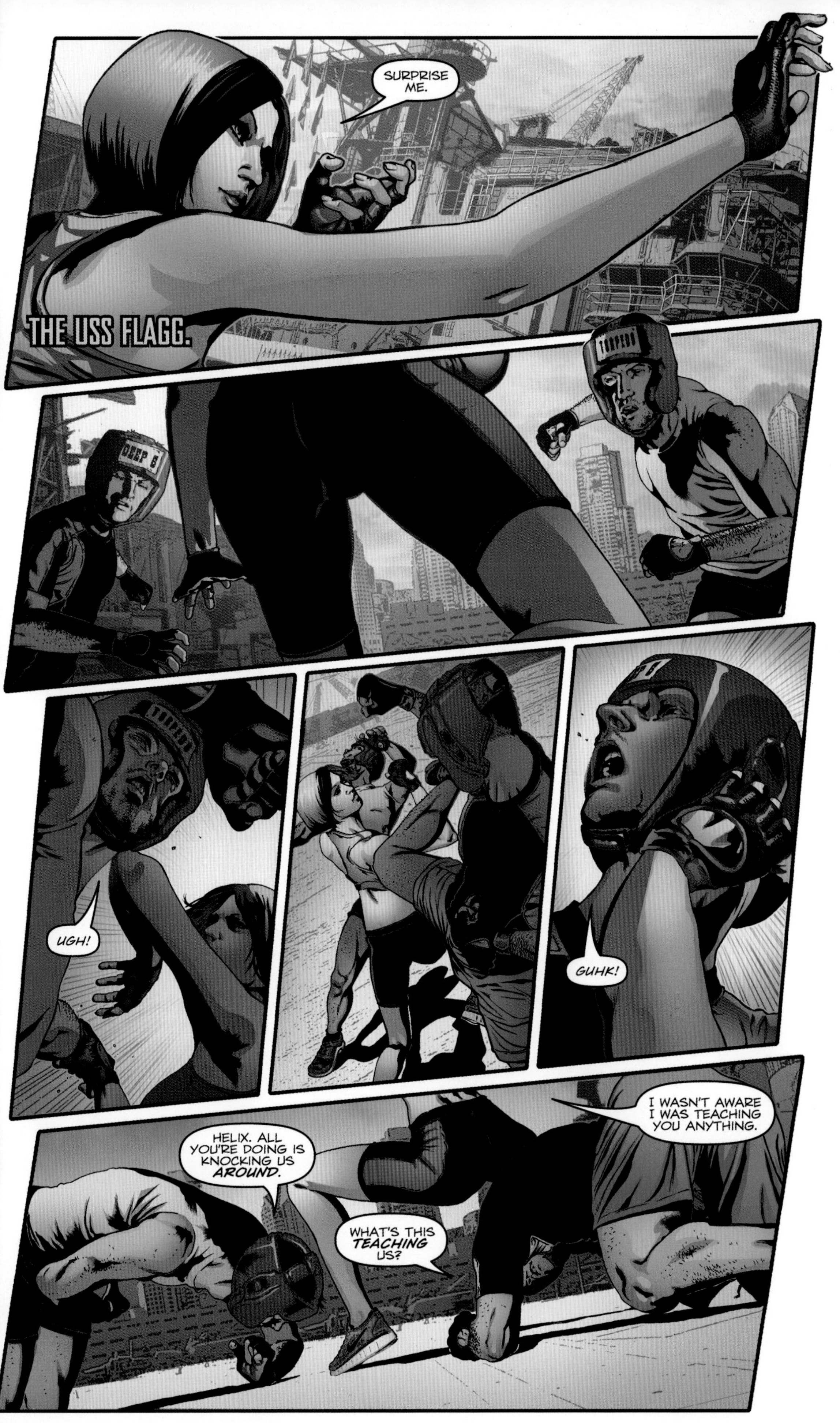
SURPRISE ME.
THE USS FLAGG.
TORPEDO
DEEP 6
UGH!
GUHK!
HELIX. ALL YOU'RE DOING IS KNOCKING US *AROUND*.
WHAT'S THIS *TEACHING* US?
I WASN'T AWARE I WAS TEACHING YOU ANYTHING.

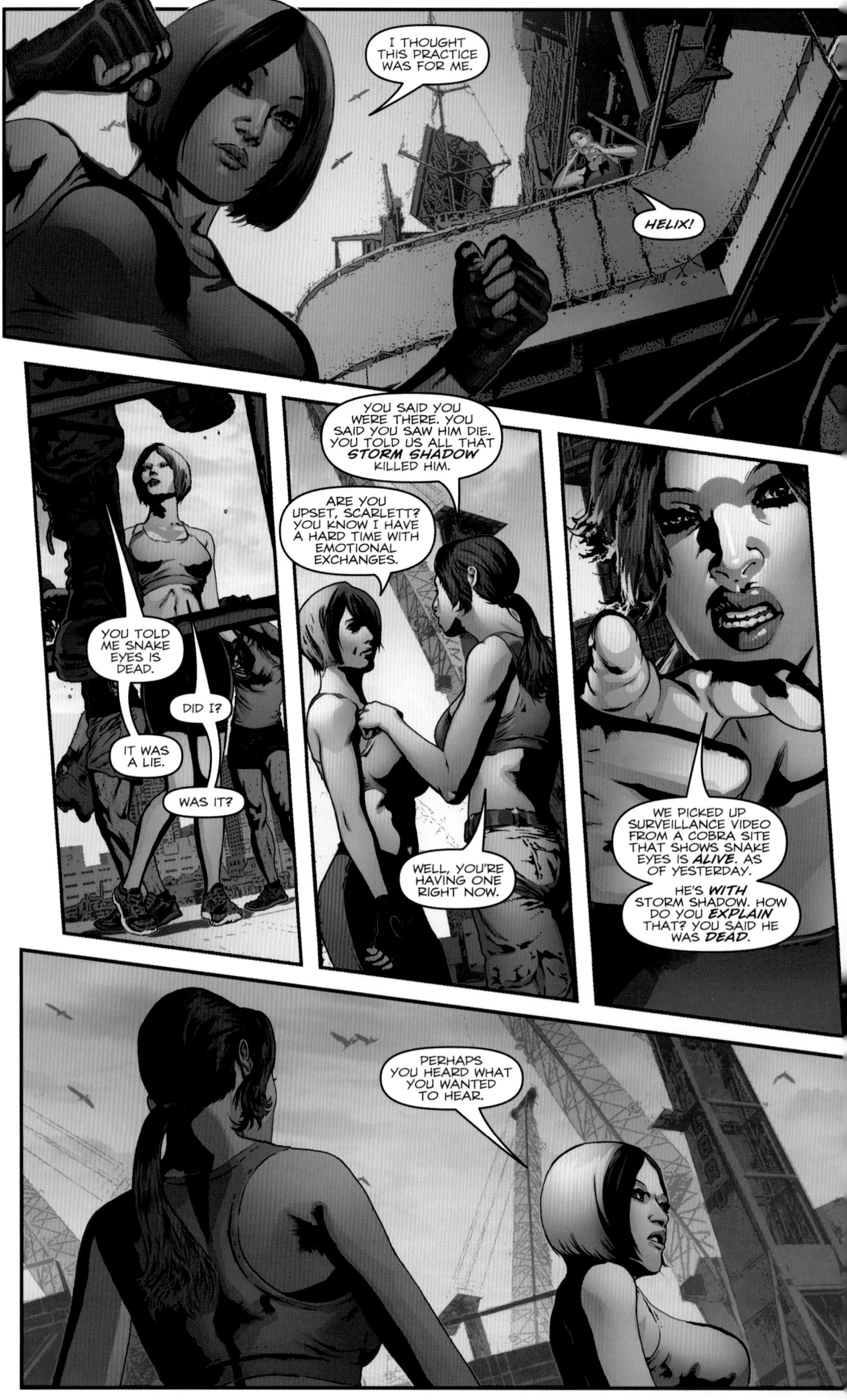

I THOUGHT THIS PRACTICE WAS FOR ME.
HELIX!
YOU TOLD ME SNAKE EYES IS DEAD.
DID I?
IT WAS A LIE.
WAS IT?
YOU SAID YOU WERE THERE. YOU SAID YOU SAW HIM DIE. YOU TOLD US ALL THAT STORM SHADOW KILLED HIM.
ARE YOU UPSET, SCARLETT? YOU KNOW I HAVE A HARD TIME WITH EMOTIONAL EXCHANGES.
WELL, YOU'RE HAVING ONE RIGHT NOW.
WE PICKED UP SURVEILLANCE VIDEO FROM A COBRA SITE THAT SHOWS SNAKE EYES IS ALIVE. AS OF YESTERDAY.
HE'S WITH STORM SHADOW. HOW DO YOU EXPLAIN THAT? YOU SAID HE WAS DEAD.
PERHAPS YOU HEARD WHAT YOU WANTED TO HEAR.

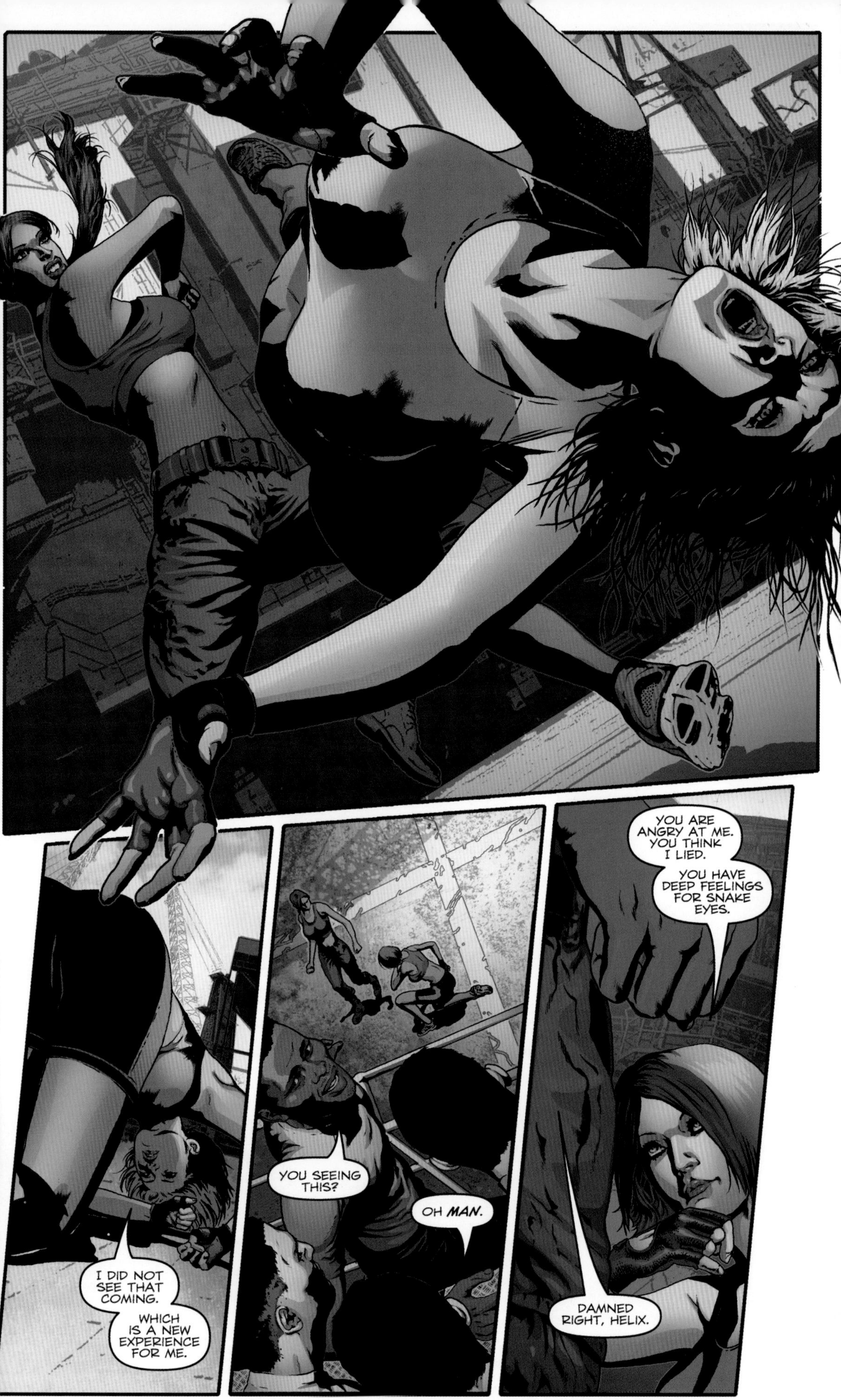
I DID NOT SEE THAT COMING.
WHICH IS A NEW EXPERIENCE FOR ME.
YOU SEEING THIS?
OH MAN.
YOU ARE ANGRY AT ME. YOU THINK I LIED.
YOU HAVE DEEP FEELINGS FOR SNAKE EYES.
DAMNED RIGHT, HELIX.

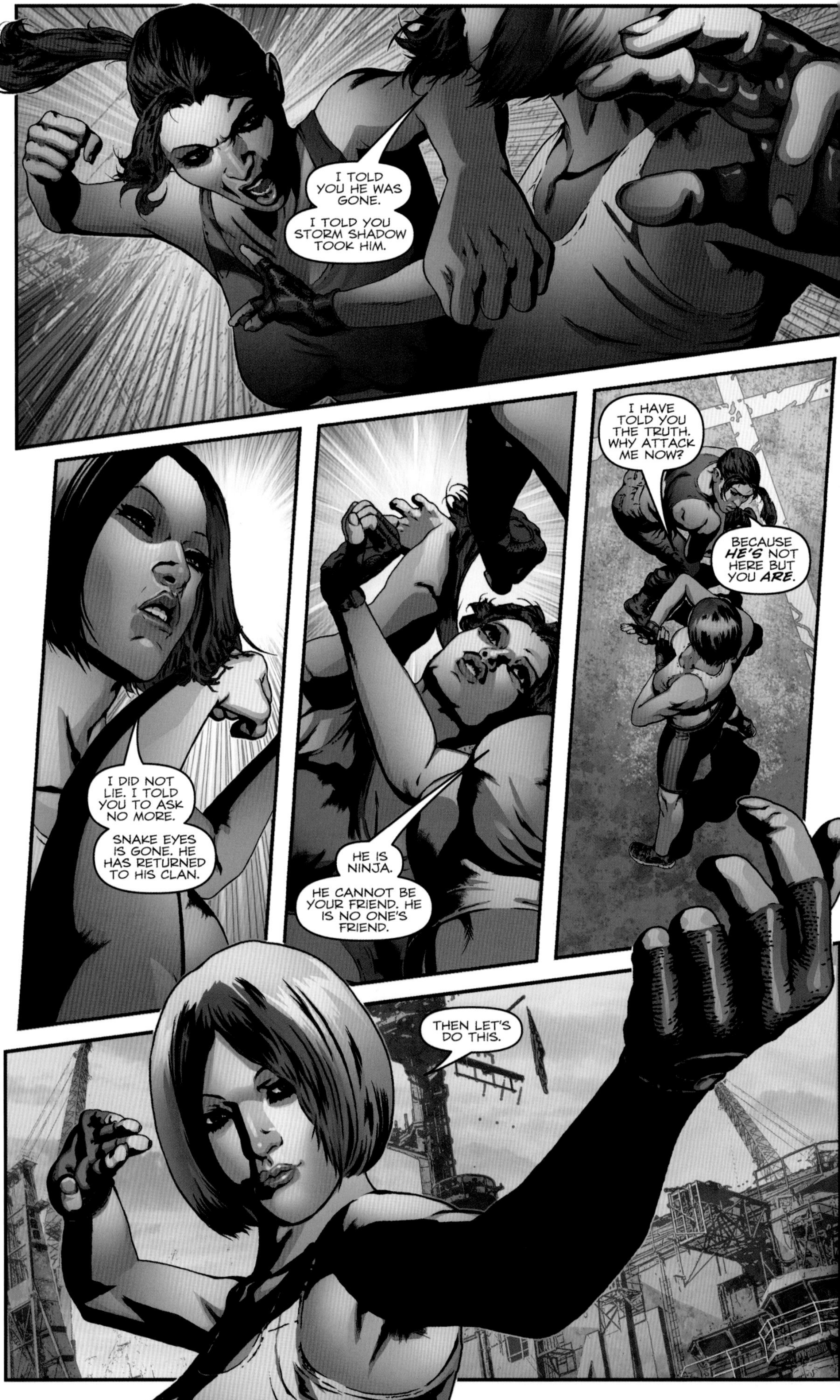
I TOLD YOU HE WAS GONE.
I TOLD YOU STORM SHADOW TOOK HIM.
I DID NOT LIE. I TOLD YOU TO ASK NO MORE.
SNAKE EYES IS GONE. HE HAS RETURNED TO HIS CLAN.
HE IS NINJA.
HE CANNOT BE YOUR FRIEND. HE IS NO ONE'S FRIEND.
I HAVE TOLD YOU THE TRUTH. WHY ATTACK ME NOW?
BECAUSE *HE'S* NOT HERE BUT YOU *ARE*.
THEN LET'S DO THIS.

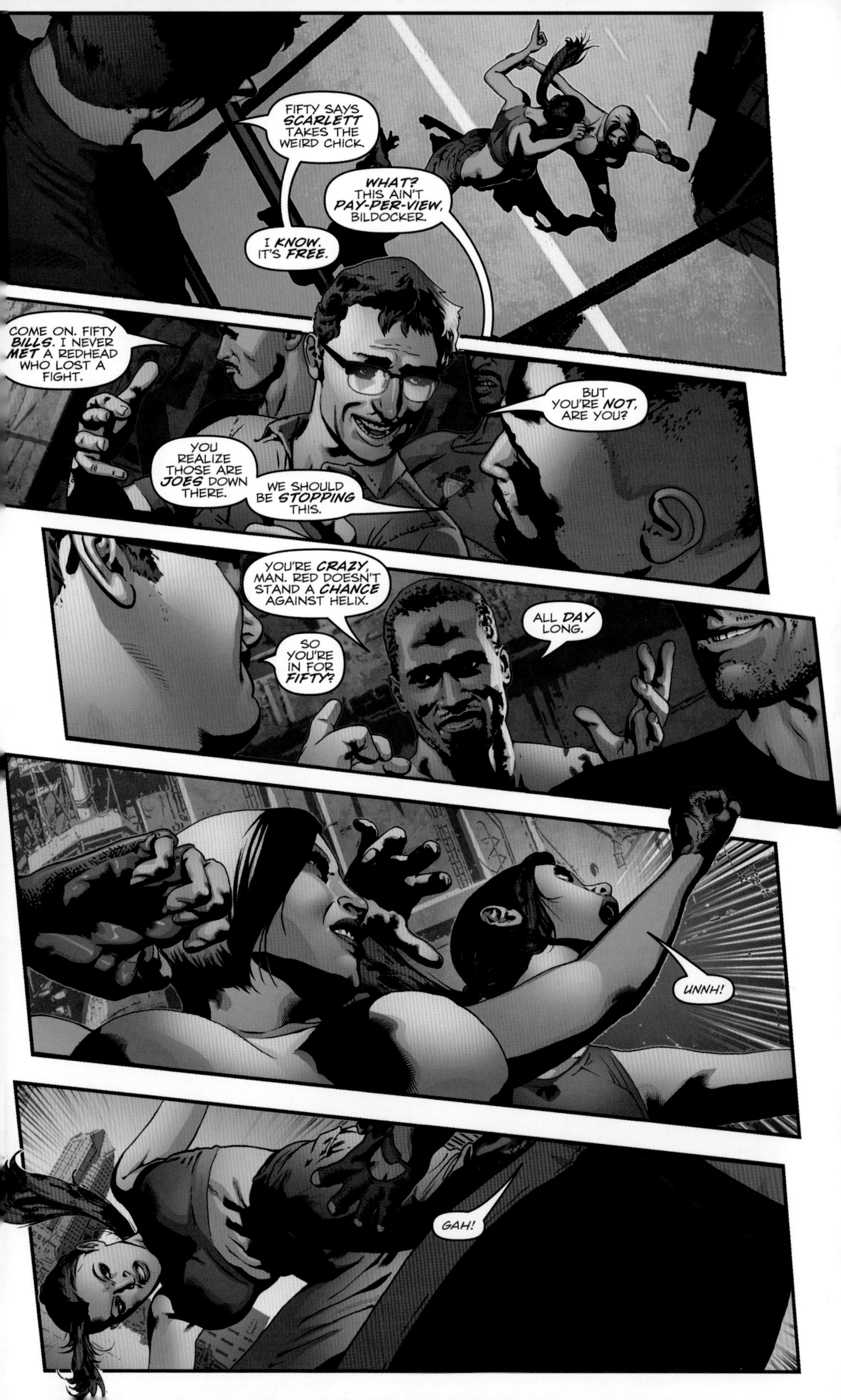
FIFTY SAYS SCARLETT TAKES THE WEIRD CHICK.
WHAT? THIS AIN'T PAY-PER-VIEW, BILDOCKER.
I KNOW. IT'S FREE.
COME ON. FIFTY BILLS. I NEVER MET A REDHEAD WHO LOST A FIGHT.
BUT YOU'RE NOT, ARE YOU?
YOU REALIZE THOSE ARE JOES DOWN THERE.
WE SHOULD BE STOPPING THIS.
YOU'RE CRAZY, MAN. RED DOESN'T STAND A CHANCE AGAINST HELIX.
SO YOU'RE IN FOR FIFTY?
ALL DAY LONG.
UNNH!
GAH!

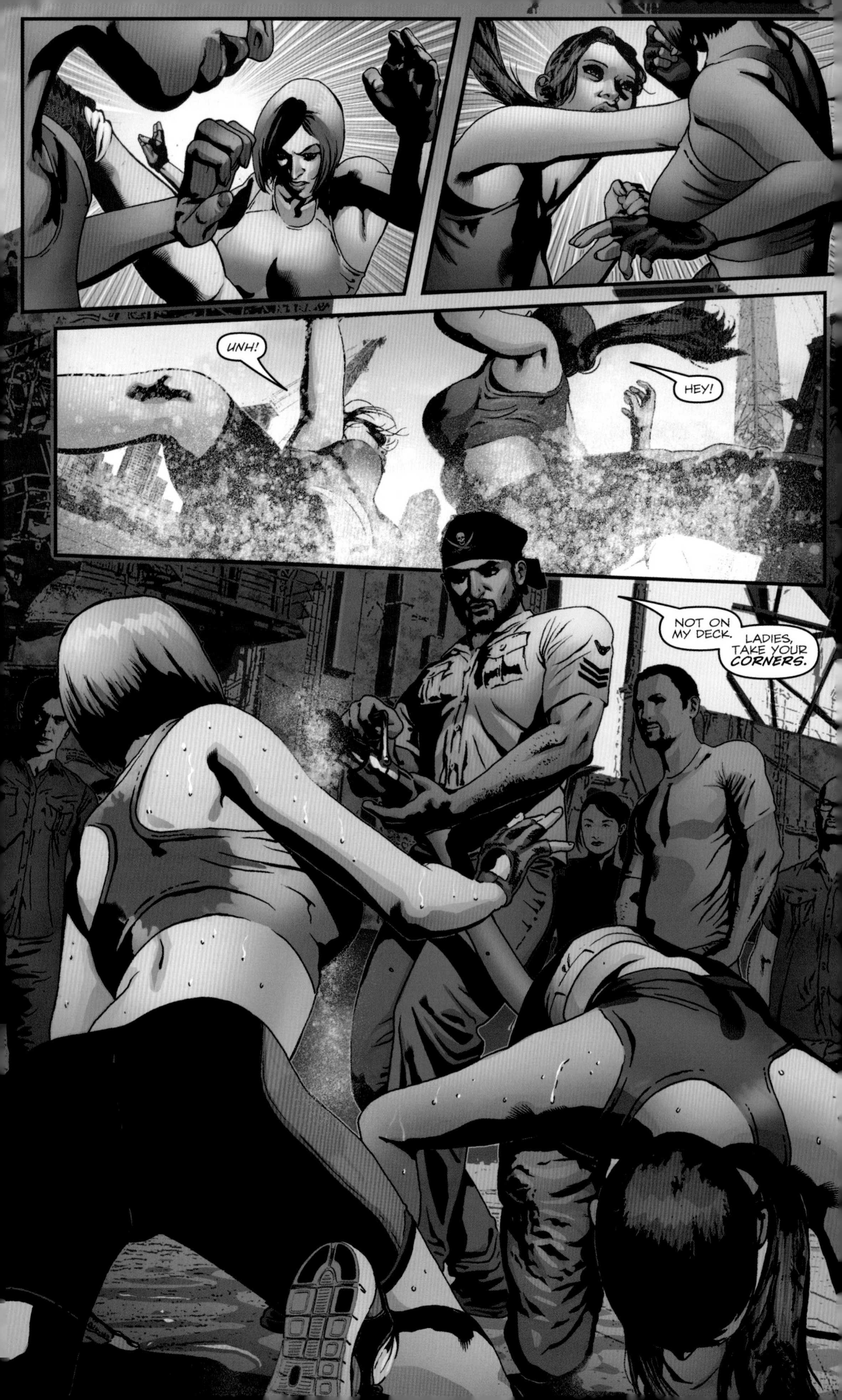
UNH!
HEY!
NOT ON MY DECK. LADIES, TAKE YOUR CORNERS.

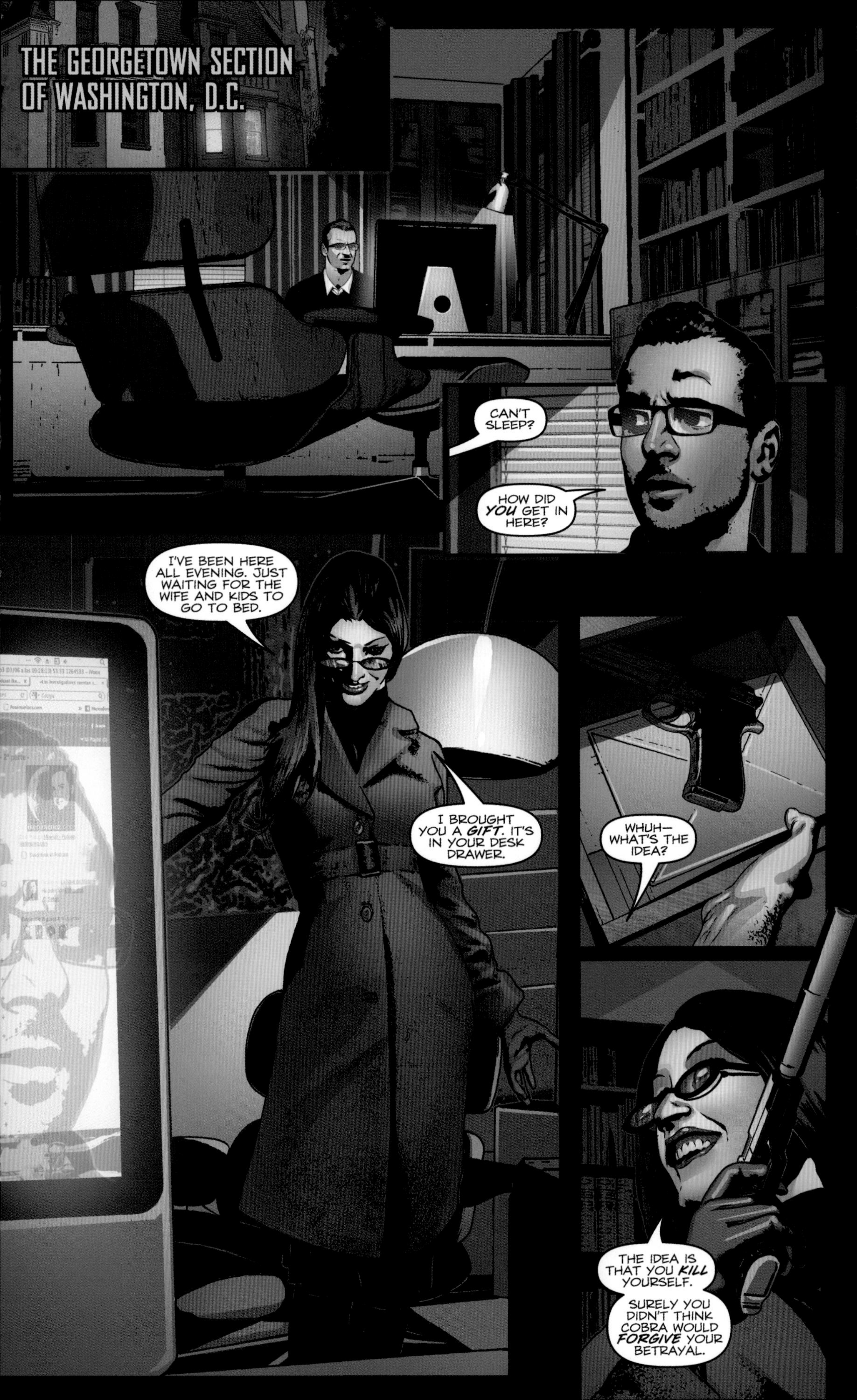
THE GEORGETOWN SECTION OF WASHINGTON, D.C.
CAN'T SLEEP?
HOW DID *YOU* GET IN HERE?
I'VE BEEN HERE ALL EVENING. JUST WAITING FOR THE WIFE AND KIDS TO GO TO BED.
I BROUGHT YOU A *GIFT*. IT'S IN YOUR DESK DRAWER.
WHUH— WHAT'S THE IDEA?
THE IDEA IS THAT YOU *KILL* YOURSELF.
SURELY YOU DIDN'T THINK COBRA WOULD *FORGIVE* YOUR BETRAYAL.

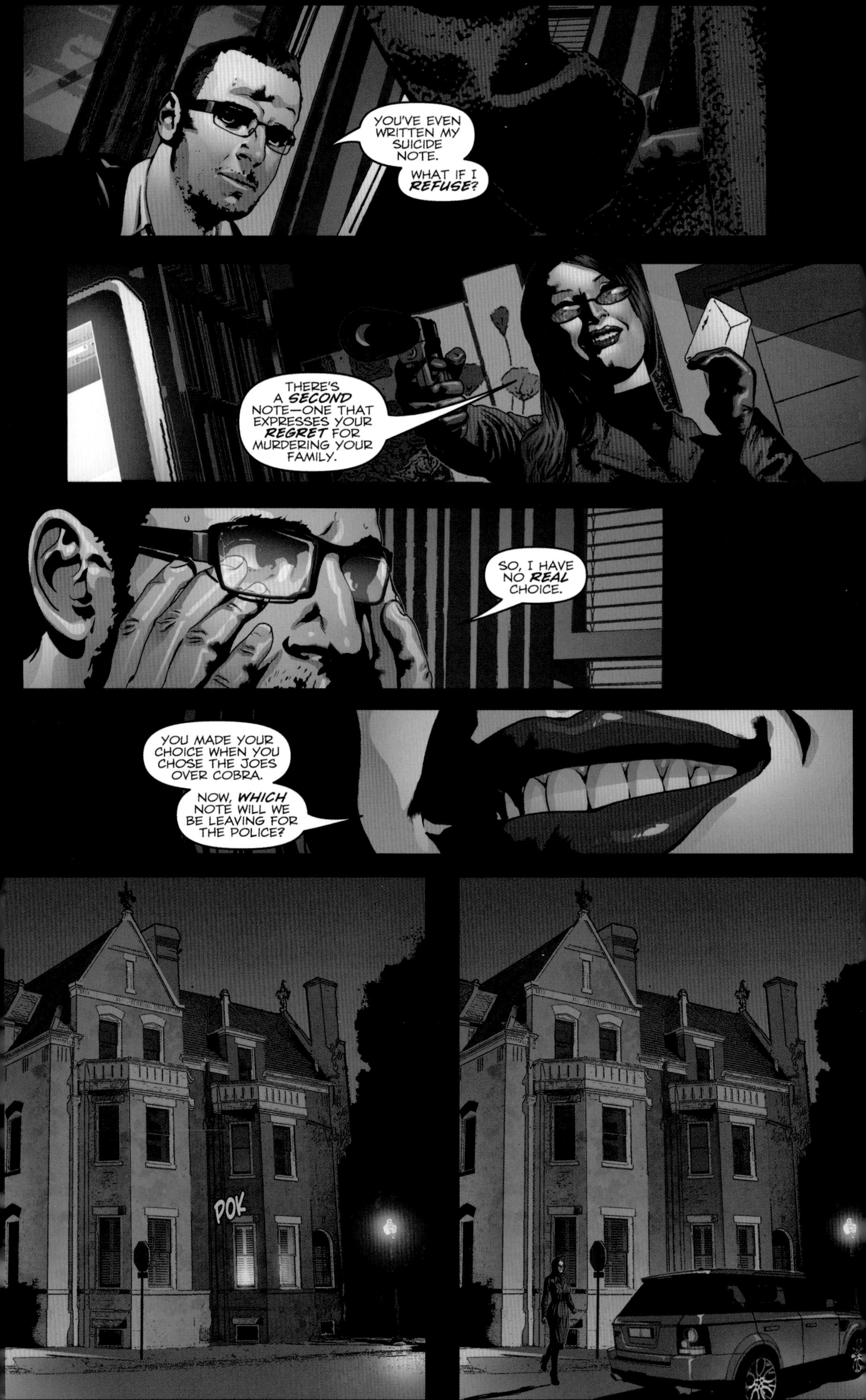
YOU'VE EVEN WRITTEN MY SUICIDE NOTE.
WHAT IF I REFUSE?
THERE'S A SECOND NOTE—ONE THAT EXPRESSES YOUR REGRET FOR MURDERING YOUR FAMILY.
SO, I HAVE NO REAL CHOICE.
YOU MADE YOUR CHOICE WHEN YOU CHOSE THE JOES OVER COBRA.
NOW, WHICH NOTE WILL WE BE LEAVING FOR THE POLICE?
POK

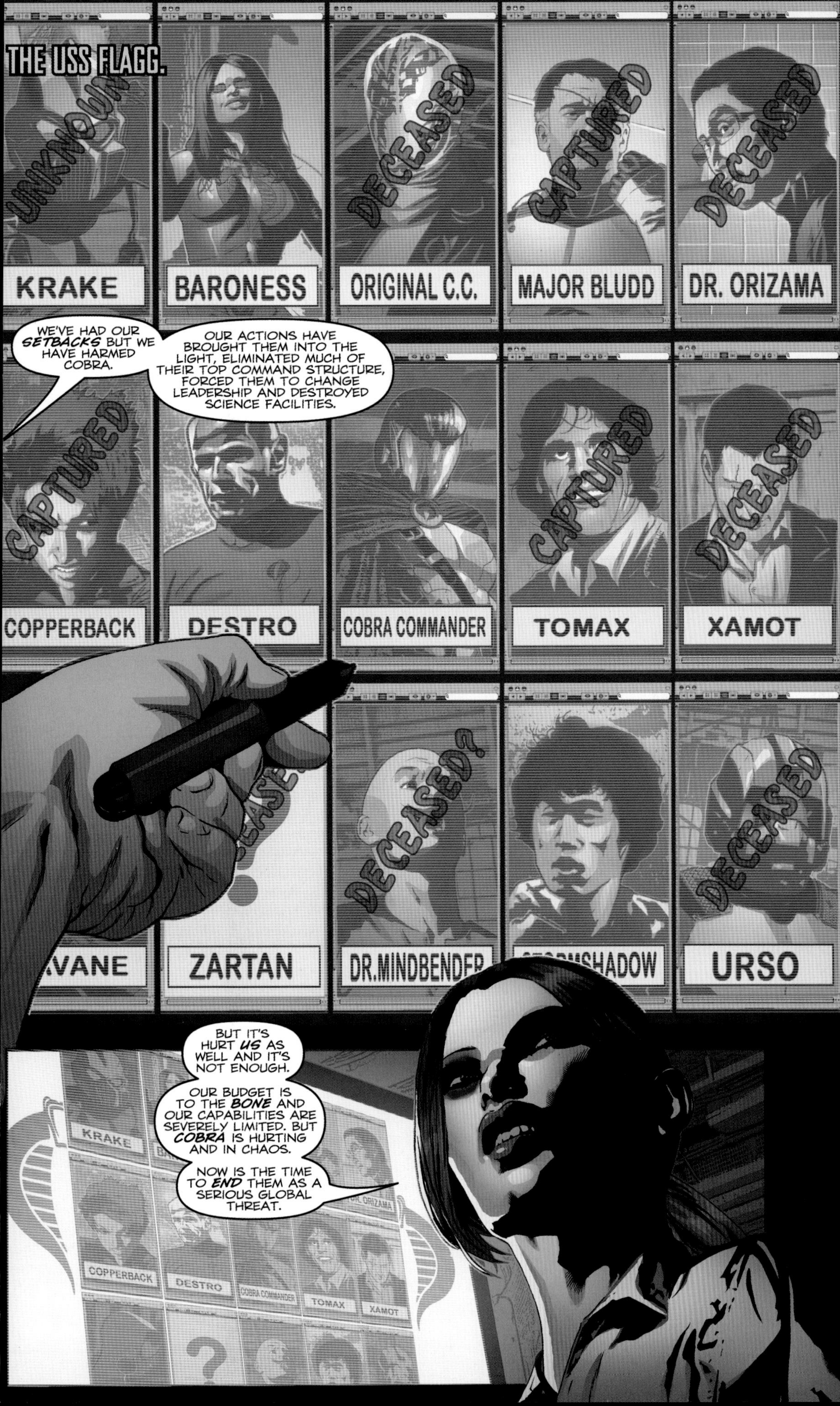

THE USS FLAGG.
UNKNOWN
KRAKE
BARONESS
DECEASED
ORIGINAL C.C.
CAPTURED
MAJOR BLUDD
DECEASED
DR. ORIZAMA
WE'VE HAD OUR SETBACKS BUT WE HAVE HARMED COBRA.
OUR ACTIONS HAVE BROUGHT THEM INTO THE LIGHT, ELIMINATED MUCH OF THEIR TOP COMMAND STRUCTURE, FORCED THEM TO CHANGE LEADERSHIP AND DESTROYED SCIENCE FACILITIES.
CAPTURED
COPPERBACK
DESTRO
COBRA COMMANDER
CAPTURED
TOMAX
DECEASED
XAMOT
DECEASED?
DR.MINDBENDER
DECEASED
URSO
ZARTAN
BUT IT'S HURT US AS WELL AND IT'S NOT ENOUGH.
OUR BUDGET IS TO THE BONE AND OUR CAPABILITIES ARE SEVERELY LIMITED. BUT COBRA IS HURTING AND IN CHAOS.
NOW IS THE TIME TO END THEM AS A SERIOUS GLOBAL THREAT.

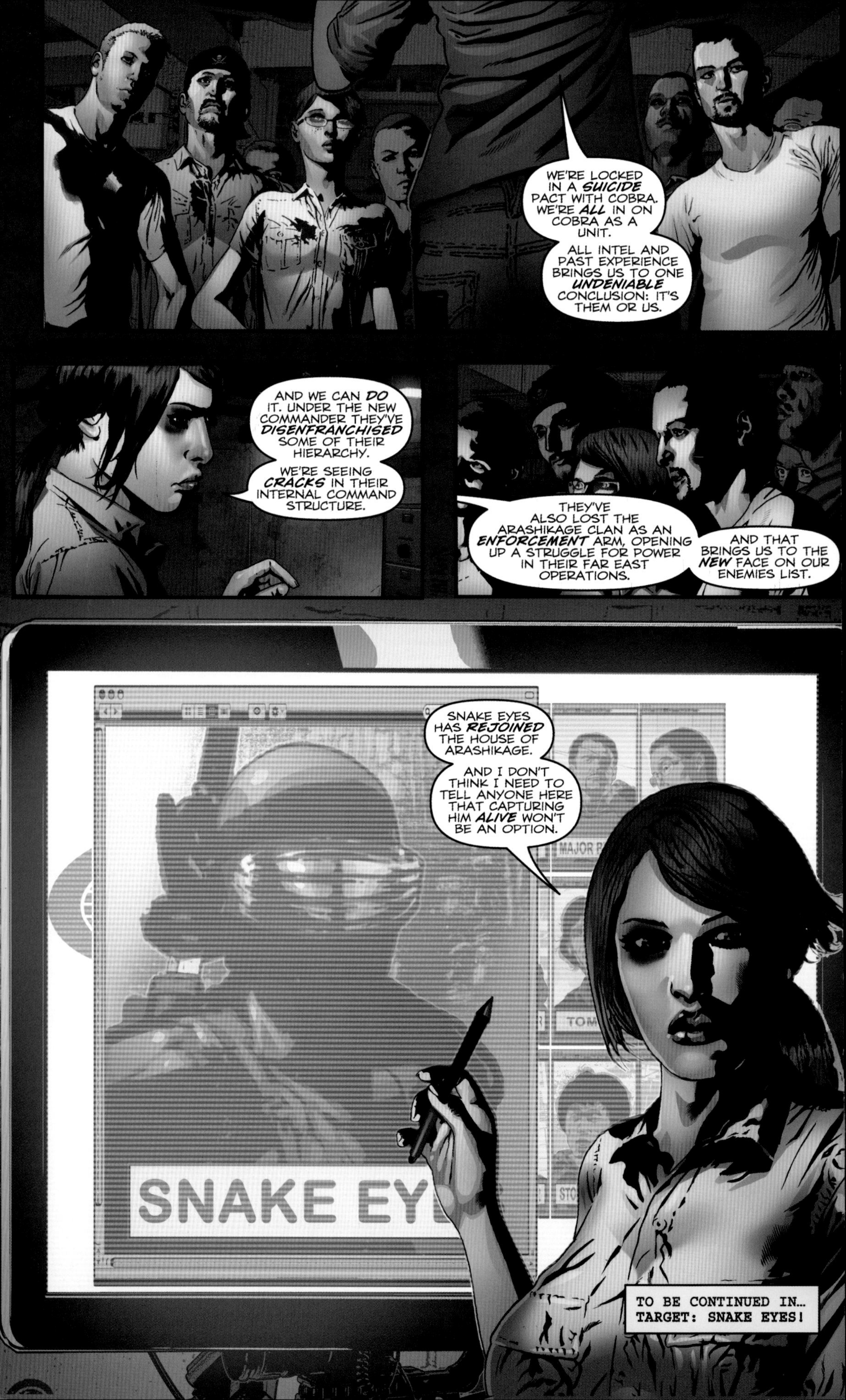
WE'RE LOCKED IN A SUICIDE PACT WITH COBRA. WE'RE ALL IN ON COBRA AS A UNIT.
ALL INTEL AND PAST EXPERIENCE BRINGS US TO ONE UNDENIABLE CONCLUSION: IT'S THEM OR US.
AND WE CAN DO IT. UNDER THE NEW COMMANDER THEY'VE DISENFRANCHISED SOME OF THEIR HIERARCHY.
WE'RE SEEING CRACKS IN THEIR INTERNAL COMMAND STRUCTURE.
THEY'VE ALSO LOST THE ARASHIKAGE CLAN AS AN ENFORCEMENT ARM, OPENING UP A STRUGGLE FOR POWER IN THEIR FAR EAST OPERATIONS.
AND THAT BRINGS US TO THE NEW FACE ON OUR ENEMIES LIST.
SNAKE EYES HAS REJOINED THE HOUSE OF ARASHIKAGE.
AND I DON'T THINK I NEED TO TELL ANYONE HERE THAT CAPTURING HIM ALIVE WON'T BE AN OPTION.
SNAKE EY
TO BE CONTINUED IN... TARGET: SNAKE EYES!

ART GALLERY

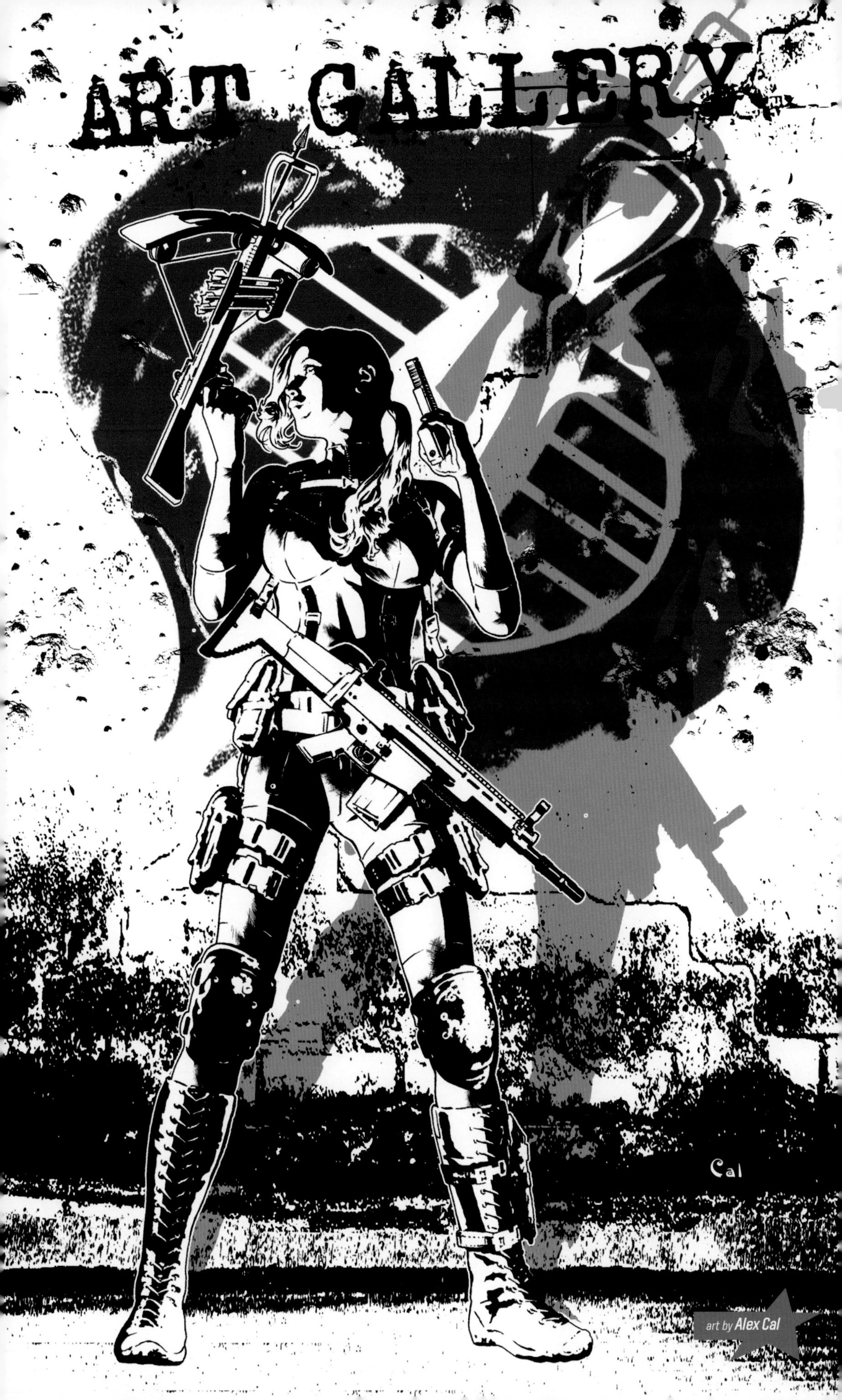
Cal

art by Alex Cal

art by **Will Rosado**
colors by **Romulo Fajardo, Jr.**

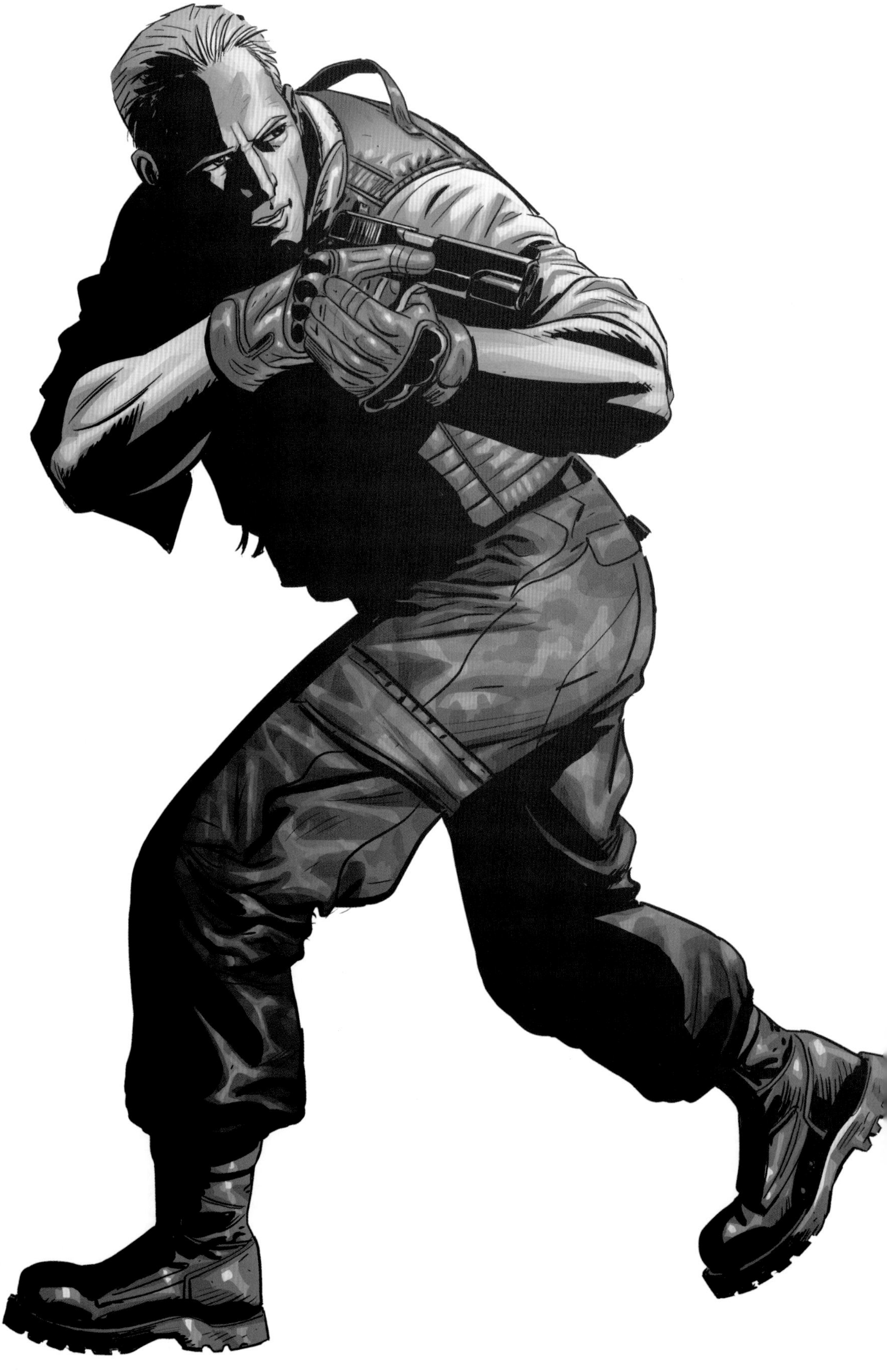

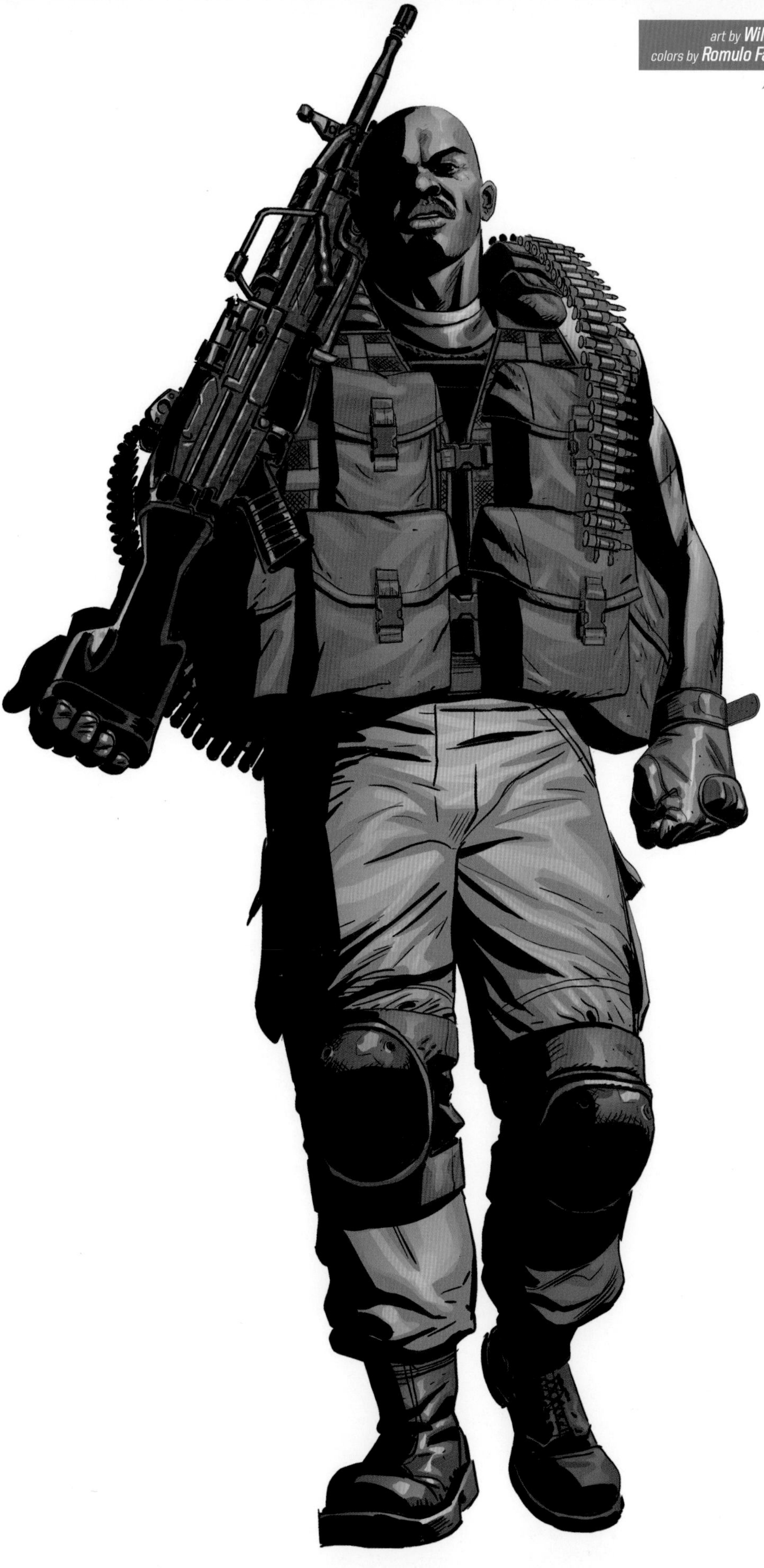

art by **Will Rosado**
colors by **Romulo Fajardo, Jr.**

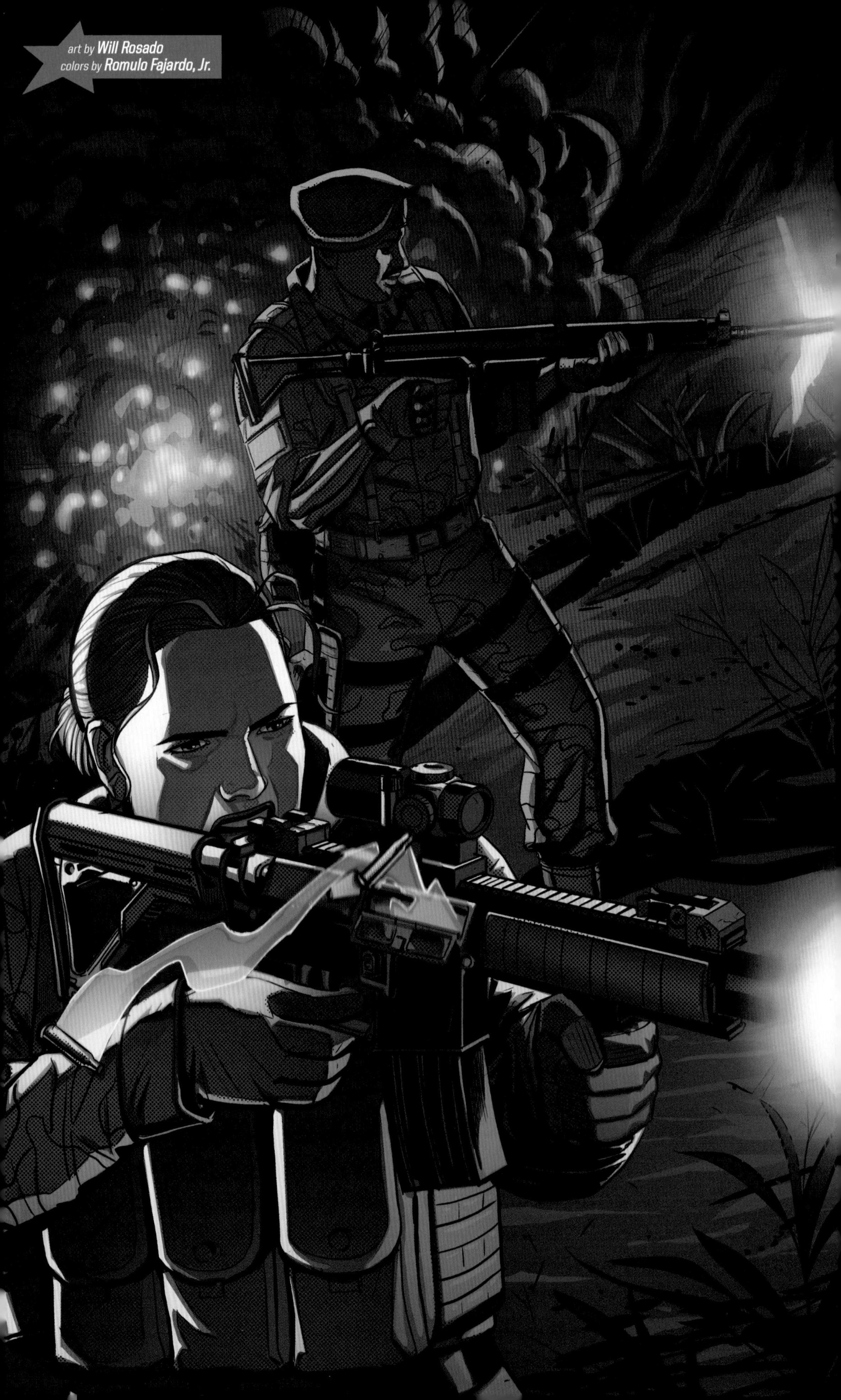
art by Will Rosado
colors by Romulo Fajardo, Jr.

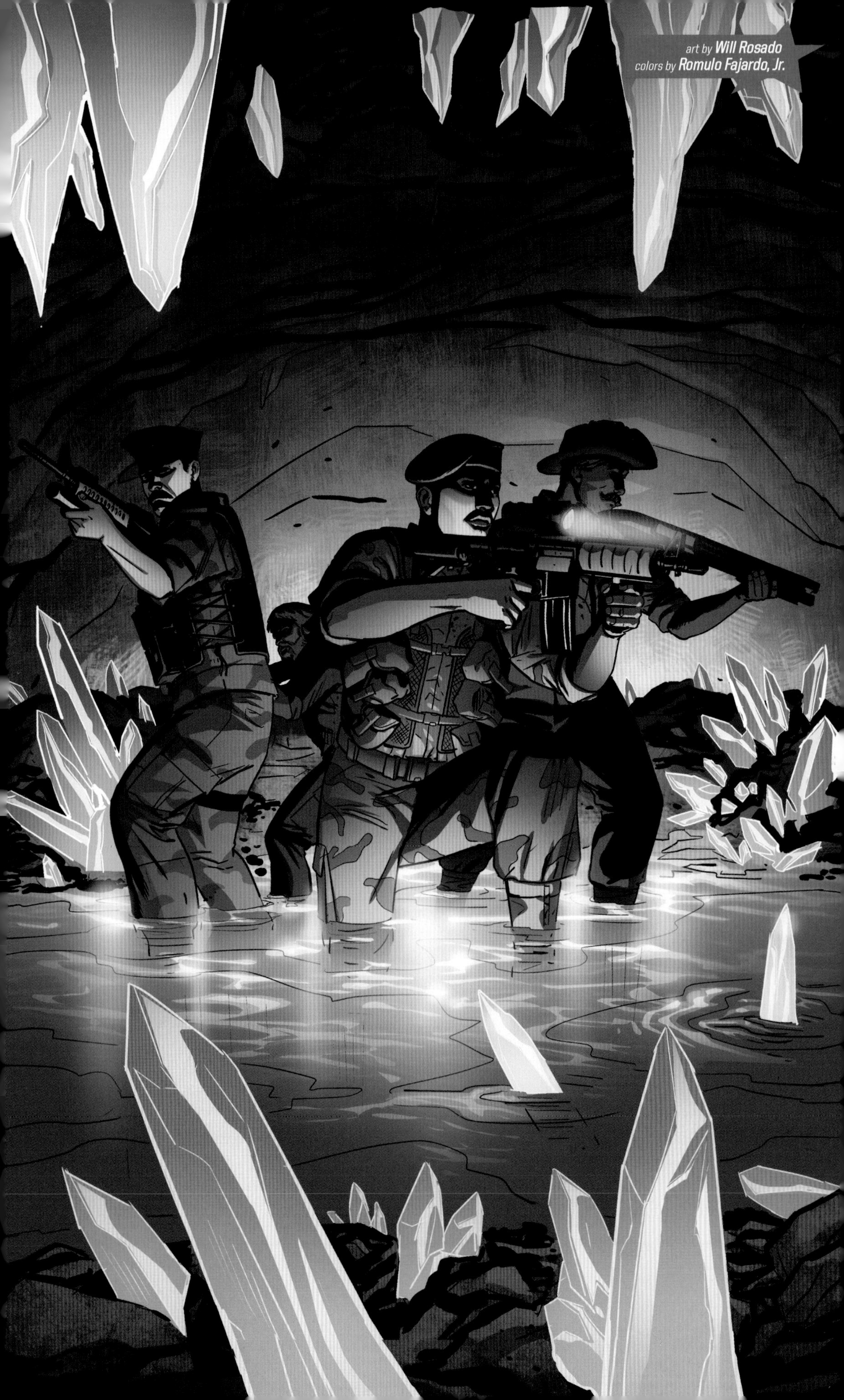
art by Will Rosado
colors by Romulo Fajardo, Jr.

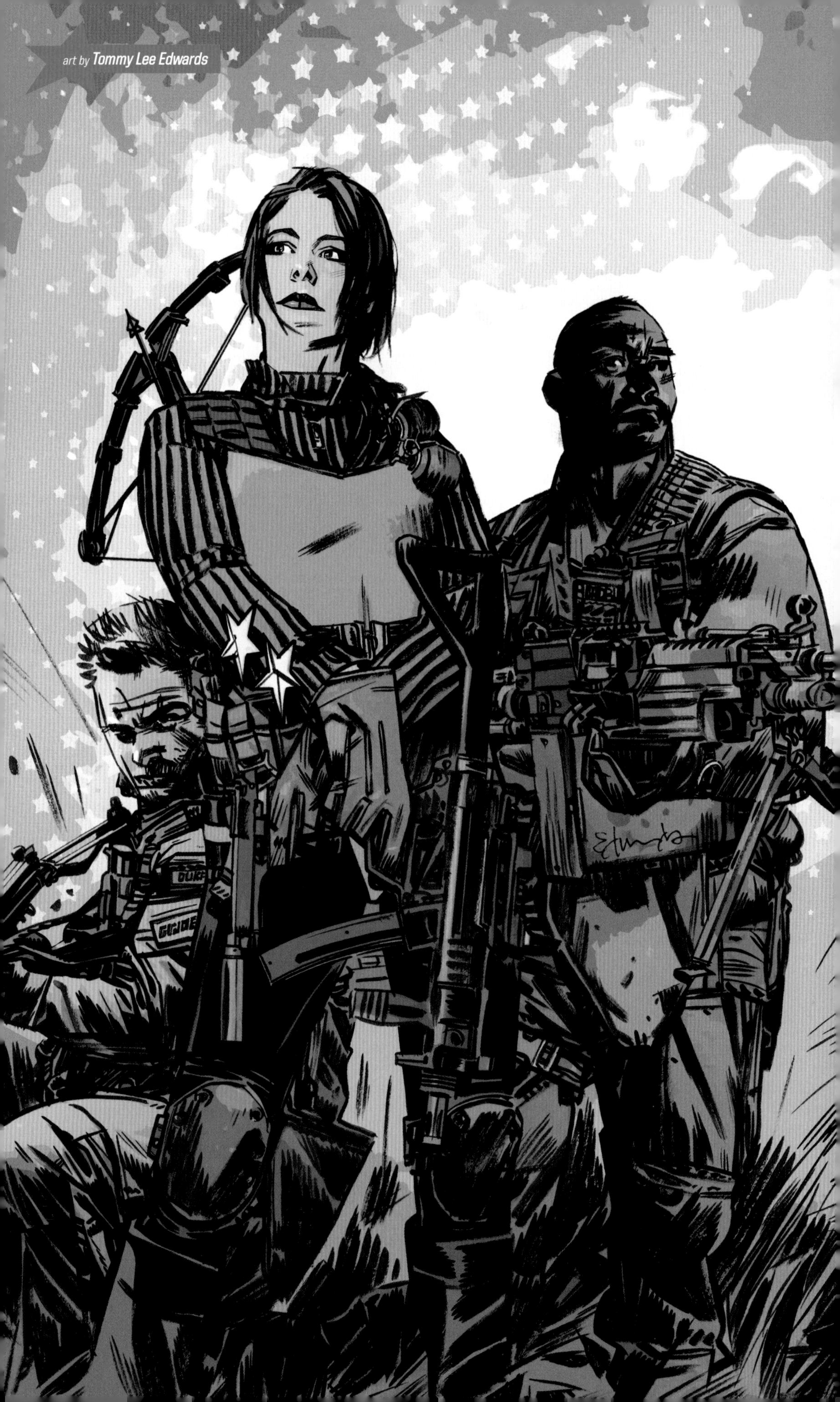

art by Tommy Lee Edwards

art by *Tommy Lee Edwards*

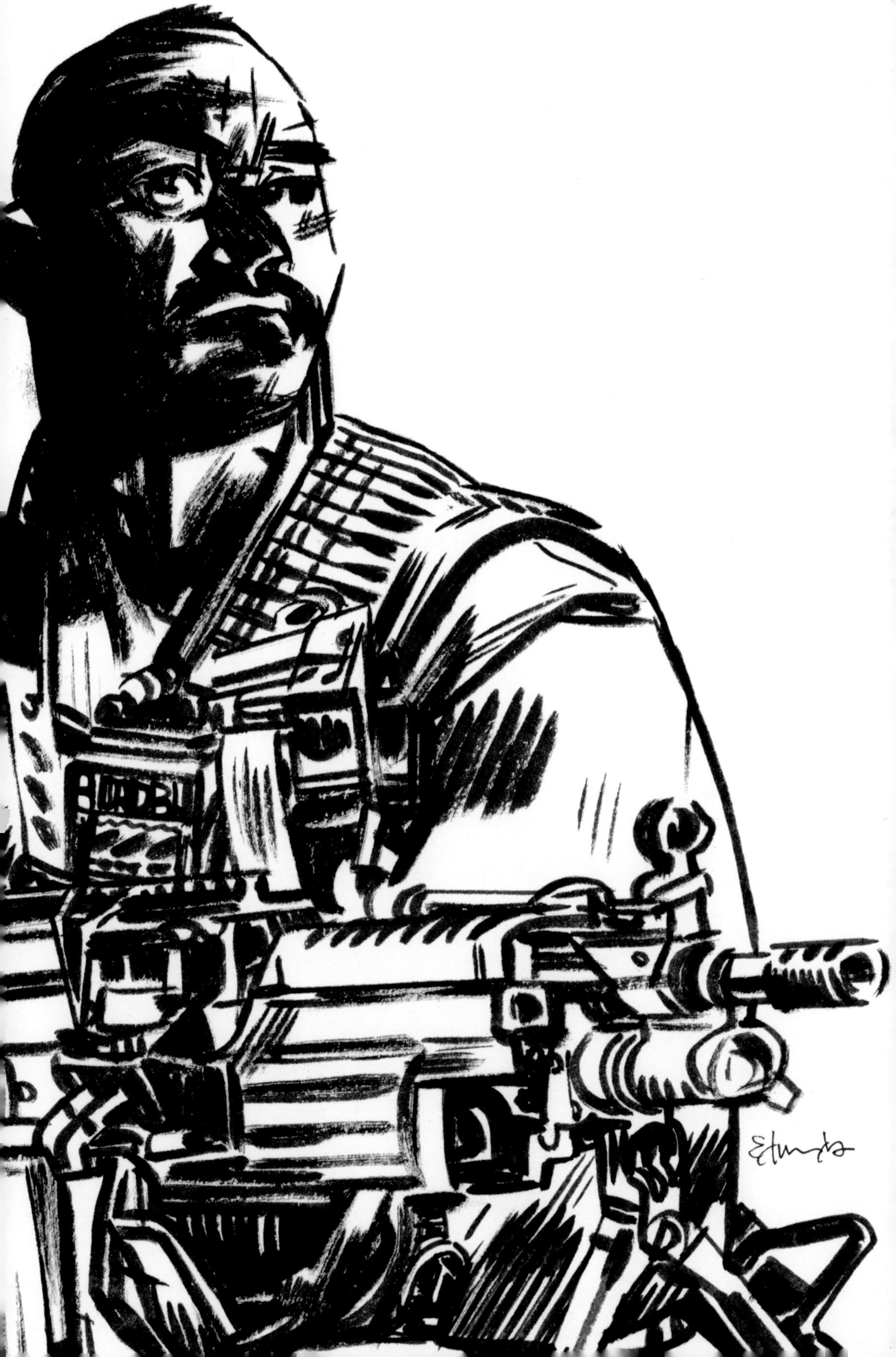

art by Tommy Lee Edwards

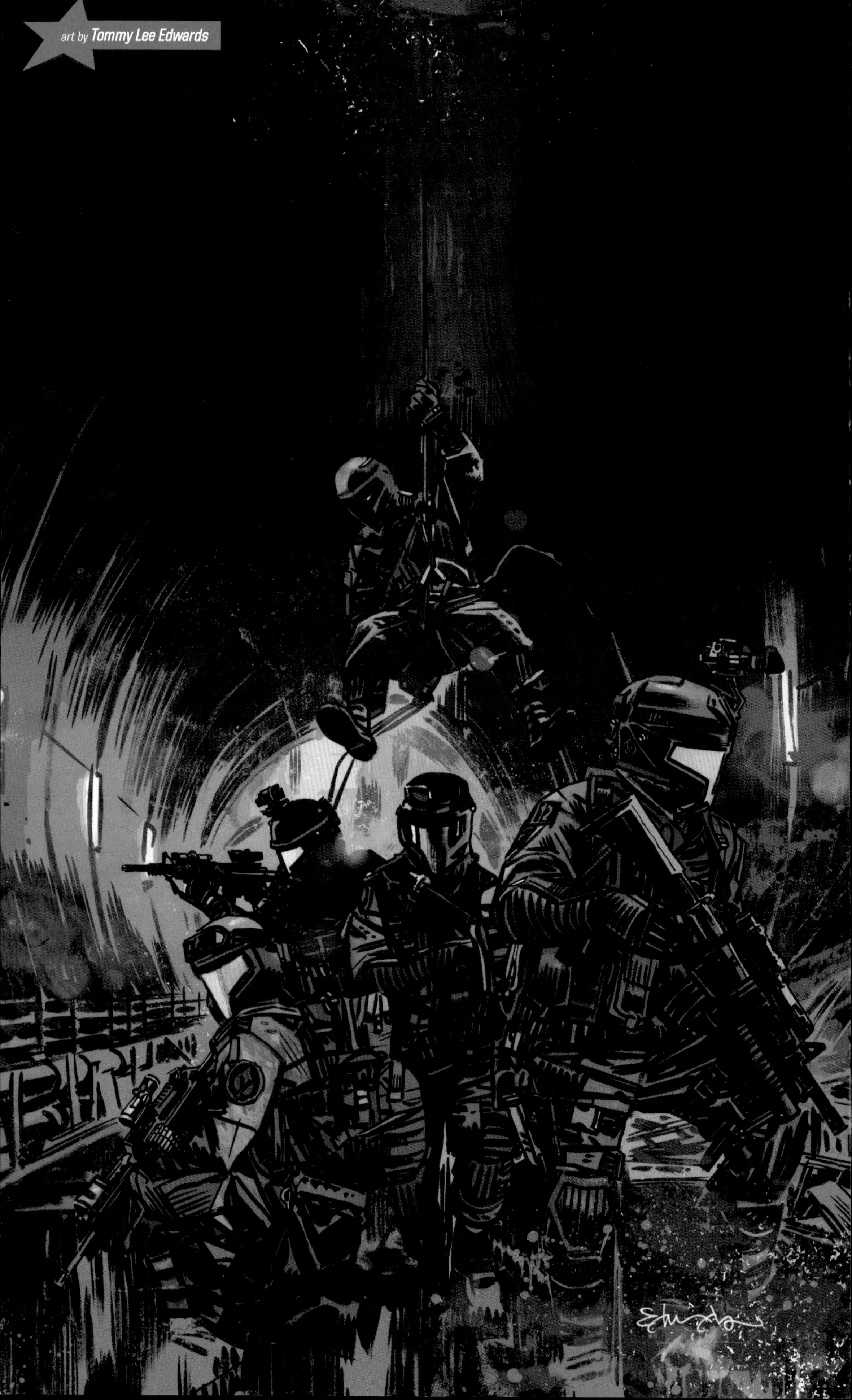

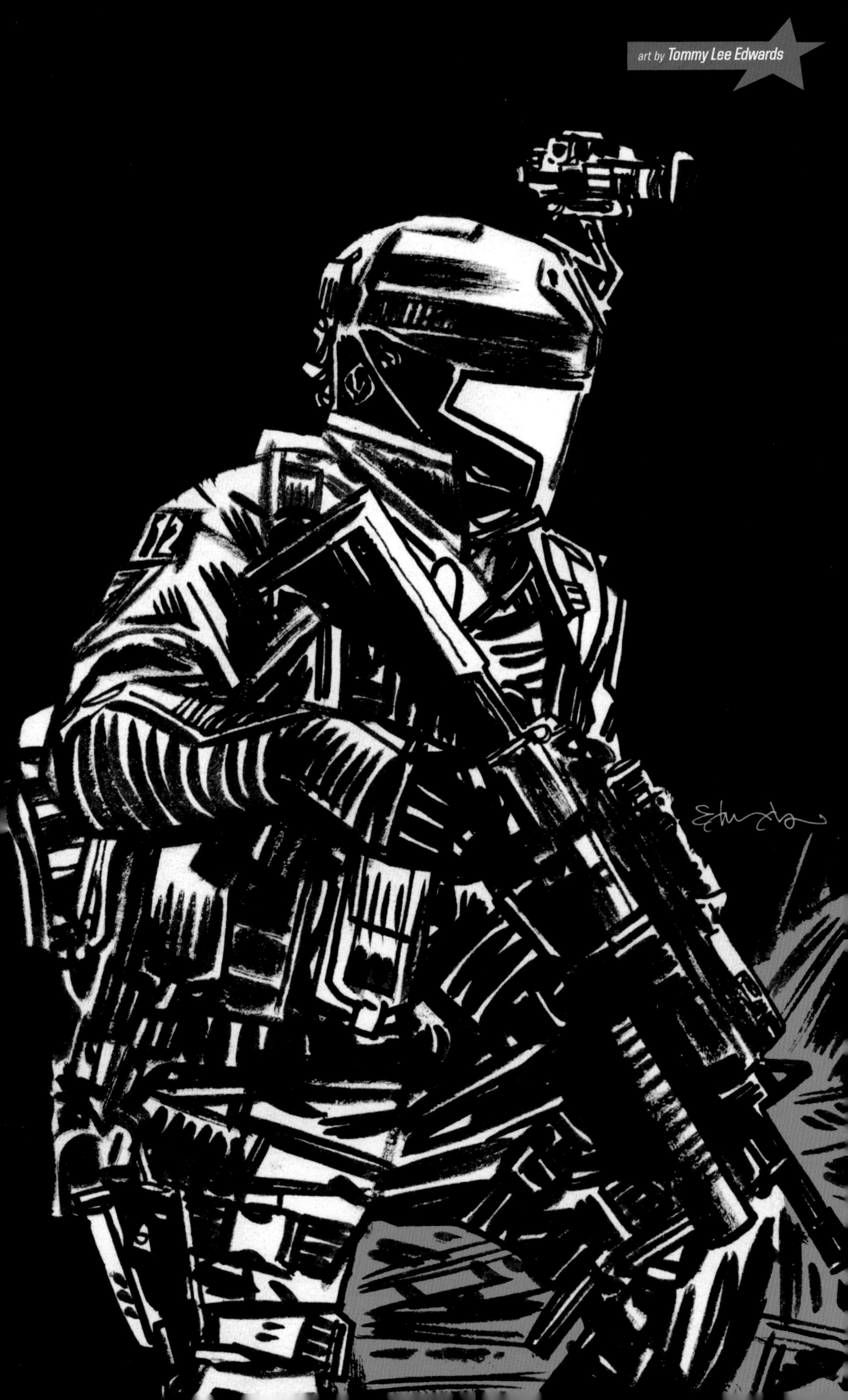

art by Tommy Lee Edwards

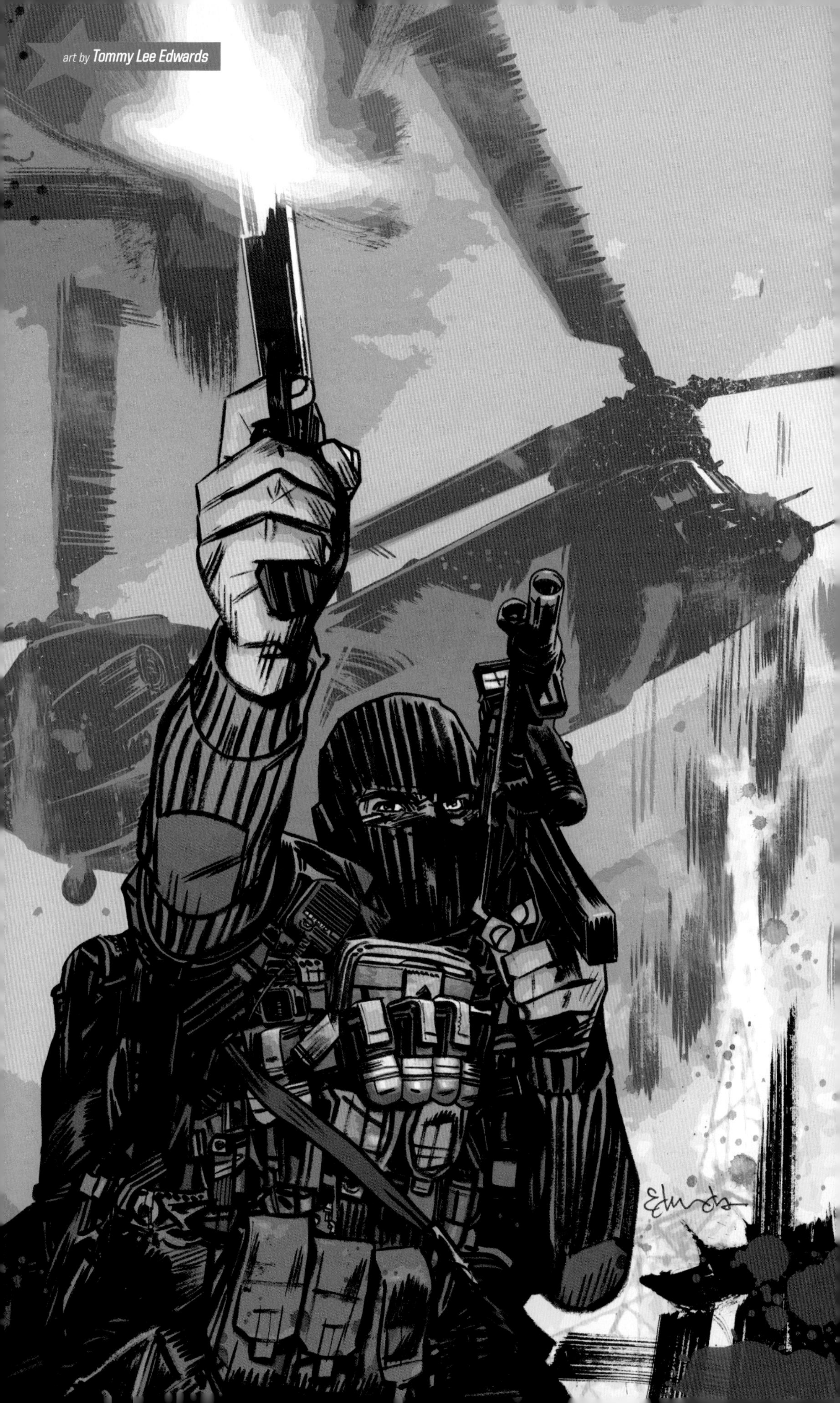

art by ***Tommy Lee Edwards***

art by Tommy Lee Edwards

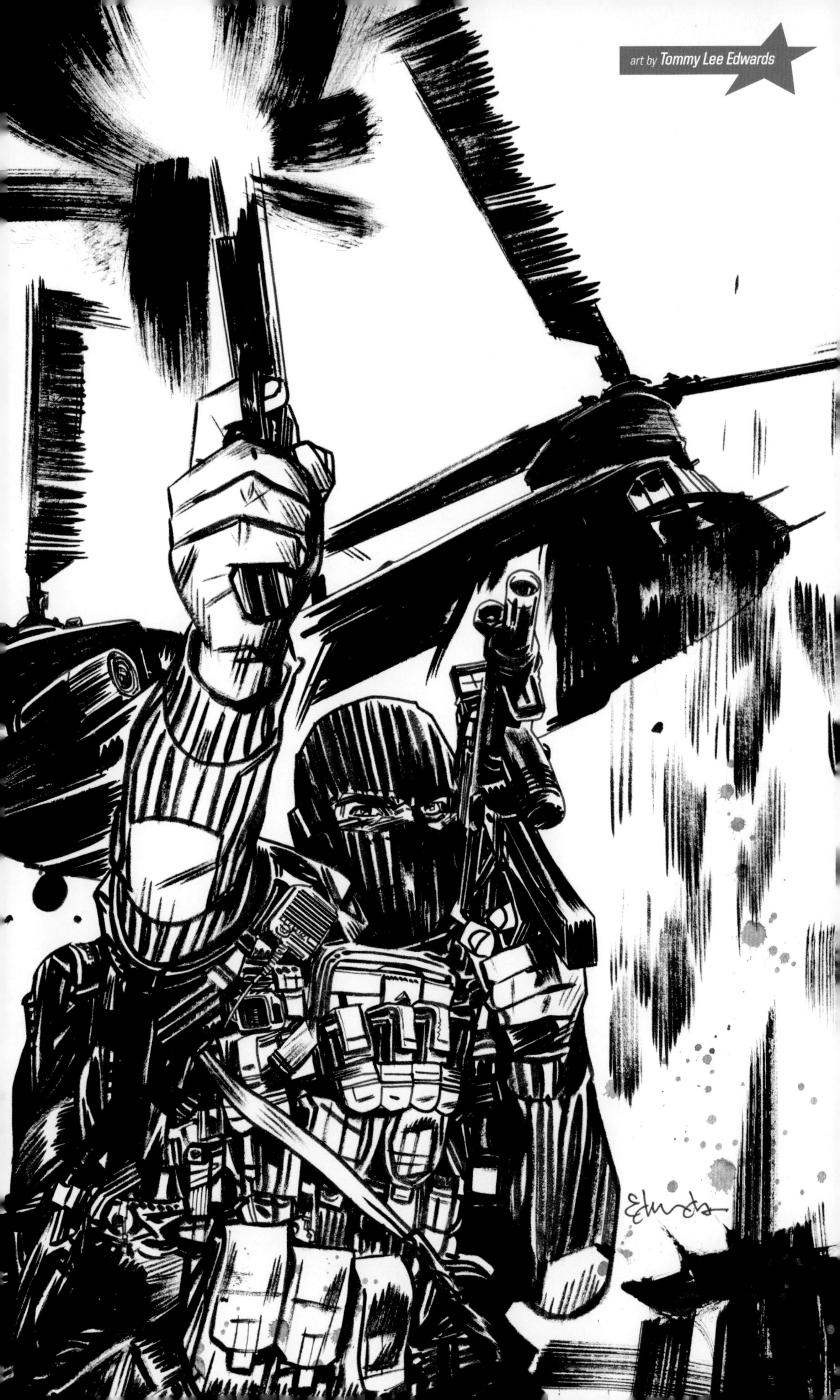

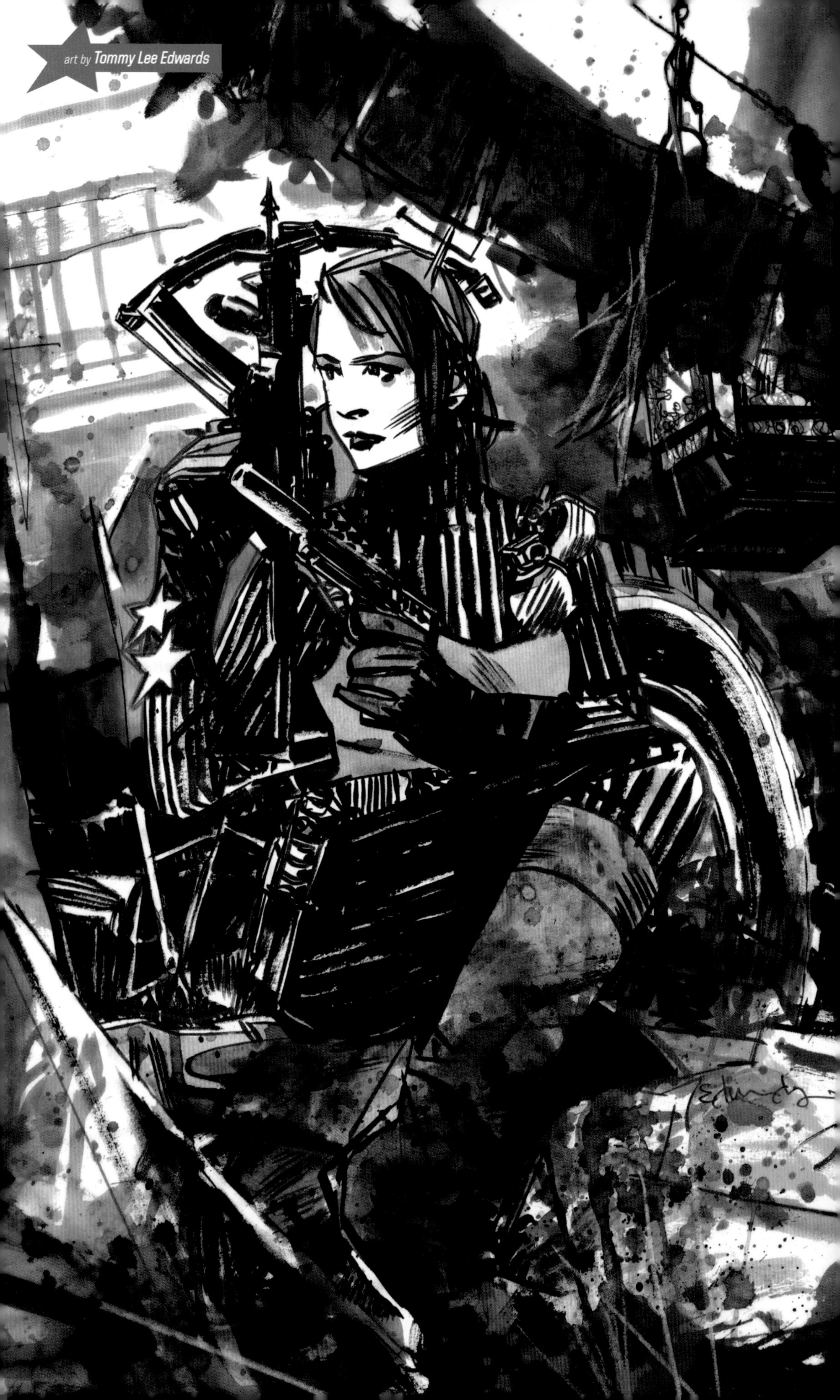
art by Tommy Lee Edwards

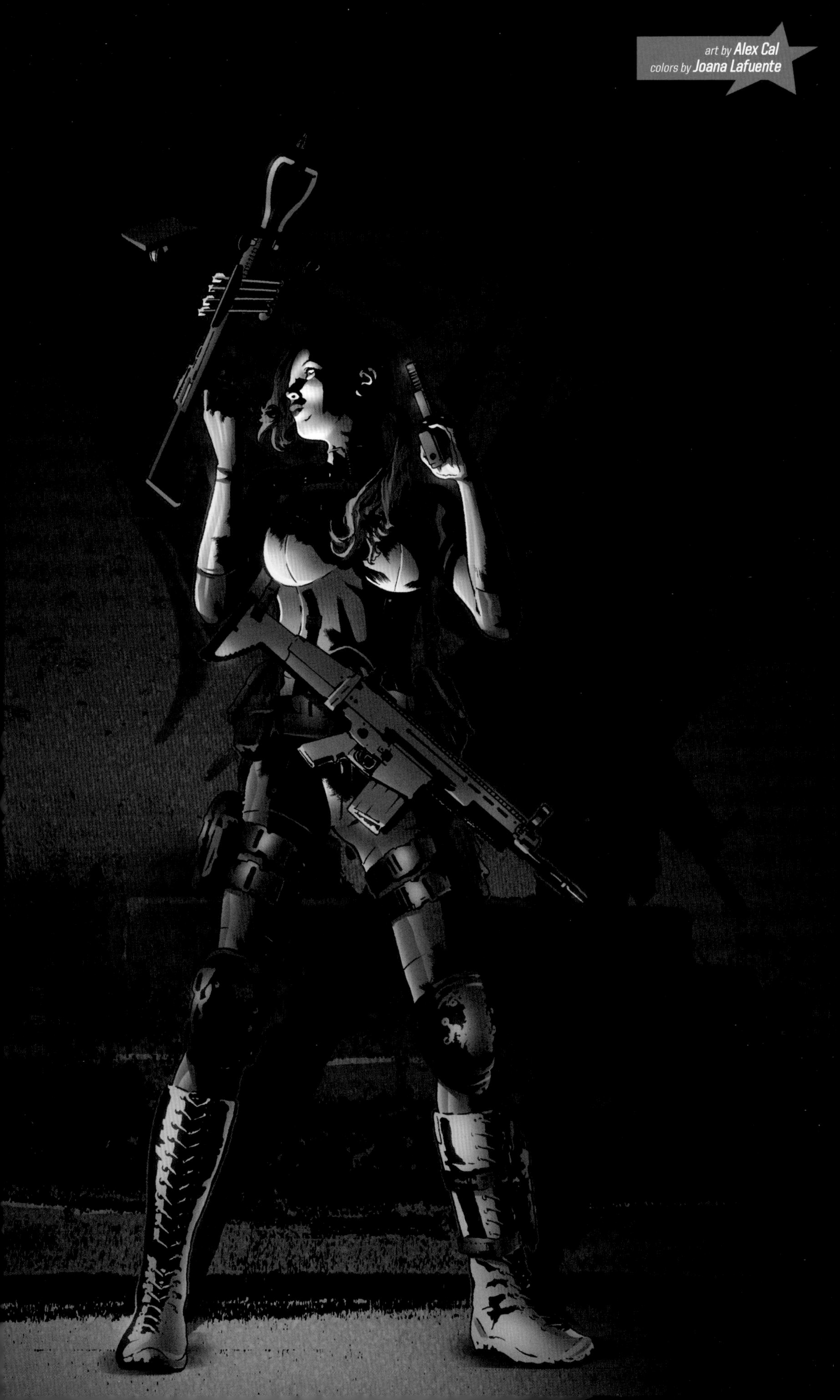
art by Alex Cal
colors by Joana Lafuente

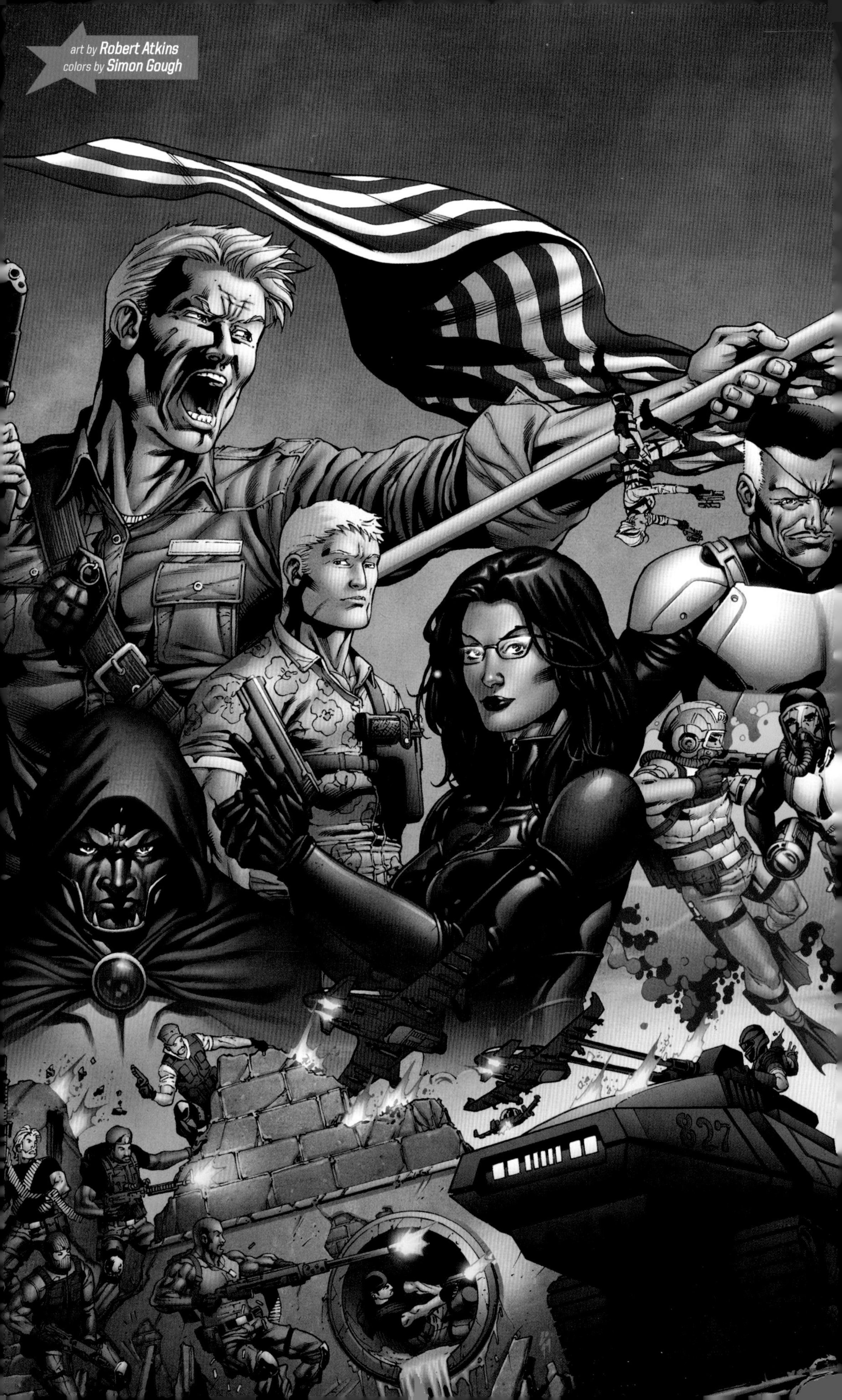
art by Robert Atkins
colors by Simon Gough
827